WORLDS APART

WORLDS APART

AN ANTHOLOGY OF SCIENCE FICTION

Chosen by

AMABEL WILLIAMS-ELLIS

and

MABLY OWEN

BLACKIE

LONDON AND GLASGOW

Other Science Fiction Anthologies
chosen by Amabel Williams-Ellis and Mably Owen:

OUT OF THIS WORLD 1
OUT OF THIS WORLD 2
OUT OF THIS WORLD 3
OUT OF THIS WORLD 4
OUT OF THIS WORLD 5
OUT OF THIS WORLD 6
OUT OF THIS WORLD 7
OUT OF THIS WORLD 8

chosen by Amabel Williams-Ellis and Michael Pearson:

OUT OF THIS WORLD 9
OUT OF THIS WORLD 10

Reprinted 1967
This reprint 1972

Blackie & Son Limited, 5 Fitzhardinge Street, London, W1H 0DL
Bishopbriggs, Glasgow G64 2NZ

ISBN 0 216 89349 6

Printed in Great Britain by R. & R. Clark, Ltd., Edinburgh

CONTENTS

	Page
DOCTOR *by Murray Leinster*	9
CONSIDER HER WAYS *by John Wyndham*	39
AN EYE FOR A WHAT? *by Damon Knight*	116
CAPTIVITY *by Zenna Henderson*	146
O'MARA'S ORPHAN *by James White*	205
NUMBER TEN Q STREET *by Helen McCloy*	246
INFRA DRACONIS *by G. Gurevich*	259
THE ENORMOUS ROOM *by H. L. Gold and Robert Krepps*	281
LAST AND FIRST MEN *by Olaf Stapledon*	353
THE ANARCHIST: *or* THE DOOM OF THE GREAT CITY *by Douglas Fawcett*	373

ACKNOWLEDGEMENTS

THE ENORMOUS ROOM by H. L. GOLD and ROBERT KREPPS
Reprinted by permission of the authors

INFRA DRACONIS by G. GUREVICH
Reprinted from the book *A Visitor from Outer Space* by permission of the Foreign Languages Publishing House in Moscow and of Central Books, Ltd.

CAPTIVITY by ZENNA HENDERSON
Copyright © 1958 by Mercury Press, Inc., from the book *Pilgrimage: The Book of the People* by Zenna Henderson. Reprinted by permission of the author and Victor Gollancz, Ltd., and of Doubleday and Company, Inc.

AN EYE FOR A WHAT? by DAMON KNIGHT
Reprinted from the book *In Deep* by permission of Victor Gollancz, Ltd., and the author's agent, E. J. Carnell

DOCTOR by MURRAY LEINSTER
Reprinted by permission of the author and E. J. Carnell, literary agent

NUMBER TEN Q STREET by HELEN MCCLOY
Reprinted from the book *Surprise, Surprise!* by permission of Victor Gollancz, Ltd.

LAST AND FIRST MEN by OLAF STAPLEDON
This extract reprinted by permission of Methuen and Co., Ltd.

O'MARA'S ORPHAN by JAMES WHITE
Copyright © 1960 by Nova Publications, Ltd., for *New Worlds Science Fiction* and reprinted by permission of the author's agent, E. J. Carnell

CONSIDER HER WAYS by JOHN WYNDHAM
Reprinted from the book *Sometime, Never* by permission of David Higham Associates, Ltd.

PREFACE

Nobody seems quite able to decide on an adequate definition of Science Fiction, although the matter is often discussed at World Science Fiction Conventions, which are attended by authors from all over the world, including the Communist countries. At a recent convention, Poul Anderson, a well known American writer, suggested a definition: 'Science Fiction is a technique for inventing new situations to explore more human experience'. Discussing new trends, a very prolific author, who has written nearly five hundred stories, said that he had worked his way 'from vampires and were-wolves to psychiatric thrillers'. (Doubtless a Czech author, who mentioned a story about a car which runs on its owner's blood, had gone through a similar progression).

One of the most noticeable trends at the moment is towards something that has always been a favourite—the political or sociological fantasy or thriller, i.e. the creation of a whole society, an entire 'World Apart'. This sort of story has changed in recent years though it has its roots far back in imaginative fiction.

Langland in his, often very amusing, *Vision of Piers Plowman*, Spenser, Sir Thomas More, Swift, H. G. Wells, all wrote about entire imaginary worlds. But, just about the time of Wells, something new and different appears. This new development can be seen in *The Anarchist*, which dates from just before Wells, and in several other tales in this collection.

What is new is that writers began to see changes in technology and science as setting off changes in society and in the individuals who make up society. At first, as Aldous Huxley points out in *Literature and Science*, the creators of Utopias or Laputas or Brobdingnags, and even the designers of machines, were technically uninventive: 'Even the most original minds are incapable of imagining a state of affairs radically unlike that with which they are familiar. Leonardo made designs for tanks and air-conditioning machines; but he was unable to imagine any sources of power different from those available at the beginning of the 16th century—the power developed by human and animal muscles and by wind and falling water . . .'

Modern writers create worlds of much greater technical intricacy, but face another difficulty, the tendency to show technical changes acting on people who haven't changed at all. The lesser writers, in fact, produce some pretty wooden versions of 'Everyman'. More subtle and perceptive S.F. authors, however, have noticed that there are both male and female human beings, and that, unlike dinosaurs, Homo Sapiens adapts to new circumstances, and adapts differently according to upbringing and temperament.

That excellent critic, Mr V. S. Pritchett, condemns writers of S.F. who 'lazily forget character and motivation' and adds 'Science Fiction is stiff with the conceits of the ivory lab'. Such authors, says Pritchett, feel that is it enough to hold the reader if 'their characters are killed by unheard of means".

Not long ago it was easy for a S.F. writer to succumb to what Pritchett goes on to call 'the ironmongery of science and technology'. The authors in this collection have none of them succumbed, but, as Bertrand Russell pointed out (in a foreword to the first anthology produced by the present editors), some of this ironmongery there must be. The essence of change has in fact been technical and, as Lord Russell says, 'Today a rocket-ship is nearer to us than Apollo's chariot, a blaster gun than Apollyon's sword, but the prime business of the story-teller remains the same. It is to myths, fantasies and symbols that mankind has always looked for support when confronted with the terrors, immensities, absurdities and paradoxes of the universe'. To the idea of 'support' we believe that Lord Russell might have added that of 'elucidation'. Surely Science Fiction at its best should provide what has been called (to quote V. S. Pritchett again) 'A humane corrective and perspective to new knowledge'.

AMABEL WILLIAMS-ELLIS
MABLY OWEN

DOCTOR

MURRAY LEINSTER

Isolated in space with chlorophage aboard (a destroyer which had devastated the planet Kamerun and could annihilate mankind) it seemed at first that the STAR QUEEN had no choice but to dive into the nearest sun.

There were suns which were near by, and there were stars which were so far away that no way of telling their distance had any meaning. The suns had planets, most of which did not matter, but the ones that did count had seas and continents, and the continents had cities and highways and spaceports. And people.

The people paid no attention to their insignificance. They built ships which went through emptiness beyond imagining, and they landed upon planets and rebuilt them to their own liking. Suns flamed terribly, resenting their impertinence, and storms swept across the planets they pre-empted, but the people built more strongly and were secure. Everything in the universe was bigger or stronger than the people, but they ignored the fact. They went about the businesses they had contrived for themselves.

They were not afraid of anything until somewhere on a certain small planet an infinitesimal single molecule changed itself.

It was one molecule among unthinkably many, upon one planet of one solar system among uncountable star clusters. It was not exactly alive, but it acted as if it were, in which it was like all the important matter of the cosmos. It was actually a combination of two complicated substances not too firmly joined together. When one of the parts changed, it became a new molecule. But, like the original one, it was still capable of a process called autocatalysis. It practised that process and catalysed other molecules into existence, which in each case were duplicates of itself. Then mankind had to take notice, though it ignored flaming suns and monstrous storms and emptiness past belief.

Men called the new molecule a virus and gave it a name. They called it and its duplicates 'chlorophage'. And chlorophage was, to people, the most terrifying thing in the universe.

In a strictly temporary orbit around the planet Altaira, the *Star Queen* floated, while lift-ships brought passengers and cargo up to it. The ship was too large to be landed economically at an unimportant spaceport like Altaira. It was a very modern ship and it made the Regulus-to-Cassim run, which is five hundred light-years, in only fifty days of Earthtime.

Now the lift-ships were busy. There was an unusual number of passengers to board the *Star Queen* at Altaira and an unusual number of them were women and children. The children tended to podginess and the women had the dieted look of the wives of well-to-do men. Most of them looked red-eyed, as if they had been crying.

One by one the lift-ships hooked on to the airlock of the *Star Queen* and delivered passengers and cargo to the ship. Presently the last of them was hooked on, and the last batch of passengers came through to the liner, and the ship's doctor watched them stream past him.

His air was negligent, but he was actually impatient. Like most doctors, Nordenfeld approved of lean children and wiry women. They had fewer things wrong with them and they responded better to treatment. Well, he was the doctor of the *Star Queen* and he had much authority. He had exerted it back on Regulus to insist that a shipment of botanical specimens for Cassim travel in quarantine—to be exact, in the ship's practically unused hospital compartment—and he was prepared to exercise authority over the passengers.

He had a sheaf of health slips from the examiners on the ground below. There was one slip for each passenger. It certified that so-and-so had been examined and could safely be admitted to the *Star Queen*'s air, her four restaurants, her two swimming pools, her recreation areas and the six levels of passenger cabins the ship contained.

He impatiently watched the people go by. Health slips or no health slips, he looked them over. A characteristic gait or a typical complexion tint, or even a certain lack of hair lustre, could tell him things that ground physicians might miss. In such a case the passenger would go back down again. It was not desirable to have deaths on a liner in space. Of course nobody was ever refused passage because of chlorophage. If it were ever discovered, the discovery would already be too late. But the health regulations for space travel were very, very strict.

He looked twice at a young woman as she passed. Despite applied complexion, there was a trace of waxiness in her skin. Nordenfeld had never actually seen a case of chlorophage. No doctor alive ever had. The best authorities were those who had been in Patrol ships during the quarantine of Kamerun when chlorophage was loose on that planet. They had seen beamed-up pictures of patients, but not patients themselves. The Patrol ships stayed in orbit while the planet died. Most doctors, and Nordenfeld was among them, had only seen pictures of the screens which showed the patients.

He looked sharply at the young woman. Then he glanced at her hands. They were normal. The young woman went on, unaware that for the fraction of an instant there had been the possibility of the landing of the *Star Queen* on Altaira, and the destruction of her space drive, and the establishment of a quarantine which, if justified, would mean that nobody could ever leave Altaira again, but must wait there to die. Which would not be a long wait.

A fat man puffed past. The gravity on Altaira was some five per cent under ship-normal and he felt the difference at once. But the veins at his temples were ungorged. Nordenfeld let him go by.

There appeared a white-haired, space-tanned man with a briefcase under his arm. He saw Nordenfeld and lifted a hand in greeting. The doctor knew him. He stepped aside from the passengers and stood there. His name was Jensen, and he represented a fund which invested the surplus money of insurance companies. He travelled a great deal to check on the business interests of that organization.

The doctor grunted, 'What're you doing here? I thought you'd be on the far side of the cluster.'

'Oh, I get about,' said Jensen. His manner was not quite normal. He was tense. 'I got here two weeks ago on a Q-and-C tramp from Regulus. We were a shipload of salt meat. There's romance for you! Salt meat by the spaceship load!'

The doctor grunted again. All sorts of things moved through space, naturally. The *Star Queen* carried a botanical collection for a museum and pig-beryllium and furs and enzymes and a list of items that no man could remember. He watched the passengers go by, automatically counting them against the number of health slips in his hand.

'Lots of passengers this trip,' said Jensen.

'Yes,' said the doctor, watching a man with a limp. 'Why?'

Jensen shrugged and did not answer. He was uneasy, the doctor noted. He and Jensen were as much unlike as two men could very well be, but Jensen was good company. A ship's doctor does not have much congenial society.

The file of passengers ended abruptly. There was no one in the *Star Queen*'s airlock, but the 'Connected' lights still burned and the doctor could look through into the small lift-ship from the planet down below. He frowned. He fingered the sheaf of papers.

'Unless I missed the count,' he said, annoyed, 'there's supposed to be one more passenger. I don't see——'

A door opened far back in the lift-ship. A small figure appeared. It was a little girl perhaps ten years old. She was very neatly dressed, though not quite the way a mother would have done it. She wore the carefully composed expression of a child with no adult in charge of her. She walked precisely from the lift-ship into the *Star Queen's* lock. The opening door closed briskly behind her. There was the rumbling of seals making themselves tight. The lights flickered for 'Disconnect' and then 'All Clear'. They went out, and the lift-ship had pulled away from the *Star Queen*.

'There's my missing passenger,' said the doctor.

The child looked soberly about. She saw him. 'Excuse me,' she said very politely. 'Is this the way I'm supposed to go?'

'Through that door,' said the doctor gruffly.

'Thank you,' said the little girl. She followed his direction. She vanished through the door. It closed.

There came a deep, droning sound, which was the

interplanetary drive of the *Star Queen*, building up that directional stress in space which had seemed such a triumph when it was first contrived. The ship swung gently. It would be turning out from orbit around Altaira. It swung again. The doctor knew that its astrogators were feeling for the incredibly exact pointing of its nose toward the next port which modern commercial ship operation required. An error of fractional seconds of arc would mean valuable time lost in making port some ten light-years of distance away. The drive droned and droned, building up velocity while the ship's aiming was refined and re-refined.

The drive cut off abruptly. Jensen turned white.

The doctor said impatiently, 'There's nothing wrong. Probably a message or a report should have been beamed down to the planet and somebody forgot. We'll go on in a minute.'

But Jensen stood frozen. He was very pale. The interplanetary drive stayed off. Thirty seconds. A minute. Jensen swallowed audibly. Two minutes. Three.

The steady, monotonous drone began again. It continued interminably, as if while it was off the ship's head had swung wide of its destination and the whole business of lining up for a jump in overdrive had to be done all over again.

Then came that 'Ping-g-g-g!' and the sensation of spiral fall which meant overdrive. The droning ceased.

Jensen breathed again. The ship's doctor looked at him sharply. Jensen had been taut. Now the tensions had left his body, but he looked as if he were going to shiver. Instead, he mopped a suddenly streaming forehead.

'I think,' said Jensen in a strange voice, 'that I'll have a drink. Or several. Will you join me?'

Nordenfeld searched his face. A ship's doctor has many duties in space. Passengers can have many things wrong with them, and in the absolute isolation of overdrive they can be remarkably affected by each other.

'I'll be at the fourth-level bar in twenty minutes,' said Nordenfeld. 'Can you wait that long?'

'I probably won't wait to have a drink,' said Jensen. 'But I'll be there.'

The doctor nodded curtly. He went away. He made no guesses, though he'd just observed the new passengers carefully and was fully aware of the strict health regulations that affect space travel. As a physician he knew that the most deadly thing in the universe was chlorophage and that the planet Kamerun was only one solar system away. It had been a stop for the *Star Queen* until four years ago. He puzzled over Jensen's tenseness and the relief he'd displayed when the overdrive field came on. But he didn't guess. Chlorophage didn't enter his mind.

Not until later.

He saw the little girl who had come out of the airlock last of all the passengers. She sat on a sofa as if someone had told her to wait there until something or other was arranged. Doctor Nordenfeld barely glanced at her. He had known Jensen for a considerable time. Jensen had been a passenger on the *Star Queen* half a dozen times, and he shouldn't have been upset by the temporary stoppage of an interplanetary drive. Nordenfeld divided people into two classes, those who were not and those who were worth talking to. There weren't many of the latter. Jensen was.

He filed away the health slips. Then, thinking of Jensen's pallor, he asked what had happened to make the *Star Queen* interrupt her slow-speed drive away from orbit around Altaira.

The purser told him. But the purser was fussily concerned because there were so many extra passengers from

Altaira. He might not be able to take on the expected number of passengers at the next stop-over point. It would be bad business to have to refuse passengers! It would give the space line a bad name.

Then the air officer stopped Nordenfeld as he was about to join Jensen in the fourth-level bar. It was time for a medical inspection of the quarter-acre of Banthyan jungle which purified and renewed the air of the ship. Nordenfeld was expected to check the complex ecological system of the air room. Specifically, he was expected to look for and identify any patches of colourlessness appearing on the foliage of the jungle plants the *Star Queen* carried through space.

The air officer was discreet and Nordenfeld was silent about the ultimate reason for the inspection. Nobody liked to think about it. But if a particular kind of bleaching appeared, as if the chlorophyll of the leaves were being devoured by something too small to be seen by an optical microscope—why, that would be chlorophage. It would also be a death sentence for the *Star Queen* and everybody in her.

But the jungle passed medical inspection. The plants grew lushly in soil which periodically was flushed with hydroponic solution and then drained away again. The UV lamps were properly distributed and the different quarters of the air room were alternately lighted and darkened. And there were no colourless patches. A steady wind blew through the air room and had its excess moisture and unpleasing smells wrung out before it recirculated through the ship. Doctor Nordenfeld authorized the trimming of some liana-like growths which were developing woody tissue at the expense of leaves.

The air officer also told him about the reason for the turning off of the interplanetary drive. He considered it a very curious happening.

The doctor left the air room and passed the place where the little girl—the last passenger to board the *Star Queen* —waited patiently for somebody to arrange something. Doctor Nordenfeld took a lift to the fourth level and went into the bar where Jensen should be waiting.

He was. He had an empty glass before him. Nordenfeld sat down and dialled for a drink. He had an indefinite feeling that something was wrong, but he couldn't put his finger on it. There are always things going wrong for a ship's doctor, though. There are so many demands on his patience that he is usually short of it.

Jensen watched him sip at his drink.

'A bad day?' he asked. He'd got over his own tension.

Nordenfeld shrugged, but his scowl deepened. 'There are a lot of new passengers.' He realized that he was trying to explain his feelings to himself. 'They'll come to me feeling miserable. I have to tell each one that if they feel heavy and depressed, it may be the gravity-constant of the ship, which is greater than their home planet. If they feel light-headed and giddy, it may be because the gravity-constant of the ship is less than they're used to. But it doesn't make them feel better, so they come back for a second assurance. I'll be overwhelmed with such complaints within two hours.'

Jensen waited. Then he said casually—too casually, 'Does anybody ever suspect chlorophage?'

'No,' said Nordenfeld shortly.

Jensen fidgeted. He sipped. Then he said, 'What's the news from Kamerun, anyhow?'

'There isn't any,' said Nordenfeld. 'Naturally! Why ask?'

'I just wondered,' said Jensen. After a moment: 'What was the last news?'

'There hasn't been a message from Kamerun in two years,' said Nordenfeld curtly. 'There's no sign of anything green anywhere on the planet. It's considered to be —uninhabited.'

Jensen licked his lips. 'That's what I understood. Yes.'

Nordenfeld drank half his drink and said unpleasantly, 'There were thirty million people on Kamerun when the chlorophage appeared. At first it was apparently a virus which fed on the chlorophyll of plants. They died. Then it was discovered that it could also feed on haemoglobin, which is chemically close to chlorophyll. Haemoglobin is the red colouring matter of the blood. When the virus consumed it, people began to die. Kamerun doctors found that the chlorophage virus was transmitted by contact, by inhalation, by ingestion. It travelled as dust particles and on the feet of insects, and it was in drinking water and the air one breathed. The doctors on Kamerun warned spaceships off and the Patrol put a quarantine fleet in orbit around it to keep anybody from leaving. And nobody left. And everybody died. *And* so did every living thing that had chlorophyll in its leaves or haemoglobin in its blood, or that needed plant or animal tissues to feed on. There's not a person left alive on Kamerun, not an animal or bird or insect, not a fish or a tree, or plant or seed or blade of grass. There's no longer a quarantine fleet there. Nobody'll go there and there's nobody left to leave. But there are beacon satellites to record any calls and to warn any fool against landing. If the chlorophage got loose and was carried about by spaceships, it could kill the other forty billion humans in the galaxy, together with every green plant or animal with haemoglobin in its blood.'

'That,' said Jensen, and tried to smile, 'sounds final.'

'It isn't,' Nordenfeld told him. 'If there's something in the universe which can kill every living thing except its maker, that something should be killed. There should be research going on about the chlorophage. It would be deadly dangerous work, but it should be done. A quarantine won't stop contagion. It can only hinder it. That's useful, but not enough.'

Jensen moistened his lips.

Nordenfeld said abruptly. 'I've answered your questions. Now what's on your mind and what has it to do with chlorophage?'

Jensen started. He went very pale.

'It's too late to do anything about it,' said Nordenfeld. 'It's probably nonsense anyhow. But what is it?'

Jensen stammered out his story. It explained why there were so many passengers for the *Star Queen*. It even explained his departure from Altaira. But it was only a rumour—the kind of rumour that starts up untraceably and can never be verified. This one was officially denied by the Altairan planetary government. But it was widely believed by the sort of people who usually were well informed. Those who could sent their families up to the *Star Queen*. And that was why Jensen had been tense and worried until the liner had actually left Altaira behind. Then he felt safe.

Nordenfeld's jaw set as Jensen told his tale. He made no comment, but when Jensen was through he nodded and went away, leaving his drink unfinished. Jensen couldn't see his face; it was hard as granite.

And Nordenfeld, the ship's doctor of the *Star Queen*, went into the nearest bathroom and was violently sick. It was a reaction to what he'd just learned.

There were stars which were so far away that their distance didn't mean anything. There were planets beyond counting in a single star cluster, let alone the galaxy. There were comets and gas clouds in space, and worlds where there was life, and other worlds where life was impossible. The quantity of matter which was associated with life was infinitesimal, and the quantity associated with consciousness—animal life—was so much less that the difference couldn't be expressed. But the amount of animal life which could reason was so minute by comparison that the nearest ratio would be that of a single atom to a sun. Mankind, in fact, was the least impressive fraction of the smallest category of substance in the galaxy.

But men did curious things.

There was the cutting-off of the *Star Queen*'s short-distance drive before she'd got well away from Altaira. There had been a lift-ship locked to the liner's passenger airlock. When the last passenger entered the big ship—a little girl—the airlocks disconnected and the lift-ship pulled swiftly away.

It was not quite two miles from the *Star Queen* when its emergency airlocks opened and spacesuited figures plunged out of it to emptiness. Simultaneously, the ports of the lift-ship glowed and almost immediately the whole plating turned cherry-red, crimson, and then orange, from unlimited heat developed within it.

The lift-ship went incandescent and ruptured and there was a spout of white-hot air, and then it turned blue-white and puffed itself to nothing in metallic steam. Where it had been, there was only shining gas, which cooled. Beyond it there were figures in spacesuits which tried to swim away from it.

The *Star Queen*'s control room, obviously, saw the happening. The lift-ship's atomic pile had flared out of control and melted down the ship. It had developed something like sixty thousand degrees Fahrenheit when it ceased to flare. It did not blow up; it only vaporized.

But the process must have begun within seconds after the lift-ship broke contact with the *Star Queen.*

In automatic reaction, the man in control of the liner cut her drive and offered to turn back and pick up the spacesuited figures in emptiness. The offer was declined with almost hysterical haste. In fact, it was barely made before the other lift-ships moved in on rescue missions. They had waited. And they were picking up castaways before the *Star Queen* resumed its merely interplanetary drive and the process of aiming for a solar system some thirty light-years away.

When the liner flicked into overdrive, more than half the floating figures had been recovered, which was remarkable. It was almost as remarkable as the flare-up of the lift-ship's atomic pile. One has to know exactly what to do to make a properly designed atomic pile vaporize metal. Somebody had known. Somebody had done it. And the other lift-ships were waiting to pick up the destroyed lift-ship's crew when it happened.

The matter of the lift-ship's destruction was fresh in Nordenfeld's mind when Jensen had told his story. The two items fitted together with an appalling completeness. They left little doubt or hope.

Nordenfeld consulted the passenger records and presently was engaged in conversation with the sober-faced, composed little girl on a sofa in one of the cabin levels of the *Star Queen.*

'You're Kathy Brand, I believe,' he said matter-of-factly. 'I understand you've been having a rather bad time of it.'

She seemed to consider.

'It hasn't been too bad,' she assured him. 'At least I've been seeing new things. I got dreadfully tired of seeing the same things all the time.'

'What things?' asked Nordenfeld. His expression was not stern now, though his inner sensations were not pleasant. He needed to talk to this child, and he had learned how to talk to children. The secret is to talk exactly as to an adult, with respect and interest.

'There weren't any windows,' she explained, 'and my father couldn't play with me, and all the toys and books were ruined by the water. It was dreadfully tedious. There weren't any other children, you see. And presently there weren't any grown-ups but my father.'

Nordenfeld only looked more interested. He'd been almost sure ever since knowing of the lift-ship's destruction and listening to Jensen's account of the rumour the government of Altaira denied. He was horribly sure now.

'How long were you in the place that hadn't any windows?'

'Oh, dreadfully long!' she said. 'Since I was only six years old! Almost half my life!' She smiled brightly at him. 'I remember looking out of windows and even playing out-of-doors, but my father and mother said I had to live in this place. My father talked to me often and often. He was very nice. But he had to wear that funny suit and keep the glass over his face because he didn't live in the room. The glass was because he went under the water, you know.'

Nordenfeld asked carefully conversational-sounding questions. Kathy Brand, now aged ten, had been taken by her father to live in a big room without any windows. It hadn't any doors, either. There were plants in it, and there were bluish lights to shine on the plants, and there was a place in one corner where there was water. When her father came in to talk to her, he came up out of the water wearing the funny suit with glass over his face. He went out the same way. There was a place in the wall where she could look out into another room, and at first her mother used to come and smile at her through the glass, and she talked into something she held in her hand, and her voice came inside. But later she stopped coming.

There was only one possible kind of place which would answer Kathy's description. When she was six years old she had been put into some university's aseptic-environment room. And she had stayed there. Such rooms were designed for biological research. They were built and then made sterile of all bacterial life and afterward entered through a tank of antiseptic. Anyone who entered wore a suit which was made germ-free by its passage through the antiseptic, and he did not breathe the air of the aseptic room, but air which was supplied him through a hose, the exhaled-air hose also passing under the antiseptic outside. No germ or microbe or virus could possibly get into such a room without being bathed in corrosive fluid which would kill it. So long as there was someone alive outside to take care of her, a little girl could live there and defy even chlorophage.

And Kathy Brand had done it. But, on the other hand, Kamerun was the only planet where it would be necessary, and it was the only world from which a father would land his small daughter on another planet's spaceport. There was no doubt. Nordenfeld grimly imagined someone—he would have had to be a microbiologist even to attempt it—fighting to survive and defeat the chlorophage while he kept his little girl in an aseptic-environment room.

She explained quite pleasantly as Nordenfeld asked more questions. There had been other people besides her father, but for a long time there had been only him. And Nordenfeld computed that somehow she'd been kept alive on the dead planet Kamerun for four long years.

Recently, though—very recently—her father told her that they were leaving. Wearing his funny, antiseptic-wetted suit, he'd enclosed her in a plastic bag with a tank attached to it. Air flowed from the tank into the bag and out through a hose that was all wetted inside. She breathed quite comfortably.

It made sense. An air tank could be heated and its contents sterilized to supply germ-free—or virus-free—air. And Kathy's father took an axe and chopped away a wall of the room. He picked her up, still inside the plastic bag, and carried her out. There was nobody about. There was no grass. There were no trees. Nothing moved.

Here Kathy's account was vague, but Nordenfeld could guess at the strangeness of a dead planet to the child who barely remembered anything but the walls of an aseptic-environment room.

Her father carried her to a little ship, said Kathy, and they talked a lot after the ship took off. He told her that he was taking her to a place where she could run about out-doors and play, but he had to go somewhere else. He did mysterious things which to Nordenfeld meant a most scrupulous decontamination of a small spaceship's interior and its airlock. Its outer surface would reach a temperature at which no organic material could remain uncooked.

And finally, said Kathy, her father had opened a door and told her to step out and say good-bye, and she did, and the ship went away—her father still wearing his funny suit—and people came and asked her questions she did not understand.

Kathy's narrative fitted perfectly into the rumour Jensen said circulated among usually well-informed people on Altaira. They believed, said Jensen, that a small spaceship had appeared in the sky above Altaira's spaceport. It ignored all calls, landed swiftly, opened an airlock and let someone out, and plunged for the sky again. And the story said that radar telescopes immediately searched for and found the ship in space. They trailed it, calling vainly for it to identify itself, while it drove at top speed for Altaira's sun.

It reached the sun and dived in.

Nordenfeld reached the skipper on intercom vision-phone. Jensen had been called there to repeat his tale to the skipper.

'I've talked to the child,' said Nordenfeld grimly, 'and I'm putting her into isolation quarters in the hospital compartment. She's from Kamerun. She was kept in an aseptic-environment room at some university or other. She says her father looked after her. I get an impression of a last-ditch fight by microbiologists against the chlorophage. They lost it. Apparently her father landed her on Altaira and dived into the sun. From her story, he took every possible precaution to keep her from contagion or carrying contagion with her to Altaira. Maybe he succeeded. There's no way to tell—yet.'

The skipper listened in silence.

Jensen said thinly, 'Then the story about the landing was true.'

'Yes. The authorities isolated her, and then shipped her off on the *Star Queen*. Your well-informed friends, Jensen, didn't know what their government was going to do!' Nordenfeld paused, and said more coldly still, 'They didn't handle it right. They should have killed her, painlessly but at once. Her body should have been immersed, with everything that touched it, in full-strength nitric acid. The same acid should have saturated the place where the ship landed and every place she walked. Every room she entered, and every hall she passed through, should have been doused with nitric and then burned. It would still not have been all one could wish. The air she breathed couldn't be recaptured and heated white-hot. But the chances for Altaira's population to go on living would be improved. Instead, they isolated her and they shipped her off with us—and thought they were accomplishing something by destroying the lift-ship that had her in an airtight compartment until she could walk into the *Star Queen*'s lock!'

The skipper said heavily, 'Do you think she's brought chlorophage on board?'

'I've no idea,' said Nordenfeld. 'If she did, it's too late to do anything but drive the *Star Queen* into the nearest sun. . . . No. Before that, one should give warning that she was aground on Altaira. No ship should land there. No ship should take off. Altaira should be blocked off from the rest of the galaxy like Kamerun was. And to the same end result.'

Jensen said unsteadily; 'There'll be trouble if this is known on the ship. There'll be some unwilling to sacrifice themselves.'

'Sacrifice?' said Nordenfeld. 'They're dead! But before they lie down, they can keep everybody they care about from dying too! Would you want to land and have your wife and family die of it?'

The skipper said in the same heavy voice, 'What are the probabilities? You say there was an effort to keep her from contagion. What are the odds?'

'Bad,' said Nordenfeld. 'The man tried, for the child's sake. But I doubt if he managed to make a completely aseptic transfer from the room she lived in to the spaceport on Altaira. The authorities on Altaira should have known it. They should have killed her and destroyed everything she'd touched. And *still* the odds would have been bad!'

Jensen said, 'But you can't do that, Nordenfeld! Not now!'

'I shall take every measure that seems likely to be useful.' Then Nordenfeld snapped, 'Damnation, man! Do you realize that this chlorophage can wipe out the human race if it really gets loose? Do you think I'll let sentiment keep me from doing what has to be done?'

He flicked off the vision-phone.

The *StarQueen* came out of overdrive. Her skipper arranged for it to be done at the time when the largest possible number of her passengers and crew would be asleep. Those who were awake, of course, felt the peculiar inaudible sensation which one subjectively translated into sound. They felt the momentary giddiness which—having no natural parallel—feels like the sensation of treading on a stair-step that isn't there, combined with a twisting sensation, so it is like a spiral fall. The passengers who were awake were mostly in the bars, and the bartenders explained that the ship had shifted overdrive generators and there was nothing to it.

Those who were asleep started up awake, but there was nothing in their surroundings to cause alarm. Some blinked in the darkness of their cabins and perhaps turned on the cabin lights, but everything seemed normal. They turned off the lights again. Some babies cried and had to be soothed. But there was nothing except awakening to alarm anybody. Babies went back to sleep and mothers returned to their beds and—such awakenings being customary—went back to sleep also.

It was natural enough. There were vague and commonplace noises, together making an indefinite hum. Fans circulated the ship's purified and reinvigorated air. Service motors turned in remote parts of the hull. Cooks and bakers moved about in the kitchens. Nobody could tell by any physical sensation that the *Star Queen* was not in overdrive, except in the control room.

There the stars could be seen. They were unthinkably remote. The ship was light-years from any place where humans lived. She did not drive. Her skipper had a family on Cassim. He would not land a plague ship which might destroy them. The executive officer had a small son. If his return meant that small son's death as well as his own, he would not return. All through the ship, the officers who had to know the situation recognized that if chlorophage had got into the *Star Queen*, the ship must not land anywhere. Nobody could survive. Nobody must attempt it.

So the huge liner hung in the emptiness between the stars, waiting until it could be known definitely that chlorophage was aboard or that with absolute certainty it was absent. The answer was up to Doctor Nordenfeld.

He had isolated himself with Kathy in the ship's hospital compartment. Since the ship was built it had been used once by a grown man who developed mumps, and once by an adolescent boy who developed a raging fever which antibiotics stopped. Health measures for space travel were strict. The hospital compartment had only been used those two times.

On this voyage it had been used to contain an assortment of botanical specimens from a planet seventy light-years beyond Regulus. They were on their way to the botanical research laboratory on Cassim. As a routine precaution they'd been placed in the hospital, which could be fumigated when they were taken out. Now the doctor had piled them on one side of the compartment, which he had divided in half with a transparent plastic sheet. He stayed in that side. Kathy occupied the other.

She had some flowering plants to look at and admire. They'd come from the air room and she was delighted with their colouring and beauty. But Doctor Nordenfeld had put them there as a continuing test for chlorophage. If Kathy carried that murderous virus on her person, the flowering plants would die of it—probably even before she did.

It was a scrupulously scientific test for the deadly stuff. Completely sealed off except for a circulator to freshen the air she breathed, Kathy was settled with toys and picture books. It was an improvised but well-designed germproof room. The air for Kathy to breathe was sterilized before it reached her. The air she had breathed was sterilized as it left her plastic-sided residence. It should be the perfection of protection for the ship—if it was not already too late.

The vision-phone buzzed. Doctor Nordenfeld stirred in his chair and flipped the switch. The *Star Queen*'s skipper looked at him out of the screen.

'I've cut the overdrive,' said the skipper. 'The passengers haven't been told.'

'Very sensible,' said the doctor.

'When will we know?'

'That we can go on living? When the other possibility is exhausted.'

'Then, how will we know?' asked the skipper stonily.

Doctor Nordenfeld ticked off the possibilities. He bent down a finger. 'One, her father took great pains. Maybe he did manage an aseptic transfer from a germ-free room to Altaira. Kathy may not have been exposed to the chlorophage. If she hasn't, no bleached spots will show up on the air-room foliage or among the flowering plants in the room with her. Nobody in the crew or among the passengers will die.'

He bent down a second finger. 'It is probably more

likely that white spots will appear on the plants in the air room *and* here, and people will start to die. That will mean Kathy brought contagion here the instant she arrived, and almost certainly that Altaira will become like Kamerun—uninhabited. In such a case we are finished.'

He bent down a third finger. 'Not so likely, but preferable, white spots may appear on the foliage inside the plastic with Kathy, but not in the ship's air room. In that case she was exposed, but the virus was incubating when she came on board, and only developed and spread after she was isolated. Possibly, in such a case, we can save the passengers and crew, but the ship will probably have to be melted down in space. It would be tricky, but it might be done.'

The skipper hesitated. 'If that last happened, she——'

'I will take whatever measures are necessary,' said Doctor Nordenfeld. 'To save your conscience, we won't discuss them. They should have been taken on Altaira.'

He reached over and flipped off the phone. Then he looked up and into the other part of the ship's hospital space. Kathy came out from behind a screen, where she'd made ready for bed. She was beaming. She had a large picture book under one arm and a doll under the other.

'It's all right for me to have these with me, isn't it, Doctor Nordenfeld?' she asked hopefully. 'I didn't have any picture books but one, and it got worn out. And my doll—it was dreadful how shabby she was!'

The doctor frowned. She smiled at him. He said, 'After all, picture books are made to be looked at and dolls to be played with.'

She skipped to the tiny hospital bed on the far side of the presumably virusproof partition. She climbed into it and zestfully arranged the doll to share it. She placed the book within easy reach.

She said, 'I think my father would say you were very nice, Doctor Nordenfeld, to look after me so well.'

'No-o-o-o,' said the doctor in a detached voice. 'I'm just doing what anybody ought to do.'

She snuggled down under the covers. He looked at his watch and shrugged. It was very easy to confuse official night with official day, in space. Everybody else was asleep. He'd been putting Kathy through tests which began with measurements of pulse and respiration and temperature and went on from there. Kathy managed them herself, under his direction.

He settled down with one of the medical books he had brought into the isolation section with him. Its title was *Decontamination of Infectious Material from Different Planets*. He read it grimly.

The time came when the *Star Queen* should have come out of overdrive with the sun Circe blazing fiercely near by, and a green planet with ice caps to be approached on interplanetary drive. There should have been droning, comforting drive noises to assure the passengers—who naturally could not see beyond the ship's steel walls—that they were within a mere few million miles of a world where sunshine was normal, and skies were higher than ship's ceilings, and there were fascinating things to see and do.

Some of the passengers packed their luggage and put it outside their cabins to be picked up for landing. But no stewards came for it. Presently there was an explanation. The ship had run under maximum speed and the planetfall would be delayed.

The passengers were disappointed but not concerned. The luggage vanished into cabins again.

The *Star Queen* floated in space among a thousand thousand million stars. Her astrogators had computed a course to the nearest star into which to drive the *Star Queen*, but it would not be used unless there was mutiny among the crew. It would be better to go in remote orbit around Circe III and give the news of chlorophage on Altaira, if Doctor Nordenfeld reported it on the ship.

Time passed. One day. Two. Three. Then Jensen called the hospital compartment on vision-phone. His expression was dazed. Nordenfeld saw the interior of the control room behind Jensen. He said, 'You're a passenger, Jensen. How is it you're in the control room?'

Jensen moistened his lips. 'The skipper thought I'd better not associate with the other passengers. I've stayed with the officers the past few days. We—the ones who know what's in prospect—we're keeping separate from the others so—nobody will let anything out by accident.'

'Very wise. When the skipper comes back on duty, ask him to call me. I've something interesting to tell him.'

'He's—checking something now,' said Jensen. His voice was thin and reedy. 'The—air officer reports there are white patches on the plants in the air room. They're growing. Fast. He told me to tell you. He's—gone to make sure.'

'No need,' said Nordenfeld bitterly.

He swung the vision-screen. It faced that part of the hospital space beyond the plastic sheeting. There were potted flowering plants there. They had pleased Kathy. They shared her air. And there were white patches on their leaves.

'I thought,' said Nordenfeld with an odd mirthless levity, 'that the skipper'd be interested. It is of no importance whatever now, but I accomplished something remarkable. Kathy's father didn't manage an aseptic transfer.

She brought the chlorophage with her. But I confined it. The plants on the far side of that plastic sheet show the chlorophage patches plainly. I expect Kathy to show signs of anaemia shortly. I'd decided that drastic measures would have to be taken, and it looked as if they might work, because I've confined the virus. It's there where Kathy is, but it isn't where I am. All the botanical specimens on my side of the sheet are untouched. The phage hasn't hit them. It is remarkable. But it doesn't matter a damn if the air room's infected. And I was so proud!'

Jensen did not respond.

Nordenfeld said ironically, 'Look what I accomplished! I protected the air plants on my side. See? They're beautifully green! No sign of infection! It means that a man can work with chlorophage! A laboratory ship could land on Kamerun and keep itself the equivalent of an aseptic-environment room while the damned chlorophage was investigated and ultimately whipped! And it doesn't matter!'

Jensen said numbly, 'We can't ever make port. We ought—we ought to——'

'We'll take the necessary measures,' Nordenfeld told him. 'Very quietly and very efficiently, with neither the crew nor the passengers knowing that Altaira sent the chlorophage on board the *Star Queen* in the hope of banishing it from there. The passengers won't know that their own officials shipped it off with them as they tried to run away . . . And I was so proud that I'd improvised an aseptic room to keep Kathy in! I sterilized the air that went into her, and I sterilized——

Then he stopped. He stopped quite short. He stared at the air unit, set up and with two pipes passing through the plastic partition which cut the hospital space in two. He turned utterly white. He went roughly to the air machine. He jerked back its cover. He put his hand inside.

Minutes later he faced back to the vision-screen from which Jensen looked apathetically at him.

'Tell the skipper to call me,' he said in a savage tone. 'Tell him to call me instantly he comes back! Before he issues any orders at all!'

He bent over the sterilizing equipment and very carefully began to disassemble it. He had it completely apart when Kathy waked. She peered at him through the plastic separation sheet.

"Good morning, Doctor Nordenfeld,' she said cheerfully.

The doctor grunted. Kathy smiled at him. She had got on very good terms with the doctor, since she'd been kept in the ship's hospital. She did not feel that she was isolated. In having the doctor where she could talk to him at any time, she had much more company than ever before. She had read her entire picture book to him and discussed her doll at length. She took it for granted that when he did not answer or frowned that he was simply busy. But he was company because she could see him.

Doctor Nordenfeld put the air apparatus together with an extremely peculiar expression on his face. It had been built for Kathy's special isolation by a ship's mechanic. It should sterilize the used air going into Kathy's part of the compartment, and it should sterilize the used air pushed out by the supplied fresh air. The hospital itself was an independent sealed unit, with its own chemical air freshener, and it had been divided into two. The air freshener was where Doctor Nordenfeld could attend to it, and the sterilizer pump simply shared the freshening with Kathy. But——

But the pipe that pumped air to Kathy was brown and discoloured from having been used for sterilizing, and the pipe that brought air back was not. It was cold. It had never been heated.

So Doctor Nordenfeld had been exposed to any contagion Kathy could spread. He hadn't been protected at all. Yet the potted plants on Kathy's side of the barrier were marked with great white splotches which grew almost as one looked, while the botanical specimens in the doctor's part of the hospital—as much infected as Kathy's could have been, by failure of the ship's mechanic to build the sterilizer to work two ways: the stacked plants, the alien plants, the strange plants from seventy light-years beyond Regulus—they were vividly green. There was no trace of chlorophage on them. Yet they had been as thoroughly exposed as Doctor Nordenfeld himself!

The doctor's hands shook. His eyes burned. He took out a surgeon's scalpel and ripped the plastic partition from floor to ceiling. Kathy watched interestedly.

'Why did you do that, Doctor Nordenfeld?' she asked.

He said in an emotionless, unnatural voice, 'I'm going to do something that it was very stupid of me not to do before. It should have been done when you were six years old, Kathy. It should have been done on Kamerun, and after that on Altaira. Now we're going to do it here. You can help me.'

The *Star Queen* had floated out of overdrive long enough to throw all distance computations off. But she swung about, and swam back, and presently she was not too far from the world where she was now many days overdue. Lift-ships started up from the planet's surface. But the *Star Queen* ordered them back.

'Get your spaceport health officer on the vision-phone,' ordered the *Star Queen*'s skipper. 'We've had chlorophage on board.'

There was a panic. Even at a distance of a hundred thousand miles, chlorophage could strike stark terror into anybody. But presently the image of the spaceport health officer appeared on the *Star Queen*'s screen.

'We're not landing,' said Doctor Nordenfeld. 'There's almost certainly an outbreak of chlorophage on Altaira, and we're going back to do something about it. It got on our ship with passengers from there. We've whipped it, but we may need some help.'

The image of the health officer aground was a mask of horror for seconds after Nordenfeld's last statement. Then his expression became incredulous, though still horrified.

'We came on to here,' said Doctor Nordenfeld, 'to get you to send word by the first possible ship to the Patrol that a quarantine must be set up on Altaira, and we need to be inspected for recovery from chlorophage infection. And we need to pass on, officially, the discovery that whipped the contagion on this ship. We were carrying botanical specimens to Cassim and we discovered that they were immune to chlorophage. That's absurd, of course. Their green colouring is the same substance as in plants under Sol-type suns anywhere. They couldn't be immune to chlorophage. So there had to be something else.'

'Was—was there?' asked the health officer.

'There was. Those specimens came from somewhere beyond Regulus. They carried, as normal symbiotes on their foliage, micro-organisms unknown both on Kamerun and Altaira. The alien bugs are almost the size of virus particles, feed on virus particles, and are carried by contact, air, and so on, as readily as virus particles themselves. We discovered that those micro-organisms devoured chlorophage. We washed them off the leaves of the plants, sprayed them in our air-room jungle, and they multiplied faster than the chlorophage. Our whole air supply is now loaded with an airborne anti-chlorophage organism which has made our crew and passengers immune. We're heading back to Altaira to turn loose our merry little bugs on that planet. It appears that they grow on certain vegetation, but they'll live anywhere there's phage to eat. We're keeping some chlorophage cultures alive so our micro-organisms don't die out for lack of food!'

The medical officer on the ground gasped. 'Keeping phage *alive*?'

'I hope you've recorded this,' said Nordenfeld. 'It's rather important. This trick should have been tried on Kamerun and Altaira and everywhere else new diseases have turned up. When there's a bug on one planet that's deadly to us, there's bound to be a bug on some other planet that's deadly to it! The same goes for any pests or vermin—the principle of natural enemies. All we have to do is find the enemies!'

There was more communication between the *Star Queen* and the spaceport on Circe III, which the *Star Queen* would not make other contact with on this trip, and presently the big liner headed back to Altaira. It was necessary for official as well as humanitarian reasons. There would need to be a health examination of the *Star Queen* to certify that it was safe for passengers to breathe her air and eat in her restaurants and swim in her swimming pools and occupy the six levels of passenger cabins she contained. This would have to be done by a Patrol ship, which would turn up at Altaira.

The *Star Queen*'s skipper would be praised by his owners for not having driven the liner into a star, and the purser would be forgiven for the confusion in his records due to off-schedule operations of the big ship, and Jensen would find in the ending of all terror of chlorophage an excellent reason to look for appreciation in the value of the investments he was checking up. And Doctor Nordenfeld. . . .

He talked very gravely to Kathy. 'I'm afraid,' he told her, 'that your father isn't coming back. What would you like to do?'

She smiled at him hopefully. 'Could I be your little girl?' she asked.

Doctor Nordenfeld grunted. 'Hm . . . I'll think about it.'

But he smiled at her. She grinned at him. And it was settled.

CONSIDER HER WAYS

JOHN WYNDHAM

Was the strange world, in which Dr. Jane Waterleigh found herself reluctantly playing a grotesque part, a nightmare? Or must it be part of the future? And could she really prevent it from coming to pass?

There was nothing but myself.

I hung in a timeless, spaceless, forceless void that was neither light, nor dark. I had entity, but no form; awareness, but no senses; mind, but no memory. I wondered, is this—this nothingness—my soul? And it seemed that I had wondered that always, and should go on wondering it for ever. . . .

But, somehow, timelessness ceased. I became aware that there *was* a force: that I was being moved, and that spacelessness had, therefore, ceased, too. There was nothing to show that I moved; I knew simply that I was being drawn. I felt happy because I knew there was something or someone to whom I wanted to be drawn. I had no other wish than to turn like a compass-needle, and then fall through the void. . . .

But I was disappointed. No smooth, swift fall followed. Instead, other forces fastened on me. I was pulled this way, and then that. I did not know how I knew it; there was no outside reference, no fixed point, no direction, even; yet I could feel that I was tugged hither and thither, as though against the resistance of some inner gyroscope. It was as if one force were in command of me for a time, only to weaken and lose me to a new force. Then I would seem to slide towards an unknown point, until I was arrested, and diverted upon another course. I wafted this way and that, with the sense of awareness continually growing firmer; and I wondered whether rival forces were fighting for me, good and evil, perhaps, or life and death. .

The sense of pulling back and forth became more definite until I was almost jerked from one course to another. Then abruptly, the feeling of struggle finished. I had a sense of travelling faster and faster still, plunging like a wandering meteorite that had been trapped at last. . . .

'All right,' said a voice. 'Resuscitation was a little retarded, for some reason. Better make a note of that on her card. What's the number? Oh, only her fourth time. Yes, certainly make a note. It's all right. Here she comes!'

It was a woman's voice speaking, with a slightly unfamiliar accent. The surface I was lying on shook under me. I opened my eyes, saw the ceiling moving along above me, and let them close. Presently, another voice, again with an unfamiliar intonation, spoke to me:

'Drink this,' she said.

A hand lifted my head, and a cup was pressed against my lips. After I had drunk the stuff I lay back with my eyes closed again. I dozed for a little while, and came out of it feeling stronger. For some minutes I lay looking up at the ceiling and wondering vaguely where I was. I could not recall any ceiling that was painted like this pinkish shade of cream. Then, suddenly, while I was still gazing up at the ceiling, I was shocked, just as if something had hit my mind a sharp blow. I was frighteningly aware that it was not just the pinkish ceiling that was unfamiliar—*everything* was unfamiliar. Where there should have been memories there was just a great gap. I had no idea who I was, or where I was; I could recall nothing of how or why I came to be here. . . . In a rush of panic I tried to sit up, but a hand pressed me back, and presently held the cup to my lips again.

'You're quite all right. Just relax,' the same voice told me, reassuringly.

I wanted to ask questions, but somehow I felt immensely weary, and everything was too much trouble. The first rush of panic subsided, leaving me lethargic. I wondered what had happened to me—had I been in an accident, perhaps? Was this the kind of thing that happened when one was badly shocked? I did not know, and now for the moment I did not care: I was being looked after. I felt so drowsy that the questions could wait.

I suppose I dozed, and it may have been for a few minutes, or for an hour. I know only that when I opened my eyes again I felt calmer—more puzzled than alarmed—and I lay for a time without moving. I had recovered enough grasp now to console myself with the thought that if there had been an accident, at least there was no pain.

Presently I gained a little more energy, and, with it, curiosity to know where I was. I rolled my head on the pillow to see more of the surroundings.

A few feet away I saw a contrivance on wheels, something between a bed and a trolley. On it, asleep with her mouth open, was the most enormous woman I had ever seen. I stared, wondering whether it was some kind of cage over her to take the weight of the covers that gave her the mountainous look, but the movement of her breathing soon showed me that it was not. Then I looked beyond her and saw two more trolleys, both supporting equally enormous women.

I studied the nearest one more closely, and discovered to my surprise that she was quite young—not more than twenty-two, or twenty-three, I guessed. Her face was a little plump, perhaps, but by no means over-fat; indeed, with her fresh, healthy young colouring and her short-cropped gold curls, she was quite pretty. I fell to wondering what curious disorder of the glands could cause such a degree of anomaly at her age.

Ten minutes or so passed, and there was a sound of brisk, businesslike footsteps approaching. A voice inquired:

'How are you feeling now?'

I rolled my head to the other side, and found myself looking into a face almost level with my own. For a moment I thought its owner must be a child, then I saw that the features under the white cap were certainly not less than thirty years old. Without waiting for a reply she reached under the bedclothes and took my pulse. Its rate appeared to satisfy her, for she nodded confidently.

'You'll be all right now, Mother,' she told me.

I stared at her, blankly.

'The car's only just outside the door there. Do you think you can walk to it?' she went on.

Bemusedly, I asked:

'What car?'

'Why, to take you home, of course,' she said, with professional patience. 'Come along now.' And she pulled away the bedclothes.

I started to move, and looked down. What I saw there held me fixed. I lifted my arm. It was like nothing so much as a plump, white bolster with a ridiculous little hand attached at the end. I stared at it in horror. Then I heard a far-off scream as I fainted. . . .

When I opened my eyes again there was a woman—a normal-sized woman—in a white overall with a stethoscope round her neck, frowning at me in perplexity. The white-capped woman I had taken for a child stood beside her, reaching only a little above her elbow.

'—I don't know, Doctor,' she was saying. 'She just suddenly screamed, and fainted.'

'What is it? What's happened to me? I know I'm not like this—I'm not, I'm not,' I said, and I could hear my own voice wailing the words.

The doctor went on looking puzzled.

'What does she mean?' she asked.

'I've no idea, Doctor,' said the small woman. 'It was quite sudden, as if she'd had some kind of shock—but I don't know why.'

'Well, she's been passed and signed off, and, anyway, she can't stay here. We need the room,' said the doctor. 'I'd better give her a sedative.'

'But what's happened? Who am I? There's something terribly wrong. I know I'm not like this. P-please t-tell me——' I implored her, and then somehow lost myself in a stammer and a muddle.

The doctor's manner became soothing. She laid a hand gently on my shoulder.

'That's all right, Mother. There's nothing to worry about. Just take things quietly. We'll soon have you back home.'

Another white-capped assistant, no taller than the first, hurried up with a syringe, and handed it to the doctor.

'No!' I protested. 'I want to know where I am. Who am I? Who are you? What's happened to me?' I tried to slap the syringe out of her hand, but both the small assistants flung themselves on my arm, and held on to it while she pressed in the needle.

It was a sedative, all right. It did not put me out, but it detached me. An odd feeling: I seemed to be floating a few feet outside myself and considering me with an unnatural calmness. I was able, or felt I was able, to evaluate matters with intelligent clarity. . . .

Evidently I was suffering from amnesia. A shock of some kind had caused me to 'lose my memory', as it is often put. Obviously it was only a very small part of my memory that had gone—just the personal part, who I was, what I was, where I lived—all the mechanism for day-to-day getting along seemed to be intact: I'd not forgotten how to talk, or how to think, and I seemed to have quite a well-stored mind to think with.

On the other hand there was a nagging conviction that everything about me was somehow *wrong*. I *knew*, somehow, that I'd never before seen the place I was in; I *knew*, too, that there was something queer about the presence of the two small nurses; above all, I *knew*, with absolute certainty, that this massive form lying here was not mine. I could not recall what face I ought to see in a mirror, not even whether it would be dark or fair, or old or young, but there was no shadow of doubt in my mind that whatever it was like, it had never topped such a shape as I had now. —And there were the other enormous young women, too. Obviously, it could not be a matter of glandular disorder in all of us, or there'd not be this talk of sending me 'home', wherever that might be. . . .

I was still arguing the situation with myself in, thanks no doubt to the sedative, a most reasonable-seeming manner, though without making any progress at all, when the ceiling above my head began to move again, and I realized I was being wheeled along. Doors opened at the end of the room, and the trolley tilted a little beneath me as we went down a gentle ramp beyond.

At the foot of the ramp, an ambulance-like car, with pink coachwork polished until it gleamed, was waiting with the rear doors open. I observed interestedly that I was playing a part in a routine procedure. A team of eight diminutive attendants carried out the task of transferring me from the trolley to a sprung couch in the ambulance as if it were a kind of drill. Two of them lingered after the rest to tuck in my coverings and place another pillow behind my head. Then they got out, closing the doors behind them, and in a minute or two we started off.

It was at this point—and possibly the sedative helped in this, too—that I began to have an increasing sense of balance and a feeling that I was perceiving the situation. Probably there *had* been an accident, as I had suspected, but obviously my error, and the chief cause of my alarm, proceeded from my assumption that I was a stage farther on than I actually was. I had assumed that after an interval I had recovered consciousness in these baffling circumstances, whereas the true state of affairs must clearly be that I had *not* recovered consciousness. I must still be in a suspended state, very likely with concussion, and this was a dream, or hallucination. Presently, I should wake up in conditions that would at least be sensible, if not necessarily familiar.

I wondered now that this consoling and stabilizing thought had not occurred to me before, and decided that it was the alarming sense of detailed reality that had thrown me into panic. It had been astonishingly stupid of me to be taken in to the extent of imagining that I was really a kind of Gulliver among rather oversize Lilliputians. It was quite characteristic of most dreams, too, that I should lack a clear knowledge of my identity, so we did not need to be surprised at that. The thing to do was to take an intelligent interest in all I observed: the whole thing must be chock-full of symbolic content which it would be most interesting to work out later.

The discovery quite altered my attitude and I looked

about me with a new attention. It struck me as odd right away that there was so much circumstantial detail, and all of it in focus—there was none of that sense of foreground in sharp relief against a muzzy, or even non-existent, background that one usually meets in a dream. Everything was presented with a most convincing, three-dimensional solidity. My own sensations, too, seemed perfectly valid. The injection, in particular, had been quite acutely authentic. The illusion of reality fascinated me into taking mental notes with some care.

The interior of the van, or ambulance, or whatever it was, was finished in the same shell-pink as the outside—except for the roof, which was powder-blue with a scatter of small silver stars. Against the front partition were mounted several cupboards, with plated handles. My couch, or stretcher, lay along the left side: on the other were two fixed seats, rather small, and upholstered in a semi-glazed material to match the colour of the rest. Two long windows on each side left little solid wall. Each of them was provided with curtains of a fine net, gathered back now in pink braid loops, and had a roller blind furled above it. Simply by turning my head on the pillow I was able to observe the passing scenery—though somewhat jerkily, for either the springing of the vehicle scarcely matched its appointments, or the road surface was bad: whichever the cause, I was glad my own couch was independently and quite comfortably sprung.

The external view did not offer a great deal of variety save in its hues. Our way was lined by buildings standing back behind some twenty yards of tidy lawn. Each block was three storeys high, about fifty yards long, and had a tiled roof of somewhat low pitch, suggesting a vaguely Italian influence. Structurally the blocks appeared identical, but each was differently coloured, with contrasting window-frames and doors, and carefully considered, uniform curtains. I could see no one behind the windows, indeed there appeared to be no one about at all except here and there a woman in overalls mowing a lawn, or tending one of the inset flower-beds.

Farther back from the road, perhaps two hundred yards away, stood larger, taller, more utilitarian-looking blocks, some of them with high, factory-type chimneys. I thought they might actually be factories of some kind, but at the distance, and because I had no more than fugitive views of them between the foreground blocks, I could not be sure.

The road itself seldom ran straight for more than a hundred yards at a stretch, and its windings made one wonder whether the builders had not been more concerned to follow a contour line than a direction. There was little other traffic, and what there was consisted of lorries, large or small, mostly large. They were painted in one primary colour or other, with only a five-fold combination of letters and figures on their sides for further identification. In design they might have been any lorries anywhere.

We continued this uneventful progress at a modest pace for some twenty minutes, until we came to a stretch where the road was under repair. The car slowed, and the workers moved to one side, out of our way. As we crawled forward over the broken surface I was able to get a good look at them. They were all women or girls dressed in denim-like trousers, sleeveless singlets, and working boots. All had their hair cut quite short, and a few wore hats. They were tall and broad-shouldered, bronzed and healthy-looking. The biceps of their arms were like a man's, and the shafts of their picks and shovels rested in the hard, strong hands of manual toilers.

They watched with concern as the car edged its way on

to the rough patch, but when it drew level with them they transferred their attention, and jostled and craned to look inside at me.

They smiled widely, showing strong white teeth in their browned faces. All of them raised their right hands, making some sign to me, still smiling. Their goodwill was so evident that I smiled back. They walked along, keeping pace with the crawling car, looking at me expectantly while their smiles faded into puzzlement. They were saying something but I could not hear the words. Some of them insistently repeated the sign. Their disappointed look made it clear that I was expected to respond with more than a smile. The only way that occurred to me was to raise my own right hand in imitation of their gesture. It was at least a qualified success; their faces brightened though a rather puzzled look remained. Then the car lurched on to the made-up road again, and their still somewhat troubled faces slid back as we speeded up to our former sedate pace. More dream symbols, of course—but certainly not one of the stock symbols from the book. What on earth, I wondered, could a party of friendly Amazons, equipped with navvying implements instead of bows, stand for in my subconscious? Something frustrated, I imagined. A suppressed desire to dominate? I did not seem to be getting much farther along that line when we passed the last of the variegated but nevertheless monotonous blocks, and ran into open country.

The flower-beds had shown me already that it was spring, and now I was able to look on healthy pastures, and neat arable fields already touched with green; there was a haze like green smoke along the trim hedges, and some of the trees in the tidily placed spinneys were in young leaf. The sun was shining with a bright benignity upon the most precise countryside I have ever seen; only the cattle dotted about the fields introduced a slight disorder into the careful dispositions. The farmhouses themselves were part of the pattern; hollow squares of neat buildings with an acre or so of vegetable garden on one side, an orchard on another, and a rickyard on a third. There was a suggestion of a doll's landscape about it—Grandma Moses, but tidied up and rationalized. I could see no random cottages, casually sited sheds, or unplanned outgrowths from the farm buildings. And what, I asked myself, should we conclude from this rather pathological exhibition of tidiness? That I was a more uncertain person than I had supposed, one who was subconsciously yearning for simplicity and security? Well, well. . . .

An open lorry which must have been travelling ahead of us turned off down a lane bordered by beautifully laid hedges, towards one of the farms. There were half a dozen young women in it, holding implements of some kind; Amazons, again. One of them, looking back, drew the attention of the rest to us. They raised their hands in the same sign that the others had made, and then waved cheerfully. I waved back.

Rather bewildering, I thought: Amazons for domination *and* this landscape, for passive security: the two did not seem to tie up very well.

We trundled on, at our unambitious pace of twenty miles an hour or so, for what I guessed to be three-quarters of an hour, with the prospect changing very little. The country undulated gently and appeared to continue like that to the foot of a line of low, blue hills many miles away. The tidy farmhouses went by with almost the regularity of milestones, though with something like twice the frequency. Occasionally there were working-parties in the fields; more rarely, one saw individuals busy about the farm, and others hoeing with tractors, but they were all too far off for me to make out any details. Presently, however, came a change.

Off to the left of the road, stretching back at right-angles to it for more than a mile, appeared a row of trees. At first I thought it just a wood, but then I noticed that the trunks were evenly spaced, and the trees themselves topped and pruned until they gave more the impression of a high fence.

The end of it came to within twenty feet of the road, where it turned, and we ran along beside it for almost half a mile until the car slowed, turned to the left and stopped in front of a pair of tall gates. There were a couple of toots on the horn.

The gates were ornamental, and possibly of wrought iron under their pink paint. The archway that they barred was stucco-covered, and painted the same colour.

Why, I inquired of myself, this prevalence of pink, which I regard as a namby-pamby colour, anyway? Flesh-colour? Symbolic of an ardency for the flesh which I had insufficiently gratified? I scarcely thought so. Not pink. Surely a burning red . . . I don't think I know anyone who can be really ardent in a pink way. . . .

While we waited, a feeling that there was something wrong with the gatehouse grew upon me. The structure was a single-storey building, standing against the left, inner side of the archway, and coloured to match it. The woodwork was pale blue, and there were white net curtains at the windows. The door opened, and a middle-aged woman in a white blouse-and-trouser suit came out. She was bare-headed, with a few grey locks in her short, dark hair. Seeing me, she raised her hand in the same sign the Amazons had used, though perfunctorily, and walked over to open the gates. It was only as she pushed them back to admit us that I suddenly saw how small she was—certainly not over four feet tall. And that explained what was wrong with the gatehouse: it was built entirely to her scale. . . .

I went on staring at her and her little house as we passed. Well, what about that? Mythology is rich in gnomes and 'little people', and they are fairly pervasive of dreams, too, so somebody, I am sure, must have decided that they are a standard symbol of something, but for the moment I did not recall what it was. Would it be repressed philoprogenitiveness, or was that too unsubtle? I stowed that away, too, for later contemplation and brought my attention back to the surroundings.

We were on our way, unhurriedly, along something more like a drive than a road, with surroundings that suggested a compromise between a public garden and a municipal housing-estate. There were wide lawns of an unblemished velvet green, set here and there with flowerbeds, delicate groups of silver birch, and occasional, larger, single trees. Among them stood pink, three-storey blocks, dotted about, seemingly to no particular plan.

A couple of the Amazon types in singlets and trousers of a faded rust-red were engaged in planting-out a bed close beside the drive, and we had to pause while they dragged their handcart full of tulips on to the grass to let us pass. They gave me the usual salute and amiable grin as we went by.

A moment later I had a feeling that something had gone wrong with my sight, for as we passed one block we came in sight of another. It was white instead of pink, but otherwise exactly similar to the rest—except that it was scaled down by at least one-third. . . .

I blinked at it and stared hard, but it continued to seem just the same size.

A little farther on, a grotesquely huge woman in pink draperies was walking slowly and heavily across a lawn.

She was accompanied by three of the small, white-suited women looking, in contrast, like children, or very animated dolls: one was involuntarily reminded of tugs fussing round a liner.

I began to feel swamped: the proliferation and combination of symbols was getting well out of my class.

The car forked to the right, and presently we drew up before a flight of steps leading to one of the pink buildings —a normal-sized building, but still not free from oddity, for the steps were divided by a central balustrade; those to the left of it were normal, those to the right, smaller and more numerous.

Three toots on the horn announced our arrival. In about ten seconds half a dozen small women appeared in the doorway and came running down the right-hand side of the steps. A door slammed as the driver got out and went to meet them. When she came into my range of view I saw that she was one of the little ones, too, but not in white as the rest were; she wore a shining pink suit like a livery that exactly matched the car.

They had a word together before they came round to open the door behind me, then a voice said brightly;

'Welcome, Mother Orchis. Welcome home.'

The couch, or stretcher, slid back on runners, and between them they lowered it to the ground. One young woman whose blouse was badged with a pink St. Andrew's cross on the left breast leaned over me. She inquired considerately:

'Do you think you can walk, Mother?'

It did not seem the moment to inquire into the form of address. I was obviously the only possible target for the question.

'Walk?' I repeated. 'Of course I can walk.' And I sat up, with about eight hands assisting me.

'Of course' had been an overstatement. I realized that by the time I had been heaved to my feet. Even with all the help that was going on around me it was an exertion which brought on heavy breathing. I looked down at the monstrous form that billowed under my pink draperies, with sickly revulsion and a feeling that whatever this particular mass of symbolism disguised, it was likely to prove a distasteful revelation later on. I tried a step. 'Walk' was scarcely the word for my progress. It felt like, and must have looked like, a slow series of forward surges. The women, at little more than my elbow height, fluttered about me like a flock of anxious hens. Once started, I was determined to go on, and I progressed with a kind of wave-motion, first across a few yards of gravel, and then, with ponderous deliberation, up the left-hand side of the steps.

There was a perceptible sense of relief and triumph all round as I reached the summit. We paused there a few moments for me to regain my breath, then we moved on into the building. A corridor led straight ahead, with three or four closed doors on each side; at the end it branched right and left. We took the left arm, and, at the end of it, I came face to face, for the first time since the hallucination had set in, with a mirror.

It took every volt of my resolution not to panic again at what I saw in it. The first few seconds of my stare were spent in fighting down a leaping hysteria.

In front of me stood an outrageous travesty: an elephantine female form, looking the more huge for its pink swathings. Mercifully, they covered everything but the head and hands, but these exposures were themselves another kind of shock, for the hands, though soft and dimpled and looking utterly out of proportion, were not uncomely, and the head and face were those of a girl.

She was pretty, too. She could not have been more than

twenty-one, if that. Her curling fair hair was touched with auburn lights, and cut in a kind of bob. The complexion of her face was pink and cream, her mouth was gentle, and red without any artifice. She looked back at me, and at the little women anxiously clustering round me, from a pair of blue-green eyes beneath lightly arched brows. And this delicate face, this little Fragonard, was set upon that monstrous body: no less outrageously might a blossom of freesia sprout from a turnip.

When I moved my lips, hers moved; when I bent my arm, hers bent; and yet, once I got the better of that threatening panic, she ceased to be a reflection. She was nothing like me, so she must be a stranger whom I was observing, though in a most bewildering way. My panic and revulsion gave way to sadness, an aching pity for her. I could weep for the shame of it. I did. I watched the tears brim over on her lower lids; mistily, I saw them overflow.

One of the little women beside me caught hold of my hand. 'Mother Orchis, dear, what's the matter?' she asked, full of concern.

I could not tell her: I had no clear idea myself. The image in the mirror shook her head, with tears running down her cheeks. Small hands patted me here and there; small, soothing voices encouraged me onward. The next door was opened for me and I was led into the room beyond, amid concerned fussing.

We entered a place that struck me as a cross between a boudoir and a ward. The boudoir impression was sustained by a great deal of pink—in the carpet, coverlets, cushions, lampshades, and filmy window-curtains; the ward motif, by an array of six divans, or couches, one of which was unoccupied.

It was a large enough room for three couches, separated by a chest, chair and table for each, to be arranged on either side without an effect of crowding, and the open space in the middle was still big enough to contain several expansive easy-chairs and a central table bearing an intricate flower-arrangement. A not-displeasing scent faintly pervaded the place, and from somewhere came the subdued sound of a string-quartet in a sentimental mood. Five of the bed-couches were already mountainously occupied. Two of my attendant party detached themselves and hurried ahead to turn back the pink satin cover on the sixth.

Faces from all the five other beds were turned towards me. Three of them smiling in welcome, the other two less committal.

'Hallo, Orchis,' one of them greeted me in a friendly tone. Then, with a touch of concern she added: 'What's the matter, dear? Did you have a bad time?'

I looked at her. She had a kindly, plumply pretty face, framed by light-brown hair as she lay back against a cushion. The face looked about twenty-three or twenty-four years old. The rest of her was a huge mound of pink satin. I couldn't make any reply, but I did my best to return her smile as we passed.

Our convoy hove to by the empty bed. After some preparation and positioning I was helped into it by all hands, and a cushion was arranged behind my head.

The exertion of my journey from the car had been considerable, and I was thankful to relax. While two of the little women pulled up the coverlet and arranged it over me, another produced a handkerchief and dabbed gently at my cheeks. She encouraged me:

'There you are, dear. Safely home again now. You'll be quite all right when you've rested a bit. Just try to sleep for a little.'

'What's the matter with her?' inquired a forthright voice from one of the other beds. 'Did she make a mess of it?'

The little woman with the handkerchief—she was the one who wore the St. Andrew's cross and appeared to be in charge of the operation—turned her head sharply.

'There's no need for that tone, Mother Hazel. Of course Mother Orchis had four beautiful babies—didn't you, dear?' she added to me. 'She's just a bit tired after the journey, that's all.'

'H'mph,' said the girl addressed, in an unaccommodating tone, but she made no further comment.

A degree of fussing continued. Presently the small woman handed me a glass of something that looked like water, but had unsuspected strength. I spluttered a little at the first taste, but quickly felt the better for it. After a little more tidying and ordering, my retinue departed leaving me propped against my cushion, with the eyes of the five other monstrous women dwelling upon me speculatively.

An awkward silence was broken by the girl who had greeted me as I came in.

'Where did they send you for your holiday, Orchis?'

'Holiday?' I asked blankly.

She and the rest stared at me in astonishment.

'I don't know what you're talking about,' I told them.

They went on staring, stupidly, stolidly.

'It can't have been much of a holiday,' observed one, obviously puzzled. 'I'll not forget my last one. They sent me to the sea, and gave me a little car so that I could get about everywhere. Everybody was lovely to us, and there were only six Mothers there, including me. Did you go by the sea, or in the mountains?'

They were determined to be inquisitive, and one would have to make some answer sooner or later. I chose what seemed the simplest way out for the moment.

'I can't remember,' I said. 'I can't remember a

thing. I seem to have lost my memory altogether.'

That was not very sympathetically received, either.

'Oh,' said the one who had been addressed as Hazel, with a degree of satisfaction. 'I thought there was something. And I suppose you can't even remember for certain whether your babies were Grade One this time, Orchis?'

'Don't be stupid, Hazel,' one of the others told her. 'Of course they were Grade One. If they'd not been, Orchis wouldn't be back here now—she'd have been re-rated as a Class Two Mother, and sent to Whitewich.' In a more kindly tone she asked me: 'When did it happen, Orchis?'

'I—I don't know,' I said. 'I can't remember anything before this morning at the hospital. It's all gone entirely.'

'Hospital!' repeated Hazel, scornfully.

'She must mean the Centre,' said the other. 'But do you mean to say you can't even remember *us*, Orchis?'

'No,' I admitted, shaking my head. 'I'm sorry, but everything before I came round in the Hosp—in the Centre, is all blank.'

'That's queer,' Hazel said, in an unsympathetic tone. 'Do they know?'

One of the others took my part.

'Of course they're bound to know. I expect they don't think that remembering or not has anything to do with having Grade One babies. And why should it, anyway? But look, Orchis——'

'Why not let her rest for a bit,' another cut in. 'I don't suppose she's feeling too good after the Centre, and the journey, and getting in here. I never do myself. Don't take any notice of them, Orchis, dear. You just go to sleep for a bit. You'll probably find it's quite all right when you wake up.'

I accepted her suggestion gratefully. The whole thing was

far too bewildering to cope with at the moment; moreover, I did feel exhausted. I thanked her for her advice, and lay back on my pillow. In so far as the closing of one's eyes can be made ostentatious, I made it so. What was more surprising was that, if one can be said to sleep within an hallucination or a dream, I slept. . . .

In the moment of waking, before opening my eyes, I had a flash of hope that I should find the illusion had spent itself. Unfortunately, it had not. A hand was shaking my shoulder gently, and the first thing that I saw was the face of the little women's leader, close to mine.

In the way of nurses, she said:

'There, Mother Orchis, dear. You'll be feeling a lot better after that nice sleep, won't you?'

Beyond her, two more of the small women were carrying a short-legged bed-tray towards me. They set it down so that it bridged me, and was convenient to reach. I stared at the load on it. It was, with no exception, the most enormous and nourishing meal I had ever seen put before one person. The first sight of it revolted me—but then I became aware of a schism within, for it did not revolt the physical form that I occupied: that, in fact, had a watering mouth, and was eager to begin. An inner part of me marvelled in a kind of semi-detachment while the rest consumed two or three fish, a whole chicken, some slices of meat, a pile of vegetables, fruit hidden under mounds of stiff cream, and more than a quart of milk, without any sense of surfeit. Occasional glances showed me that the other 'Mothers' were dealing just as thoroughly with the contents of their similar trays.

I caught one or two curious looks from them, but they were too seriously occupied to take up their inquisition again at the moment. I wondered how to fend them off later, and it occurred to me that if only I had a book or a magazine I might be able to bury myself effectively, if not very politely, in it.

When the attendants returned I asked the badged one if she could let me have something to read. The effect of such a simple request was astonishing: the two who were removing my tray all but dropped it. The one beside me gaped for an amazed moment before she collected her wits. She looked at me, first with suspicion, and then with concern.

'Not feeling quite yourself yet, dear?' she suggested.

'But I am,' I protested. 'I'm quite all right now.'

The look of concern persisted, however.

'If I were you I'd try to sleep again,' she advised.

'But I don't want to. I'd just like to read quietly,' I objected.

She patted my shoulder, a little uncertainly.

'I'm afraid you've had an exhausting time, Mother. Never mind. I'm sure it'll pass quite soon.'

I felt impatient. 'What's wrong with wanting to read?' I demanded.

She smile a smug, professional-nurse smile.

'There, there, dear. Just you try to rest a little more. Why, bless me, what on earth would a Mother want with knowing how to read?'

With that she tidied my coverlet, and bustled away, leaving me to the wide-eyed stares of my five companions. Hazel gave a kind of contemptuous snigger; otherwise there was no audible comment for several minutes.

I had reached a stage where the persistence of the hallucination was beginning to wear away my detachment. I could feel that under a little more pressure I should be losing my confidence and starting to doubt its unreality. I did not at all care for its calm continuity. Inconsequent exaggerations and jumps, foolish perspectives, indeed any of the usual dream characteristics would have been reassuring, but, instead, it continued to present obvious nonsense, with an alarming air of conviction and consequence. Effects, for instance, were unmistakably following causes. I began to have an uncomfortable feeling that were one to dig deep enough one might begin to find logical causes for the absurdities, too. The integration was far too good for mental comfort—even the fact that I had enjoyed my meal as if I were fully awake, and was consciously feeling the better for it, encouraged the disturbing quality of reality.

'Read!' Hazel said suddenly, with a scornful laugh. 'And write, too, I suppose?'

'Well, why not?' I retorted.

They all gazed at me more attentively than ever, and then exchanged meaning glances among themselves. Two of them smiled at one another. I demanded irritably: 'What on earth's wrong with that? Am I supposed not to be able to read or write, or something?'

One said kindly, soothingly:

'Orchis, dear. Don't you think it would be better if you were to ask to see the doctor? Just for a check-up?'

'No,' I told her flatly. 'There's nothing wrong with me. I'm just trying to understand. I simply ask for a book, and you all look at me as if I were mad. Why?'

After an awkward pause the same one said humouringly, and almost in the words of the little attendant:

'Orchis, dear, do try to pull yourself together. What sort of good would reading and writing be to a Mother? How could they help her to have better babies?'

'There are other things in life besides having babies,' I said, shortly.

If they had been surprised before, they were thunderstruck now. Even Hazel seemed bereft of suitable comment. Their idiotic astonishment exasperated me and made me suddenly sick of the whole nonsensical business. Temporarily, I *did* forget to be the detached observer of a dream.

'Damn it,' I broke out. 'What *is* all this rubbish? Orchis! Mother Orchis!—for God's sake! Where am I? Is this some kind of lunatic asylum?'

I stared at them, angrily, loathing the sight of them, wondering if they were all in some spiteful complicity against me. Somehow I was quite convinced in my own mind that whoever, or whatever I was, I was not a mother. I said so, forcibly, and then, to my annoyance, burst into tears.

For lack of anything else to use, I dabbed at my eyes with my sleeve. When I could see clearly again I found that four of them were looking at me with kindly concern. Hazel, however, was not.

'I said there was something queer about her,' she told the others, triumphantly. 'She's mad, that's what it is.'

The one who had been most kindly disposed before, tried again:

'But, Orchis, *of course* you are a Mother. You're a Class One Mother—with three births registered. Twelve fine Grade One babies, dear. You *can't* have forgotten that!'

For some reason I wept again. I had a feeling that something was trying to break through the blankness in my mind; but I did not know what it was, only that it made me feel intensely miserable.

'Oh, this is cruel, cruel! Why can't I stop it? Why won't it go away and leave me?' I pleaded. 'There's a horrible cruel mockery here—but I don't understand it. What's wrong with me? I'm not obsessional—I'm not—I—oh, can't somebody help me . . .?'

I kept my eyes tight shut for a time, willing with all my mind that the whole hallucination should fade and disappear.

But it did not. When I looked again they were still there, their silly, pretty faces gaping stupidly at me across the revolting mounds of pink satin.

'I'm getting out of this,' I said.

It was a tremendous effort to raise myself to a sitting position. I was aware of the rest watching me, wide-eyed, while I made it. I struggled to get my feet round and over the side of the bed, but they were all tangled in the satin coverlet and I could not reach to free them. It was the true, desperate frustration of a dream. I heard my voice pleading: 'Help me! Oh, Donald, darling, please help me. . . .'

And suddenly, as if the word 'Donald' had released a spring, something seemed to click in my head. The shutter in my mind opened, not entirely, but enough to let me know who I was. I understood, suddenly, where the cruelty had lain.

I looked at the others again. They were still staring half-bewildered, half-alarmed. I gave up the attempt to move, and lay back on my pillow again.

'You can't fool me any more,' I told them. 'I know who I am now.'

'But, Mother Orchis——' one began.

'Stop that,' I snapped at her. I seemed to have swung suddenly out of self-pity into a kind of masochistic callousness. 'I am *not* a mother,' I said harshly. 'I am just a woman who, for a short time, had a husband, and who hoped—but only hoped—that she would have babies by him.'

A pause followed that; a rather odd pause, where there should have been at least a murmur. What I had said did not seem to have registered. The faces showed no understanding; they were as uncomprehending as dolls.

Presently, the most friendly one seemed to feel an obligation to break up the silence. With a little vertical crease between her brows: 'What,' she inquired tentatively, 'what is a husband?'

I looked hard from one face to another. There was no trace of guile in any of them; nothing but puzzled speculation such as one sometimes sees in a child's eyes. I felt close to hysteria for a moment; then I took a grip of myself. Very well, then, since the hallucination would not leave me alone, I would play it at its own game, and see what came of that. I began to explain with a kind of deadpan, simple-word seriousness:

'A husband is a man whom a woman takes. . . .'

Evidently, from their expressions I was not very enlightening. However, they let me go on for three or four sentences without interruption. Then, when I paused for breath, the kindly one chipped in with a point which she evidently felt needed clearing up:

'But what,' she asked, in evident perplexity, 'what is a man?'

A cool silence hung over the room after my exposition. I had an impression I had been sent to Coventry, or semi-Coventry, by them, but I did not bother to test it. I was too much occupied trying to force the door of my memory further open, and finding that beyond a certain point it would not budge.

I knew now that I was Jane. I had been Jane Summers, and had become Jane Waterleigh when I had married Donald.

I was—had been—twenty-four when we were married: just twenty-five when Donald was killed, six months later. And there it stopped. It seemed like yesterday, but I couldn't tell. . . .

Before that, everything was perfectly clear. My parents and friends, my home, my school, my training, my job, as Dr. Summers, at the Wraychester Hospital. I could remember my first sight of Donald when they brought him in one evening with a broken leg—and all that followed....

I could remember now the face that I ought to see in a looking-glass—and it was certainly nothing like that I had seen in the corridor outside—it should be more oval, with a complexion looking faintly sun-tanned; with a smaller, neater mouth; surrounded by chestnut hair that curled naturally; with brown eyes rather wide apart and perhaps a little grave as a rule.

I knew, too, how the rest of me should look—slender, long-legged, with small, firm breasts—a nice body, but one that I had simply taken for granted until Donald gave me pride in it by loving it....

I looked down at the repulsive mound of pink satin, and shuddered. A sense of outrage came welling up. I longed for Donald to comfort and pet me and love me and tell me it would be all right; that I wasn't as I was seeing myself at all, and that it *really was* a dream. At the same time I was stricken with horror at the thought that he should ever see me gross and obese like this. And then I remembered that Donald would never see me again at all—never any more—and I was wretched and miserable, and the tears trickled down my cheeks again.

The five others just went on looking at me, wide-eyed and wondering. Half an hour passed, still in silence, then the door opened to admit a whole troop of the little women, all in white suits. I saw Hazel look at me, and then at the leader. She seemed about to speak, and then to change her mind. The little women split up, two to a couch. Standing one on each other, they stripped away the coverlet, rolled up their sleeves, and set to work at massage.

At first it was not unpleasant, and quite soothing. One lay back and relaxed. Presently, however, I liked it less: soon I found it offensive.

'Stop that!' I told the one on the right, sharply.

She paused, smiled at me amiably, though a trifle uncertainly, and then continued.

'I said stop it,' I told her, pushing her away.

Her eyes met mine. They were troubled and hurt, although a professional smile still curved her mouth.

'I mean it,' I added, curtly.

She continued to hesitate, and glanced across at her partner on the farther side of the bed.

'You, too,' I told the other. 'That'll do.'

She did not even pause in her rhythm. The one on the right plucked a decision and returned. She re-started just what I had stopped. I reached out and pushed her, harder this time. There must have been a lot more muscle in that bolster of an arm than one would have supposed. The shove carried her half across the room, and she tripped and fell.

All movement in the room suddenly ceased. Everybody stared, first at her, and then at me. The pause was brief. They all set to work again. I pushed away the girl on the left, too, though more gently. The other one picked herself up. She was crying and she looked frightened, but she set her jaw doggedly and started to come back.

'You keep away from me, you little horrors,' I told them threateningly.

That checked them. They stood off, and looked miserably at one another. The one with the badge of seniority fussed up.

'What's the trouble, Mother Orchis?' she inquired.

I told her. She looked puzzled.

'But that's quite right,' she expostulated.

'Not for me. I don't like it, and I won't have it,' I replied.

She stood awkwardly, at a loss.

Hazel's voice came from the other side of the room:

'Orchis is off her head. She's been telling us the most disgusting things. She's quite mad.'

The little woman turned to regard her, and then looked inquiringly at one of the others. When a girl confirmed with a nod and an expression of distaste she turned back to me, giving me a searching inspection.

'You two go and report,' she told my discomfited masseuses.

They were both crying now, and they went wretchedly down the room together. The one in charge gave me another thoughtful look, and then followed them.

A few minutes later all the rest had packed up and gone. The six of us were alone again. It was Hazel who broke the ensuing silence.

'That was a bitchy piece of work. The poor little devils were only doing their job,' she observed.

'If that's their job, I don't like it,' I told her.

'So you just get them a beating, poor things. But I suppose that's the lost memory again. You wouldn't remember that a Servitor who upsets a Mother is beaten, would you?' she added sarcastically.

'Beaten?' I repeated, uneasily.

'Yes, beaten,' she mimicked. 'But you don't care what becomes of them, do you? I don't know what's happened to you while you were away, but whatever it was it seems to have produced a thoroughly nasty result. I never did care for you, Orchis, though the others thought I was wrong. Well, now we all know.'

None of the rest offered any comment. The feeling that they shared her opinion was strong, but luckily I was spared confirmation by the opening of the door.

The senior attendant re-entered with half a dozen small myrmidons, but this time the group was dominated by a handsome woman of about thirty. Her appearance gave me immense relief. She was neither little, nor Amazonian, nor was she huge. Her present company made her look a little over-tall, perhaps, but I judged her at about five-foot-ten; a normal, pleasant-featured young woman with brown hair, cut somewhat short, and a pleated black skirt showing beneath a white overall. The senior attendant was almost trotting to keep up with her longer steps, and was saying something about delusions and 'only back from the Centre today, Doctor.'

The woman stopped beside my couch while the smaller women huddled together, looking at me with some misgiving. She thrust a thermometer into my mouth and held my wrist. Satisfied on both these counts, she inquired:

'Headache? Any other aches or pains?'

'No,' I told her.

She regarded me carefully. I looked back at her.

'What——?' she began.

'She's mad,' Hazel put in from the other side of the room. 'She says she's lost her memory and doesn't know us.'

'She's been talking about horrid, disgusting things,' added one of the others.

'She's got delusions. She thinks she can read and write,' Hazel supplemented.

The doctor smiled at that.

'Do you?' she asked me.

'I don't see why not—but it should be easy enough to prove,' I replied, brusquely.

She looked startled, a little taken aback, then she recovered her tolerant half-smile.

'All right,' she said, humouring me.

She pulled a small note-pad out of her pocket and offered it to me, with a pencil. The pencil felt a little odd in my hand; the fingers did not fall into place readily on it, nevertheless I wrote:

'I'm only too well aware that I have delusions—and that you are part of them.'

Hazel tittered as I handed the pad back.

The doctor's jaw did not actually drop, but her smile came right off. She looked at me very hard indeed. The rest of the room, seeing her expression, went quiet, as though I had performed some startling feat of magic. The doctor turned towards Hazel.

'What sort of things has she been telling you?' she inquired.

Hazel hesitated, then she blurted out:

'Horrible things. She's been talking about two human sexes—just as if we were like the animals. It was disgusting!'

The doctor considered a moment, then she told the senior attendant:

'Better get her along to the sick-bay. I'll examine her there.'

As she walked off there was a rush of little women to fetch a low trolley from the corner to the side of my couch. A dozen hands assisted me on to it, and then wheeled me briskly away.

'Now,' said the doctor grimly, 'let's get down to it. Who told you all this stuff about two human sexes? I want her name.'

We were alone in a small room with a gold-dotted pink wallpaper. The attendants, after transferring me from the trolley to a couch again, had taken themselves off. The doctor was sitting with a pad on her knee and a pencil at the ready. Her manner was that of an unbluffable inquisitor.

I was not feeling tactful. I told her not to be a fool.

She looked staggered, flushed with anger for a moment, and then took a hold on herself. She went on:

'After you left the Clinic you had your holiday, of course. Now, where did they send you?'

'I don't know,' I replied. 'All I can tell you is what I told the others—that this hallucination, or delusion, or whatever it is, started in that hospital place you call the Centre.'

With resolute patience she said:

'Look here, Orchis. You were perfectly normal when you left here six weeks ago. You went to the Clinic and had your babies in the ordinary way. *But* between then and now somebody has been filling your head with all this rubbish—and teaching you to read and write as well. Now you are going to tell me who that somebody was. I warn you that you won't get away with this loss of memory nonsense with me. If you are able to remember this nauseating stuff you told the others, then you're able to remember where you got it from.'

'Oh, for heaven's sake talk sense,' I told her.

She flushed again.

'I can find out from the Clinic where they sent you, and I can find out from the Rest Home who were your chief associates while you were there, but I don't want to waste time following up all your contacts, so I'm asking you to save trouble by telling me now. You might just as well. We don't want to have to *make* you talk,' she concluded, ominously.

I shook my head.

'You're on the wrong track. As far as I am concerned

this whole hallucination, including my connection with this Orchis, began somehow at the Centre—how it happened I can't tell you, and what happened to her before that just isn't there to be remembered.'

She frowned, obviously disturbed.

'What hallucination?' she inquired, carefully.

'Why, this fantastic set-up—and you, too.' I waved my hand to include it all. 'This revolting great body, all those little women, everything. Obviously it is all some projection of the subconscious—and the state of my subconscious is worrying me, for it's certainly no wish-fulfilment.'

She went on staring at me, more worried now.

'Who on earth has been telling you about the subconscious and wish-fulfilments?' she asked, uncertainly.

'I don't see why, even in an hallucination, I am expected to be an illiterate moron,' I replied.

'But a Mother doesn't know anything about such things. She doesn't need to.'

'Listen,' I said. 'I've told you, as I've told those poor grotesques in the other room, that I am *not* a Mother. What I am is just an unfortunate M.B. who is having some kind of nightmare.'

'M.B.?' she inquired, vaguely.

'Bachelor of Medicine. I practise medicine,' I told her.

She went on looking at me curiously. Her eyes wandered over my mountainous form, uncertainly.

'You are claiming to be a doctor?' she said, in an odd voice.

'Colloquially—yes,' I agreed.

There was indignation mixed with bewilderment as she protested:

'But this is sheer nonsense! You were brought up and

developed to be a Mother. You *are* a Mother. Just look at you!'

'Yes,' I said bitterly. 'Just look at me!'

There was a pause.

'It seems to me,' I suggested at last, 'that, hallucination or not, we shan't get much farther simply by going on accusing one another of talking nonsense. Suppose you explain to me what this place is, and who you think I am. It might jog my memory.'

She countered that. 'Suppose,' she said, 'that first you tell me what you *can* remember. It would give me more idea of what is puzzling you.'

'Very well,' I agreed, and launched upon a potted history of myself as far as I could recollect it—up to the time, that is to say, when Donald's aircraft crashed.

It was foolish of me to fall for that one. Of course, she had no intention of telling me anything. When she had listened to all I had to say, she went away, leaving me impotently furious.

I waited until the place quietened down. The music had been switched off. An attendant had looked in to inquire, with an air of polishing off the day's duties, whether there was anything I wanted, and presently there was nothing to be heard. I let a margin of half an hour elapse, and then struggled to get up—taking it by very easy stages this time. The greatest part of the effort was to get on to my feet from a sitting position, but I managed it at the cost of heavy breathing. Presently I crossed to the door, and found it unfastened. I held it a little open, listening. There was no sound of movement in the corridor, so I pulled it wide open, and set out to discover what I could about the place. All the doors of the rooms were shut. Putting my ear close to them I could hear regular, heavy breathing behind some but there were no other sounds in the stillness. I kept on, turning several corners, until I recognized the front door ahead of me. I tried the latch, and found that it was neither barred nor bolted. I paused again, listening for some moments, and then pulled it open and stepped outside.

The park-like garden stretched out before me, sharp-shadowed in the moonlight. Through the trees to the right was a glint of water, to the left was a house similar to the one behind me, with not a light showing in any of its windows.

I wondered what to do next. Trapped in this huge carcass, all but helpless in it, there was very little I could do, but I decided to go on and at least find out what I could while I had the chance. I went forward to the edge of the steps that I had earlier climbed from the ambulance, and started down them cautiously, holding on to the balustrade.

'Mother,' said a sharp, incisive voice behind me. 'What are you doing?'

I turned and saw one of the little women, her white suit gleaming in the moonlight. She was alone. I made no reply, but took another step down. I could have wept at the outrage of the heavy, ungainly body, and the caution it imposed on me.

'Come back. Come back at once,' she told me.

I took no notice. She came pattering down after me and laid hold of my draperies.

'Mother,' she said again. 'You must come back. You'll catch cold out here.'

I started to take another step, and she pulled at the draperies to hold me back. I leant forward against the pull. There was a sharp tearing sound as the material gave. I swung round, and lost my balance. The last thing I saw was the rest of the flight of steps coming up to meet me....

As I opened my eyes a voice said:

'That's better, but it was very naughty of you, Mother Orchis. And lucky it wasn't a lot worse. Such a silly thing to do. I'm ashamed of you—really I am.'

My head was aching, and I was exasperated to find that the whole stupid business was still going on; altogether, I was in no mood for reproachful drip. I told her to go to hell. Her small face goggled at me for a moment, and then became icily prim. She applied a piece of lint and plaster to the left side of my forehead, in silence, and then departed, stiffly.

Reluctantly, I had to admit to myself that she was perfectly right. What on earth had I been expecting to do —what on earth *could* I do, encumbered by this horrible mass of flesh? A great surge of loathing for it and a feeling of helpless frustration brought me to the verge of tears again. I longed for my own nice, slim body that pleased me and did what I asked of it. I remembered how Donald had once pointed to a young tree swaying in the wind, and introduced it to me as my twin sister. And only a day or two ago. . . .

Then, suddenly, I made a discovery which brought me struggling to sit up. The blank part of my mind had filled up. I could remember everything. . . . The effort made my head throb, so I relaxed and lay back once more, recalling it all, right up to the point where the needle was withdrawn and someone swabbed my arm. . . .

But what had happened after that? Dreams and hallucinations I had expected . . . but not the sharp-focused, detailed sense of reality . . . not this state which was like a nightmare made solid. . . .

What, what in heaven's name, had they done to me . . .?

I must have fallen asleep again, for when I opened my

eyes there was daylight outside, and a covey of little women had arrived to attend to my toilet.

They spread their sheets dexterously and rolled me this way and that with expert technique as they cleaned me up. I suffered their industry patiently, feeling the fresher for it, and glad to discover that the headache had all but gone.

When we were almost at the end of our ablutions there came a peremptory knock, and without invitation two figures, dressed in black uniforms with silver buttons, entered. They were the Amazon type, tall, broad, well set-up, and handsome. The little women dropped everything and fled with squeaks of dismay into the far corner of the room where they cowered in a huddle.

The two gave me the familiar salute. With an odd mixture of decision and deference one of them inquired:

'You are Orchis—Mother Orchis?'

'That's what they're calling me,' I admitted.

The girl hesitated, then, in a tone rather more pleading than ordering, she said:

'I have orders for your arrest, Mother. You will please come with us.'

An excited, incredulous twittering broke out among the little women in the corner. The uniformed girl quelled them with a look.

'Get the Mother dressed and make her ready,' she commanded.

The little women came out of their corner hesitantly, directing nervous, propitiatory glances towards the pair. The second one told them briskly, though not altogether unkindly:

'Come along now. Jump to it.'

They jumped.

I was almost swathed in my pink draperies again when the doctor strode in. She frowned at the two in uniform.

'What's all this? What are you doing here?' she demanded.

The leader of the two explained.

'Arrest!' exclaimed the doctor. 'Arrest a Mother! I never heard such nonsense. What's the charge?'

The uniformed girl said, a little sheepishly:

'She is accused of Reactionism.'

The doctor simply stared at her.

'A Reactionist Mother! What'll you people think of next? Go on, get out, both of you.'

The young woman protested:

'We have our orders, Doctor.'

'Rubbish. There's no authority. Have you ever heard of a Mother being arrested?'

'No, Doctor.'

'Well, you aren't going to make a precedent now. Go on.'

The uniformed girl hesitated unhappily, then an idea occurred to her.

'If you would let me have a signed refusal to surrender the Mother . . .?' she suggested helpfully.

When the two had departed, quite satisfied with their piece of paper, the doctor looked at the little women gloomily.

'You can't help tattling, you servitors, can you? Anything you happen to hear goes through the lot of you like a fire in a cornfield, and makes trouble all round. Well, if I hear any more of this I shall know where it comes from.' She turned to me. 'And you, Mother Orchis, will in future please restrict yourself to yes-and-no in the hearing of these nattering little pests. I'll see you again shortly. We want to ask you some questions,' she added, and went out, leaving a subdued, industrious silence behind her.

She returned just as the tray which held my gargantuan breakfast was being removed, and not alone. The four women who accompanied her, and looked as normal as herself, were followed by a number of little women lugging in chairs which they arranged beside my couch. When they had departed, the five women, all in white overalls, sat down and regarded me as if I were an exhibit. One appeared to be much the same age as the first doctor, two nearer fifty, and one sixty, or more.

'Now, Mother Orchis,' said the doctor, with an air of opening the proceedings, 'it is quite clear that something highly unusual has taken place. Naturally we are interested to understand just what and, if possible, why. You don't need to worry about those police this morning—it was quite improper of them to come here at all. This is simply an inquiry—a scientific inquiry—to establish what has happened.'

'You can't want to understand more than I do,' I replied. I looked at them, at the room about me, and finally at my massive prone form. 'I am aware that all this must be an hallucination, but what is troubling me most is that I have always supposed that any hallucination must be deficient in at least one dimension—must lack reality to some of the senses. But this does not. I have all my senses, and can use them. Nothing is insubstantial: I am trapped in flesh that is very palpably too, too solid. The only striking deficiency, so far as I can see, is reason—even symbolic reason.'

The four other women stared at me in astonishment. The doctor gave them a sort of now-perhaps-you'll-believe me glance, and then turned to me again.

'We'll start with a few questions,' she said.

'Before you begin,' I put in, 'I have something to add to what I told you last night. It has come back to me.'

'Perhaps the knock when you fell,' she suggested,

looking at my piece of plaster. 'What were you trying to do?'

I ignored that. 'I think I'd better tell you the missing part—it might help—a bit, anyway.'

'Very well,' she agreed. 'You told me you were—er—married, and that your—er—husband was killed soon afterwards.' She glanced at the others; their blankness of expression was somehow studious. 'It was the part after that that was missing,' she added.

'Yes,' I said. 'He was a test-pilot,' I explained to them. 'It happened six months after we were married—only one month before his contract was due to expire.

'After that, an aunt took me away for some weeks. I don't suppose I'll ever remember that part very well—I—I wasn't noticing anything very much. . . .

'But then I remember waking up one morning and suddenly seeing things differently, and telling myself that I couldn't go on like that. I knew I must have some work, something that would keep me busy.

'Dr. Hellyer, who is in charge of the Wraychester Hospital where I was working before I married, told me that he would be glad to have me with them again. So I went back, and worked very hard, so that I did not have much time to think. That would be about eight months ago, now.

'Then one day Dr. Hellyer spoke about a drug that a friend of his had succeeded in synthesizing. I don't think he was really asking for volunteers, but I offered to try it out. From what he said it sounded as if the drug might have some quite important properties. It struck me as a chance to do something useful. Sooner or later, someone would try it, and as I didn't have any ties and didn't care very much what happened, anyway, I thought I might as well be the one to try it.'

The spokesman doctor interrupted to ask:

'What was this drug?'

'It's called chuinjuatin,' I told her. 'Do you know it?'

She shook her head. One of the others put in:

'I've heard the name. What is it?'

'It's a narcotic,' I told her. 'The original form is in the leaves of a tree that grows chiefly in the South of Venezuela. The tribe of Indians who live there discovered it somehow, like others did quinine and mescalin. And in much the same way they use it for orgies. Some of them sit and chew the leaves—they have to chew about six ounces of them—and gradually they go into a zombie-like, trance state. It lasts three or four days during which they are quite helpless and incapable of doing the simplest thing for themselves, so that other members of the tribe are appointed to look after them as if they were children, and to guard them.

'It's necessary to guard them because the Indian belief is that chuinjuatin liberates the spirit from the body, setting it free to wander anywhere in space and time, and the guardian's most important job is to see that no other wandering spirit shall slip into the body while the true owner is away. When the subjects recover they claim to have had wonderful mystical experiences. There seem to be no physical ill effects, and no craving results from it. The mystical experiences, though, are said to be intense, and clearly remembered.

'Dr. Hellyer's friend had tested his synthesized chuinjuatin on a number of laboratory animals and worked out the dosage, and tolerances, and that kind of thing, but what he could not tell, of course, was what validity, if any, the reports of the mystical experiences had. Presumably they were the product of the drug's influence on the nervous system—but whether that effect produced a sensation of pleasure, ecstasy, awe, fear, horror, or any of a dozen more, it was impossible to tell without a human guinea-pig. So that was what I volunteered for.'

I stopped. I looked at their serious, puzzled faces, and at the billow of pink satin in front of me.

'In fact,' I added, 'it appears to have produced a combination of the absurd, the incomprehensible, and the grotesque.'

They were earnest women, these, not to be side-tracked. They were there to disprove an anomaly—if they could.

'I see,' said the spokeswoman with an air of preserving reasonableness, rather than meaning anything. She glanced down at a paper on which she had made a note from time to time.

'Now, can you give us the time and date at which this experiment took place?'

I could, and did, and after that the questions went on and on and on. . . .

The least satisfactory part of it from my point of view was that even though my answers caused them to grow more uncertain of themselves as we went on, they did at least get them; whereas when I put a question it was usually evaded, or answered perfunctorily, as an unimportant digression.

They went on steadily, and only broke off when my next meal arrived. Then they went away, leaving me thankfully in peace—but little the wiser. I half expected them to return, but when they did not I fell into a doze from which I was awakened by the incursion of a cluster of the little women, once more. They brought a trolley with them, and in a short time were wheeling me out of the building on it —but not by the way I had arrived. This time we went down a ramp where another, or the same, pink ambulance waited at the bottom. When they had me safely loaded aboard, three of them climbed in, too, to keep me company. They were chattering as they did so, and they kept it up inconsequently, and mostly incomprehensively, for the whole hour and a half of the journey that ensued.

The countryside differed little from what I had already seen. Once we were outside the gates there were the same tidy fields and standardized farms. The occasional built-up areas were not extensive and consisted of the same types of blocks close by, and we ran on the same, not very good, road surfaces. There were groups of the Amazon types, and, more rarely, individuals, to be seen at work in the fields; the sparse traffic was lorries, large or small, and occasional buses, but with never a private car to be seen. My illusion, I reflected, was remarkably consistent in its details. Not a single group of Amazons, for instance, failed to raise its right hands in friendly, respectful greeting to the pink car.

Once, we crossed a cutting. Looking down from the bridge I thought at first that we were over the dried bed of a canal, but then I noticed a post leaning at a crazy angle among the grass and weeds: most of its attachments had fallen off, but there were enough left to identify it as a railway-signal.

We passed through one concentration of identical blocks which was in size, though in no other way, quite a town, and then, two or three miles farther on, ran through an ornamental gateway into a kind of park.

In one way it was not unlike the estate we had left, for everything was meticulously tended; the lawns like velvet, the flower-beds vivid with spring blossoms, but it differed essentially in that the buildings were not blocks. They were houses, quite small for the most part, and varied in style, often no larger than roomy cottages. The place had a subduing effect on my small companions; for the first time they left off chattering, and gazed about them with obvious awe.

The driver stopped once to inquire the way of an overalled Amazon who was striding along with a hod on her shoulder. She directed us, and gave me a cheerful, respectful grin through the window, and presently we drew up again in front of a neat little two-storey Regency-style house.

This time there was no trolley. The little women, assisted by the driver, fussed over helping me out, and then half-supported me into the house, in a kind of buttressing formation.

Inside, I was manoeuvred with some difficulty through a door on the left, and found myself in a beautiful room, elegantly decorated and furnished in the period style of the house. A white-haired woman in a purple silk dress was sitting in a wing-chair beside a wood fire. Both her face and her hands told of considerable age, but she looked at me from keen, lively eyes.

'Welcome, my dear,' she said, in a voice which had no trace of the quaver I half-expected.

Her glance went to a chair. Then she looked at me again, and thought better of it.

'I expect you'd be more comfortable on the couch,' she suggested.

I regarded the couch—a genuine Georgian piece, I thought—doubtfully.

'Will it stand it?' I wondered.

'Oh, I think so,' she said, but not too certainly.

The retinue deposited me there carefully, and stood by, with anxious expressions. When it was clear that though it creaked it was probably going to hold, the old lady shooed them away, and rang a little silver bell. A diminutive figure, a perfect parlourmaid three-foot-ten in height, entered.

'The brown sherry, please, Mildred,' instructed the old lady. 'You'll take sherry, my dear?' she added to me.

'Y-yes—yes, thank you,' I said, faintly. After a pause I added: 'You will excuse me, Mrs.—er—Miss——?'

'Oh, I should have introduced myself. My name is Laura—not Miss, or Mrs., just Laura. You, I know, are Orchis—Mother Orchis.'

'So they tell me,' I owned, distastefully.

We studied one another. For the first time since the hallucination had set in I saw sympathy, even pity, in someone else's eyes. I looked round the room again, noticing the perfection of details.

'This is—I'm not mad, am I?' I asked.

She shook her head slowly, but before she could reply the miniature parlourmaid returned, bearing a cut-glass decanter and glasses on a silver tray. As she poured out a glass for each of us I saw the old lady glance from her to me and back again, as though comparing us. There was a curious, uninterpretable expression on her face. I made an effort.

'Shouldn't it be Madeira?' I suggested.

She looked surprised, and then smiled, and nodded appreciatively.

'I think you have accomplished the purpose of this visit in one sentence,' she said.

The parlourmaid left, and we raised our glasses. The old lady sipped at hers and then placed it on an occasional table beside her.

'Nevertheless,' she went on, 'we had better go into it a little more. Did they tell you why they have sent you to me, my dear?'

'No,' I shook my head.

'It is because I am a historian,' she informed me. 'Access to history is a privilege. It is not granted to many of us nowadays—and then somewhat reluctantly. Fortunately, a feeling that no branches of knowledge should be allowed to perish entirely still exists—though some of them are pursued at the cost of a certain political suspicion.' She smiled deprecatingly, and then went on. 'So when confirmation is required it is necessary to appeal to a specialist. Did they give you any report on their diagnosis?'

I shook my head again.

'I thought not. So like the profession, isn't it? Well, I'll tell you what they told me on the telephone from the Mothers' Home, and we shall have a better idea of what we are about. I was informed that you have been interviewed by several doctors whom you have interested, puzzled—and I suspect, distressed—very much, poor things. None of them has more than a minimum smattering of history, you see. Well, briefly, two of them are of the opinion that you are suffering from delusions of a schizophrenic nature: and three are inclined to think you are a genuine case of transferred personality. It is an extremely rare condition. There are not more than three reliably documented cases, and one that is more debatable, they tell me; but of those confirmed two are associated with the drug chuinjuatin, and the third with a drug of very similar properties.

'Now, the majority of three found your answers coherent for the most part, and felt that they were authentically circumstantial. That is to say that nothing you told them conflicted directly with what they know, but, since they know so little outside their professional field, they found a great deal of the rest both hard to believe and impossible to check. Therefore I, with my better means of checking, have been asked for my opinion.'

She paused, and looked me thoughtfully over.

'I rather think,' she added, 'that this is going to be one

of the most curiously interesting things that has happened to me in my quite long life.—Your glass is empty, my dear.'

'Transferred personality,' I repeated wonderingly, as I held out my glass. 'Now, if *that* were possible——'

'Oh, there's no doubt about the *possibility*. Those three cases I mentioned are fully authenticated.'

'It might be that—almost,' I admitted. 'At least, in some ways it might be—but not in others. There *is* this nightmare quality. *You* seem perfectly normal to me, but look at me, myself—and at your little maid! There's certainly an element of delusion. I *seem* to be here, like this, and talking to you—but it can't really be so, so where am I?'

'I can understand, better than most, I think, how unreal this must seem to you. In fact, I have spent so much of my time in books that it sometimes seems unreal to me—as if I did not quite belong anywhere. Now, tell me, my dear, when were you born?'

I told her. She thought for a moment.

'H'm,' she said. 'George the Sixth—but you'd not remember the second big war?'

'No,' I agreed.

'But you might remember the coronation of the next monarch? Whose was that?'

'Elizabeth—Elizabeth the Second. My mother took me to see the procession,' I told her.

'Do you remember anything about it?'

'Not a lot really—except that it rained, nearly all day,' I admitted.

We went on like that for a little while, then she smiled, reassuringly.

'Well, I don't think we need any more to establish our point. I've heard about that coronation before—at second-hand. It must have been a wonderful scene in the abbey.'

She mused for a moment, and gave a little sigh. 'You've been very patient with me, my dear. It is only fair that you should have your turn—but I'm afraid you must prepare yourself for some shocks.'

'I think I must be inured after my last thirty-six hours or what has appeared to be thirty-six hours,' I told her.

'I doubt it,' she said, looking at me seriously.

'Tell me,' I asked her. 'Please explain it all—if you can.'

'Your glass, my dear. Then I'll get the crux of it over.' She poured for each of us, then she asked:

'What strikes you as the oddest feature of your experience, so far?'

I considered. 'There's so much——'

'Might it not be that you have not seen a single man?' she suggested.

I thought back. I remembered the wondering tone of one of the Mothers asking: 'What is a man?'

'That's certainly one of them,' I agreed. 'Where are they?'

She shook her head, watching me steadily.

'There aren't any, my dear. Not any more. None at all.'

I simply went on staring at her. Her expression was perfectly serious and sympathetic. There was no trace of guile there, or deception, while I struggled with the idea. At last I managed:

'But—but that's impossible! There must be some somewhere. . . . You couldn't—I mean, how?—I mean. . . .' My expostulation trailed off in confusion.

She shook her head.

'I know it must seem impossible to you, Jane—may I call you Jane? But it is so. I am an old woman now, nearly eighty, and in all my long life I have never seen a man—save in old pictures and photographs. Drink your sherry, my dear. It will do you good.' She paused. 'I'm afraid this upsets you.'

I obeyed, too bewildered for further comment at the moment, protesting inwardly, yet not altogether disbelieving, for certainly I had not seen one man, nor sign of any. She went on quietly, giving me time to collect my wits.

'I can understand a little how you must feel. I haven't had to learn all my history entirely from books, you see. When I was a girl, sixteen or seventeen, I used to listen a lot to my grandmother. She was as old then as I am now, but her memory of her youth was still very good. I was able almost to see the places she talked about—but they were part of such a different world that it was difficult for me to understand how she felt. When she spoke about the young man she had been engaged to, tears would roll down her cheeks, even then—not just for him, of course, but for the whole world that she had known as a girl. I was sorry for her, although I could not really understand how she felt. How should I? But now that I am old, too, and have read so much, I am perhaps a little nearer to understanding her feelings, I think.' She looked at me curiously. 'And you, my dear. Perhaps you, too, were engaged to be married?'

'I was married—for a little time,' I told her.

She contemplated that for some seconds, then:

'It must be a very strange experience to be owned,' she remarked, reflectively.

'Owned?' I exclaimed, in astonishment.

'Ruled by a husband,' she explained, sympathetically.

I stared at her.

'But it—it wasn't like that—it wasn't like that at all,' I protested. 'It was——' But there I broke off, with tears too close. To sheer her away I asked:

'But what happened? What on earth happened to the men?'

'They all died,' she told me. 'They fell sick. Nobody could do anything for them, so they died. In little more than a year they were all gone—all but a very few.'

'But surely—surely everything would collapse?'

'Oh, yes. Very largely it did. It was very bad. There was a dreadful lot of starvation. The industrial parts were the worst hit, of course. In the more backward countries and in rural areas women were able to turn to the land and till it to keep themselves and their children alive, but almost all the large organizations broke down entirely. Transport ceased very soon: petrol ran out, and no coal was being mined. It was quite a dreadful state of affairs because although there were a great many women, and they had outnumbered the men, in fact, they had only really been important as consumers and spenders of money. So when the crisis came it turned out that scarcely any of them knew how to do any of the important things because they had nearly all been owned by men, and had to lead their lives as pets and parasites.'

I started to protest, but her frail hand waved me aside.

'It wasn't their fault—not entirely,' she explained. 'They were caught up in a process, and everything conspired against their escape. It was a long process, going right back to the eleventh century, in Southern France. The Romantic conception started there as an elegant and amusing fashion for the leisured classes. Gradually, as time went on, it permeated through most levels of society, but it was not until the latter part of the nineteenth century that its commercial possibilities were intelligently perceived, and not until the twentieth that it was really exploited.

'At the beginning of the twentieth century women were starting to have their chance to lead useful, creative, interesting lives. But that did not suit commerce: it needed them much more as mass consumers than as producers—

except on the most routine levels. So Romance was adopted and developed as a weapon against their further progress and to promote consumption, and it was used intensively.

'Women must never for a moment be allowed to forget their sex, and to compete as equals. Everything had to have a "feminine angle" which must be different from the masculine angle, and be dinned in without ceasing. It would have been unpopular for manufacturers actually to issue an order "back to the kitchen", but there were other ways. A profession without a difference, called "housewife", could be invented. The kitchen could be glorified and made more expensive; it could be made to seem desirable, and it could be shown that the way to realize this heart's desire was through marriage. So the presses turned out, by the hundred thousand a week, journals which concentrated the attention of women ceaselessly and relentlessly upon selling themselves to some man in order that they might achieve some small, uneconomic unit of a home upon which money could be spent.

'Whole trades adopted the romantic approach and the glamour was spread thicker and thicker in the articles, the write-ups, and most of all in the advertisements. Romance found a place in everything that women might buy from underclothes to motor-cycles, from "health" foods to kitchen stoves, from deodorants to foreign travel, until soon they were too bemused to be amused any more.

'The air was filled with frustrated moanings. Women maundered in front of microphones yearning only to "surrender", and "give themselves", to adore and to be adored. The cinema most of all maintained the propaganda, persuading the main and important part of their audience, which was female, that nothing in life was worth achieving but dewy-eyed passivity in the strong arms of Romance. The pressure became such that the majority of young women spent all their leisure time dreaming of Romance, and the means of securing it. They were brought to a state of honestly believing that to be owned by some man and set down in a little brick box to buy all the things that the manufacturers wanted them to buy would be the highest form of bliss that life could offer.'

'But——' I began to protest again. The old lady was now well launched, however, and swept on without a check.

'All this could not help distorting society, of course. The divorce-rate went up. Real life simply could not come near to providing the degree of romantic glamour which was being represented as every girl's proper inheritance. There was probably, in the aggregate, more disappointment, disillusion, and dissatisfaction among women than there had ever been before. Yet, with this ridiculous and ornamental ideal grained-in by unceasing propaganda, what could a conscientious idealist do but take steps to break up the short-weight marriage she had made, and seek elsewhere for the ideal which was hers, she understood, by right?

'It was a wretched state of affairs brought about by deliberately promoted dissatisfaction; a kind of rat-race with, somewhere safely out of reach, the glamorized romantic ideal always luring. Perhaps an exceptional few almost attained it, but, for all except those very few, it was a cruel, tantalizing sham on which they spent themselves, and of course their money, in vain.'

This time I did get in my protest.

'But it wasn't like that. Some of what you say may be true—but that's all the superficial part. It didn't feel a bit like the way you put it. I was in it. I *know.*'

She shook her head reprovingly.

'There is such a thing as being too close to make a proper evaluation. At a distance we were able to see more clearly. We can perceive it for what it was—a gross and heartless exploitation of the weaker-willed majority. Some women of education and resolution were able to withstand it, of course, but at a cost. There must always be a painful price for resisting majority pressure—even they could not always altogether escape the feeling that they might be wrong, and that the rat-racers were having the better time of it.

'You see, the great hopes for the emancipation of women with which the century had started had been outflanked. Purchasing-power had passed into the hands of the ill-educated and highly-suggestible. The desire for Romance is essentially a selfish wish, and when it is encouraged to dominate every other it breaks down all corporate loyalties. The individual woman thus separated from, and yet at the same time thrust into competition with, all other women was almost defenceless; she became the prey of organized suggestion. When it was represented to her that the lack of certain goods or amenities would be fatal to Romance she became alarmed and, thus, eminently exploitable. She could only believe what she was told, and spent a great deal of time worrying about whether she was doing all the right things to encourage Romance. Thus, she became, in a new, subtler way, more exploited, more dependent, and less creative than she had ever been before.'

'Well,' I said, 'this is the most curiously unrecognizable account of my world that I have ever heard—it's like something copied, but with all the proportions wrong. And as for "less creative"—well, perhaps families were smaller, but women still went on having babies. The population was still increasing.'

The old lady's eyes dwelt on me a moment.

'You are undoubtedly a thought-child of your time, in some ways,' she observed. 'What makes you think there is anything creative about having babies? Would you call a plant-pot creative because seeds grow in it? It is a mechanical operation—and, like most mechanical operations, is most easily performed by the least intelligent. Now, bringing up a child, educating, helping her to become a *person*, that *is* creative. But unfortunately, in the time we are speaking of, women had, in the main, been successfully conditioned into bringing up their daughters to be unintelligent consumers, like themselves.'

'But,' I said helplessly, 'I *know* the time. It's my time. This is all distorted.'

'The perspective of history must be truer,' she told me again, unimpressed, and went on: 'But if what happened *had* to happen, then it chose a fortunate time to happen. A hundred years earlier, even fifty years earlier, it would very likely have meant extinction. Fifty years later might easily have been too late—it might have come upon a world in which *all* women had profitably restricted themselves to domesticity and consumership. Luckily, however, in the middle of the century some women were still entering the professions, and by far the greatest number of professional women was to be found in medicine—which is to say that they were only really numerous in, and skilled in, the very profession which immediately became of vital importance if we were to survive at all.

'I have no medical knowledge, so I cannot give you any details of the steps they took. All I can tell you is that there was intensive research on lines which will probably be more obvious to you than they are to me.

'A species, even our species, has great will to survive, and the doctors saw to it that the will had the means of expression. Through all the hunger, and the chaos, and the other privations, babies somehow continued to be born. That had to be. Reconstruction could wait: the priority was the new generation that would help in the reconstruction, and then inherit it. So babies were born: the girl babies lived, the boy babies died. That was distressing, and wasteful, too, and so, presently, only girl babies were born—again, the means by which that could be achieved will be easier for you to understand than for me.

'It is, they tell me, not nearly so remarkable as it would appear at first sight. The locust, it seems, will continue to produce female locusts without male, or any other kind of assistance; the aphis, too, is able to go on breeding alone and in seclusion, certainly for eight generations, perhaps more. So it would be a poor thing if we, with all our knowledge and powers of research to assist us, should find ourselves inferior to the locust and the aphis in this respect, would it not?'

She paused, looking at me somewhat quizzically for my response. Perhaps she expected amazed—or possibly shocked—disbelief. If so, I disappointed her: technical achievements have ceased to arouse simple wonder since atomic physics showed how the barriers fall before the pressure of a good brains team. One can take it that most things are possible: whether they are desirable, or worth doing, is a different matter—and one that seemed to me particularly pertinent to her question. I asked her:

'And what is it that you have achieved?'

'Survival,' she said, simply.

'Materially,' I agreed, 'I suppose you have. But when it has cost all the rest, when love, art, poetry, excitement, and physical joy have all been sacrificed to mere continued existence, what is left but a soulless waste? What reason is there any longer for survival?'

'As to the reason, I don't know—except that survival is a desire common to all species. I am quite sure that the *reason* for that desire was no clearer in the twentieth century than it is now. But, for the rest, why should you assume that they are gone? Did not Sappho write poetry?

And your assumption that the possession of a soul depends upon a duality of sexes surprises me: it has so often been held that the two are in some sort of conflict, has it not?'

'As an historian who must have studied men, women, and motives you should have taken my meaning better,' I told her.

She shook her head, with reproof. 'You are so much the conditioned product of your age, my dear. They told you, on all levels, from the works of Freud to that of the most nugatory magazines for women, that it was sex, civilized into romantic love, that made the world go round—and you believed them. But the world continues to go round for others, too—for the insects, the fish, the birds, the animals—and how much do you suppose they know of romantic love, even in brief mating-seasons? They hoodwinked you, my dear. Between them they channelled your interests and ambitions along courses that were socially convenient, economically profitable, and almost harmless.'

I shook my head.

'I just don't believe it. Oh, yes, you know something of my world—from the outside. But you don't understand it, or feel it.'

'That's your conditioning, my dear,' she told me, calmly.

Her repeated assumption irritated me. I asked:

'Suppose I were to believe what you say, what is it, then, that *does* make the world go round?'

'That's simple, my dear. It is the will to power. We have that as babies; we have it still in old age. It occurs in men and women alike. It is more fundamental, and more desirable, than sex; I tell you, you were misled—exploited, sublimated for economic convenience.

'After the disease had struck, women ceased, for the first time in history, to be an exploited class. Without male rulers to confuse and divert them they began to perceive that all true power resides in the female principle. The male had served only one brief useful purpose; for the rest of his life he was a painful and costly parasite.

'As they became aware of power, the doctors grasped it. In twenty years they were in full control. With them were the few women engineers, architects, lawyers, administrators, some teachers, and so on, but it was the doctors who held the keys of life and death. The future was in their hands and, as things began gradually to revive, they, together with the other professions, remained the dominant class and became known as the Doctorate. It assumed authority; it made the laws; it enforced them.

'There was opposition, of course. Neither the memory of the old days, nor the effect of twenty years of lawlessness, could be wiped out at once, but the doctors had the whip hand—any woman who wanted a child had to come to them, and they saw to it that she was satisfactorily settled in a community. The roving gangs dwindled away, and gradually order was restored.

'Later on, they faced better-organized opposition. There was a party which contended that the disease which had struck down the men had run its course, and the balance could, and should, be restored—they were known as Reactionists, and they became an embarrassment.

'Most of the Council of the Doctorate still had clear memories of a system which used every weakness of women, and had been no more than a mere civilized culmination of their exploitation through the ages. They remembered how they themselves had only grudgingly been allowed to qualify for their careers. They were now in command: they felt no obligation to surrender their power and authority, and eventually, no doubt, their freedom to a creature whom they had proved to be biologically, and in all other ways, expendable. They refused unanimously to take a step that would lead to corporate suicide, and the Reactionists were proscribed as a subversive criminal organization.

'That, however, was just a palliative. It quickly became clear that they were attacking a symptom and neglecting the cause. The Council was driven to realize that it had an unbalanced society at its hands—a society that was capable of continuity, but was in structure, you might say, little more than the residue of a vanished form. It could not continue in that truncated shape, and as long as it tried to disaffection would increase. Therefore, if power was to become stable, a new form suitable to the circumstances must be found.

'In deciding the shape it should take, the natural tendencies of the little-educated and uneducated woman were carefully considered—such qualities as her feeling for hierarchical principles and her disposition to respect artificial distinctions. You will no doubt recollect that in your own time any fool of a woman whose husband was ennobled or honoured at once acquired increased respect and envy from other women though she remained the same fool; and also, that any gathering or society of unoccupied women would soon become obsessionally enmeshed in the creation and preservation of social distinctions. Allied to this is the high value they usually place upon a feeling of security. Important, too, is the capacity for devoted self-sacrifice, and slavery to conscience within the canons of any local convention. We are naturally very biddable creatures. Most of us are happiest when we are being orthodox, however odd our customs may appear to an outsider; the difficulty in handling us lies chiefly in establishing the required standards of orthodoxy.

'Obviously, the broad outline of a system which was

going to stand any chance of success, would have to provide scope for these and other characteristic traits. It must be a scheme where the interplay of forces would preserve equilibrium and respect for authority. The details of such an organization, however, were less easy to determine.

'An extensive study of social forms and orders was undertaken but for several years every plan put forward was rejected as in some way unsuitable. The architecture of that finally chosen was said, though I do not know with how much truth, to have been inspired by the Bible—a book at that time still unprohibited, and the source of much unrest—I am told that it ran something like: "Go to the ant, thou sluggard; consider her ways."

'The Council appears to have felt that this advice, suitably modified, could be expected to lead to a state of affairs which would provide most of the requisite characteristics.

'A four-class system was chosen as the basis, and strong differentiations were gradually introduced. These, now that they have become well established, greatly help to ensure stability—there is scope for ambition within one's class, but none for passing from one class to another. Thus, we have the Doctorate—the educated ruling-class, fifty per cent of whom are actually of the medical profession. The Mothers, whose title is self-explanatory. The Servitors who are numerous and, for psychological reasons, small. The Workers, who are physically and muscularly strong, to do the heavier work. All the three lower classes respect the authority of the Doctorate. Both the employed classes revere the Mothers. The Servitors consider themselves more favoured in their tasks than the Workers; and the Workers tend to regard the puniness of the Servitors with a semi-affectionate contempt.

'So you see a balance has been struck, and though it works somewhat crudely as yet, no doubt it will improve.

It seems likely, for instance, that it would be advantageous to introduce sub-divisions into the Servitor class before long, and the police are thought by some to be put at a disadvantage by having no more than a little education to distinguish them from the ordinary Worker. . . .'

She went on explaining with increasing detail while the enormity of the whole process gradually grew upon me.

'Ants!' I broke in, suddenly. 'The ant-nest! You've taken *that* for your model?'

She looked surprised, either at my tone, or the fact that what she was saying had taken so long to register.

'And why not?' she asked. 'Surely it is one of the most enduring social patterns that nature has evolved—though of course some adaptation——'

'You're—are you telling me that only the Mothers have children?' I demanded.

'Oh, members of the Doctorate do, too, when they wish,' she assured me.

'But—but——'

'The Council decides the ratios,' she went on to explain. 'The doctors at the clinic examine the babies and allocate them suitably to the different classes. After that, of course, it is just a matter of seeing to their specialized feeding, glandular control, and proper training.'

'But,' I objected wildly, 'what's it *for*? Where's the sense in it? What's the good of being alive, like that?'

'Well, what *is* the sense in being alive? You tell me,' she suggested.

'But we're *meant* to love and be loved, to have babies we love by people we love.'

'There's your conditioning again; glorifying and romanticizing primitive animalism. Surely you consider that we are superior to the animals?'

'Of course I do, but——'

'Love, you say, but what can you know of the love there can be between mother and daughter when there are no men to introduce jealousy? Do you know of any purer sentiment than the love of a girl for her little sisters?'

'But you don't understand,' I protested again. 'How should you understand a love that colours the whole world? How it centres in your heart and reaches out from there to pervade your whole being, how it can affect everything you are, everything you touch, everything you hear. . . . It can hurt dreadfully, I know, oh, I know, but it can run like sunlight in your veins. . . . It can make you a garden out of a slum; brocade out of rags; music out of a speaking voice. It can show you a whole universe in someone else's eyes. Oh, you don't understand . . . you don't know . . . you can't. . . . Oh, Donald, darling, how can I show her what she's never even guessed at . . . ?'

There was an uncertain pause, but presently she said:

'Naturally, in your form of society it was necessary for you to be given such a conditioned reaction, but you can scarcely expect us to surrender our freedom, to connive at our own re-subjection, by calling our oppressors into existence again.'

'Oh, you *won't* understand. It was only the more stupid men and women who were continually at war with one another. Lots of us were complementary. We were pairs who formed units.'

She smiled. 'My dear, either you are surprisingly ill-informed on your own period, or else the stupidity you speak of was astonishingly dominant. Neither as myself, nor as an historian, can I consider that we should be justified in resurrecting such a state of affairs. A primitive stage of our development has now given way to a civilized era. Woman, who is the vessel of life, had the misfortune to find man necessary for a time, but now she does no longer.

Are you suggesting that such a useless and dangerous encumbrance ought to be preserved, out of sheer sentimentality? I will admit that we have lost some minor conveniences—you will have noticed, I expect, that we are less inventive mechanically, and tend to copy the patterns we have inherited; but that troubles us very little; our interests lie not in the inorganic, but in the organic and the sentient. Perhaps men could show us how to travel twice as fast, or how to fly to the moon, or how to kill more people more quickly; but it does not seem to us that such kinds of knowledge would be good payment for re-enslaving ourselves. No, our kind of world suits us better—all of us except a few Reactionists. You have seen our Servitors. They are a little timid in manner, perhaps, but are they oppressed, or sad? Don't they chatter among themselves as brightly and perkily as sparrows? And the Workers—those you called the Amazons—don't they look strong, healthy, and cheerful?'

'But you're robbing them all—robbing them of their birthright.'

'You mustn't give me cant, my dear. Did not your social system conspire to rob a woman of her "birthright" unless she married? You not only let her know it, but you socially rubbed it in: here, our Servitors and Workers do not know it, and they are not worried by a sense of inadequacy. Motherhood is the function of the Mothers, and understood as such.'

I shook my head. 'Nevertheless, they *are* being robbed. A woman has a right to love——'

For once she was a little impatient as she cut me short.

'You keep repeating to me the propaganda of your age. The love you talk about, my dear, existed in your little sheltered part of the world by polite and profitable convention. You were scarcely ever allowed to see its other face, unglamorized by Romance. *You* were never openly bought and sold, like livestock; *you* never had to sell yourself to the first-comer in order to live; *you* did not happen to be one of the women who through the centuries have screamed in agony and suffered and died under invaders in a sacked city—nor were you ever flung into a pit of fire to be saved from them; *you* were never compelled to suttee upon your dead husband's pyre; *you* did not have to spend your whole life imprisoned in a harem; *you* were never part of the cargo of a slave-ship; *you* never retained your own life only at the pleasure of your lord and master. . . .

'That is the other side—the age-long side. There is going to be no more of such things. They are finished at last. Dare you suggest that we should call them back, to suffer them all again?'

'But most of these things had already gone,' I protested. 'The world was getting better.'

'Was it?' she said. 'I wonder if the women of Berlin thought so when it fell? Was it, indeed?—Or was it on the edge of a new barbarism?'

'But if you can only get rid of evil by throwing out the good too, what is there left?'

'There is a great deal. Man was only a means to an end. We needed him in order to have babies. The rest of his vitality accounted for all the misery in the world. We are a great deal better off without him.'

'So you really consider that you've improved on nature?' I suggested.

'Tcha!' she said, impatient with my tone. 'Civilization *is* improvement on nature. Would you want to live in a cave, and have most of your babies die in infancy?'

'There are some things, some fundamental things——' I began, but she checked me, holding up her hand for silence.

Outside, the long shadows had crept across the lawns. In the evening quiet I could hear a choir of women's voices singing, a little distance away. We listened for some minutes until the song was finished.

'Beautiful!' said the old lady. 'Could angels themselves sing more sweetly! They sound happy enough, don't they? Our own lovely children—two of my granddaughters are there among them. They *are* happy, and they've reason to be happy; they're not growing up into a world where they must gamble on the goodwill of some man to keep them; they'll never need to be servile before a lord and master; they'll never stand in danger of rape and butchery, either. Listen to them!'

Another song had started and came lilting lightly to us out of the dusk.

'Why are you crying?' the old lady asked me as it ended.

'I know it's stupid—I don't really believe any of this is what it seems to be—so I suppose I'm crying for all you would have lost if it were true,' I told her. 'There should be lovers out there under the trees; they should be listening hand in hand to that song while they watch the moon rise. But there are no lovers now, there won't be any more. . . .' I looked back at her.

'Did you ever read the lines: "Full many a flower is born to blush unseen, and waste its sweetness on the desert air?" Can't you feel the forlornness of this world you've made? Do you *really* not understand?' I asked.

'I know you've only seen a little of us, but do *you* not begin to understand what it can be like when women are no longer forced to fight one another for the favours of men?' she countered.

We talked on while the dusk gave way to darkness and the lights of other houses started to twinkle through the trees. Her reading had been wide. It had given her even an affection for some periods of the past, but her approval of her own era was unshaken. She felt no aridity in it. Always it was my 'conditioning' which prevented me from seeing that the golden age of woman had begun at last.

'You cling to too many myths,' she told me. 'You speak of a full life, and your instance is some unfortunate woman hugging her chains in a suburban villa. Full life, fiddlesticks! But it was convenient for the traders that she could be made to think so. A truly full life would be an exceedingly short one, in any form of society.'

And so on . . .

At length, the little parlourmaid reappeared to say that my attendants were ready to leave when it should be convenient. But there was one thing I very much wanted to know before I left. I put the question to the old lady.

'Please tell me. How did it—how could it—happen?'

'Simply by accident, my dear—though it was the kind of accident that was entirely the product of its time. A piece of research which showed unexpected, secondary results, that's all.'

'But how?'

'Rather curiously—almost irrelevantly, you might say. Did you ever hear of a man called Perrigan?'

'Perrigan?' I repeated. 'I don't think so, it's an uncommon name.'

'It became very commonly known indeed,' she assured me. 'Doctor Perrigan was a biologist, and his concern was the extermination of rats—particularly the brown rat, which used to do a great deal of expensive damage.

'His approach to the problem was to find a disease which would attack them fatally. In order to produce it he took as his basis a virus infection often fatal to rabbits—or, rather, a group of virus infections that were highly selective, and also unstable since they were highly liable to mutation. Indeed, there was so much variation in the strains that when infection of rabbits in Australia was tried, it was only at the sixth attempt that it was successful; all the earlier strains died out as the rabbits developed immunity. It was tried in other places, too, though with indifferent success until a still more effective strain was started in France, and ran through the rabbit population of Europe.

'Well, taking some of these viruses as a basis, Perrigan induced new mutations by irradiation and other means, and succeeded in producing a variant that would attack rats. That was not enough, however, and he continued his work until he had a strain that had enough of its ancestral selectivity to attack only the brown rat, and with great virulence.

'In that way he settled the question of a long-standing pest, for there are no brown rats now. But something went amiss. It is still an open question whether the successful virus mutated again, or whether one of his earlier experimental viruses was accidentally liberated by escaped "carrier" rats, but that's academic. The important thing is that somehow a strain capable of attacking human beings got loose, and that it was already widely disseminated before it was traced—also, that once it was free, it spread with devastating speed; too fast for any effective steps to be taken to check it.

'The majority of women were found to be immune; and of the ten per cent or so whom it attacked over eighty per cent recovered. Among men, however, there was almost no immunity, and the few recoveries were only partial. A few men were preserved by the most elaborate precautions but they could not be kept confined for ever, and in the end the virus, which had a remarkable capacity for dormancy, got them too.'

Inevitably several questions of professional interest occurred to me, but for an answer she shook her head.

'I'm afraid I can't help you there. Possibly the medical people will be willing to explain,' she said, but her expression was doubtful.

I manoeuvred myself into a sitting position on the side of the couch.

'I see,' I said. 'Just an accident—yes, I suppose one could scarcely think of it happening in any other way.'

'Unless,' she remarked, 'unless one were to look upon it as divine intervention.'

'Isn't that a little impious?'

'I was thinking of the Death of the Firstborn,' she said, reflectively.

There did not seem to be an immediate answer to that. Instead, I asked:

'Can you honestly tell me that you never have the feeling that you are living in a dreary kind of nightmare?'

'Never,' she said. 'There *was* a nightmare—but it's over now. Listen!'

The voices of the choir, reinforced now by an orchestra, reached us distantly out of the darkened garden. No, they were not dreary: they even sounded almost exultant—but then, poor things, how were they to understand . . .?

My attendants arrived and helped me to my feet. I thanked the old lady for her patience with me and her kindness. But she shook her head.

'My dear, it is I who am indebted to you. In a short time I have learnt more about the conditioning of women in a mixed society than all my books were able to tell me in the rest of my long life. I hope, my dear, that the doctors will find some way of enabling you to forget it, and live happily here with us.'

At the door I paused and turned, still helpfully shored up by my attendants.

'Laura,' I said, using her name for the first time. 'So many of your arguments are right—yet, over all, you're, oh, so *wrong*. Did you never read of lovers? Did you never, as a girl, sigh for a Romeo who would say: "It is the east, and Laura is the sun!"?'

'I think not. Though I have read the play. A pretty, idealized tale—I wonder how much heartbreak it has given to how many would-be Juliets? But I would set a question against yours, my dear Jane. Did you ever see Goya's cycle of pictures called "The Horrors of War"?'

The pink car did not return me to the 'Home'. Our destination turned out to be a more austere and hospital-like building where I was fussed into a bed in a room alone. In the morning, after my massive breakfast, three new doctors visited me. Their manner was more social than professional, and we chatted amiably for half an hour. They had evidently been fully informed on my conversation with the old lady, and they were not averse to answering my questions. Indeed, they found some amusement in many of them, though I found none, for there was nothing consolingly vague in what they told me—it all sounded too disturbingly practicable, once the technique had been worked out. At the end of that time, however, their mood changed. One of them, with an air of getting down to business, said:

'You will understand that you present us with a problem. Your fellow-Mothers, of course, are scarcely susceptible to Reactionist disaffection—though you have in quite a short time managed to disgust and bewilder them considerably—but on others less stable your influence might be more serious. It is not just a matter of what you may say, your difference from the rest is implicit in your whole attitude. You cannot help that, and, frankly, we do not see how you, as a woman of education, could possibly adapt yourself to the placid, unthinking acceptance that is expected of a Mother. You would quickly feel frustrated beyond endurance. Furthermore, it is clear that the conditioning you have had under your system prevents you from feeling any goodwill towards ours.'

I took that straight; simply as a judgement without bias. Moreover, I could not dispute it. The prospect of spending the rest of my life in pink, scented, soft-musicked illiteracy, interrupted, one gathered, only by the production of quadruplet daughters at regular intervals, would certainly have me violently unhinged in a very short time.

'And so—what?' I asked. 'Can you reduce this great carcass to normal shape and size?'

She shook her head. 'I imagine not—though I don't know that it has ever been attempted. But even if it were possible, you would be just as much of a misfit in the Doctorate—and far more of a liability as a Reactionist influence.'

I could understand that, too.

'What, then?' I inquired.

She hesitated, then she said gently:

'The only practicable proposal we can make is that you should agree to a hypnotic treatment which will remove your memory.'

As the meaning of that came home to me I had to fight off a rush of panic. After all, I told myself, they were being reasonable with me. I must do my best to respond sensibly. Nevertheless, some minutes must have passed before I answered, unsteadily:

'You are asking me to commit suicide. My mind *is* my memories: they are me. If I lose them I shall die, just as surely as if you were to kill my—this body.'

They did not dispute that. How could they?

There is just one thing that makes my life worth living—knowing that you loved me, my sweet, sweet Donald. It is only in my memory that you live now. If you ever leave there you will die again—and for ever.

'No!' I told them. 'No! No!'

At intervals during the day small servitors staggered in under the weight of my meals. Between their visits I had only my thoughts to occupy me, and they were not good company.

'Frankly,' one of the doctors had put it to me, not unsympathetically, 'we can see no alternative. For years after it happened the annual figures of mental breakdowns were our greatest worry—even though the women then could keep themselves fully occupied with the tremendous amount of work that had to be done, so many of them could not adjust. And we can't even offer you work.'

I knew that it was a fair warning she was giving me—and I knew that, unless the hallucination which seemed to grow more real all the time could soon be induced to dissolve, I was trapped.

During the long day and the following night I tried my hardest to get back to the objectivity I had managed earlier, but I failed. The whole dialectic was too strong for me now; my senses too consciously aware of my surroundings; the air of consequence and coherence too convincingly persistent. . . .

When they had let me have twenty-four hours to think it over, the same trio visited me again.

'I think,' I told them, 'that I understand better now. What you are offering me is painless oblivion, in place of a breakdown followed by oblivion—and you see no other choice.'

'We don't,' admitted the spokeswoman, and the other two nodded. 'But, of course, for the hypnosis we shall need your co-operation.'

'I realize that,' I told her, 'and I also see now that in the circumstances it would be obstinately futile to withhold it. So I—I—yes, I'm willing to give it—but on one condition.'

They looked at me questioningly.

'It is this,' I explained, 'that you will try one other course first. I want you to give me an injection of chuinjuatin. I want it in precisely the same strength as I had it before—I can tell you the dose.

'You see, whether this is an intense hallucination, or whether it is some kind of projection which makes it seem very similar, it must have something to do with that drug. I'm sure it must—nothing remotely like this has ever happened to me before. So, I thought that if I could repeat the condition—or, would you say believe myself to be repeating the condition?—there may be just a chance . . . I don't know. It may be simply silly . . . but even if nothing comes of it, it can't make things worse in any way now, can it? So, will you let me try it . . .?'

The three of them considered for some moments.

'I can see no reason why not . . .' said one.

The spokeswoman nodded.

'I shouldn't think there'll be any difficulty with authorization in the circumstances,' she agreed. 'If you want to try, well, it's fair to let you, but—I'd not count on it too much. . . .'

In the afternoon half a dozen small servitors arrived, bustling round, making me and the room ready, with anxious industry. Presently there came one more, scarcely tall enough to see over the trolley of bottles, trays and phials which she pushed to my bedside.

The three doctors entered together. One of the little servitors began rolling up my sleeve. The doctor who had done most of the talking looked at me, kindly, but seriously.

'This is a sheer gamble, you know that?' she said.

'I know. But it's my only chance. I'm willing to take it.'

She nodded, picked up the syringe, and charged it while the little servitor swabbed my monstrous arm. She approached the bedside, and hesitated.

'Go on,' I told her. 'What is there for me here, anyway?'

She nodded, and pressed in the needle. . . .

*

Now, I have written the foregoing for a purpose. I shall deposit it with my bank, where it will remain unread unless it should be needed.

I have spoken of it to no one. The report on the effect of chuinjuatin—the one that I made to Dr. Hellyer where I described my sensation as simply one of floating in space—was false. The foregoing was my true experience.

I concealed it because after I came round, when I found that I was back in my own body in my normal world, the experience haunted me as vividly as if it had been actuality. The details were too sharp, too vivid, for me to get them out of my mind. It overhung me all the time, like a threat. It would not leave me alone. . . .

I did not dare to tell Dr. Hellyer how it worried me—he would have put me under treatment. If my other friends did not take it seriously enough to recommend treatment, too, then they would have laughed over it, and amused themselves at my expense interpreting the symbolism. So I kept it to myself.

As I went over parts of it again and again in detail, I grew angry with myself for not asking the old lady for more facts, things like dates, and details that could be verified. If, for instance, the thing should, by her account, have started two or three years ago, then the whole sense of threat would fall to pieces: it would all be discredited. But it had not occurred to me to ask that crucial question. . . . And then, as I went on thinking about it, I remembered that there was one, just one, piece of information that I could check, and I made inquiries. I wish now that I had not, but I felt forced to. . . .

So I have discovered that:

There *is* a Dr. Perrigan, he *is* a biologist, he *does* work with rabbits and rats. . . .

He is quite well known in his field. He has published papers on pest-control in a number of journals. It is no secret that he is evolving new strains of myxomatosis intended to attack rats; indeed, he has already developed a group of them and calls them mucosimorbus, though he has not yet succeeded in making them either stable or selective enough for general use. . . .

But I had never heard of this man or his work until his name was mentioned by the old lady in my 'hallucination'. . . .

I have given a great deal of thought to this whole matter. What sort of experience is it that I have recorded above? If it should be a kind of pre-vision of an inevitable, predestined future, then nothing anyone could do would change it. But that does not seem to me to make sense: it is what has happened, and is happening now, that determines the future. Therefore, there must be a great number of *possible* futures, each a possible consequence of what is being done now. It seems to me that under chuinjuatin I saw *one* of those futures. . . .

It was, I think, a warning of what *may* happen—unless it is prevented. . . .

The whole idea is so repulsive, so misconceived, it amounts to such a monstrous aberration of the normal course, that failure to heed the warning would be neglect of duty to one's kind.

I shall, therefore, on my own responsibility and without taking any other person into my confidence, do my best to ensure that such a state as I have described *cannot* come about.

Should it happen that any other person is unjustly accused of doing, or of assisting me to do, what I intend to do, this document must stand in his defence. That is why I have written it.

It is my own unaided decision that Dr. Perrigan must not be permitted to continue his work.

(Signed) JANE WATERLEIGH.

*

The solicitor stared at the signature for some moments; then he nodded. 'And so,' he said, 'she then took the car and drove over to Perrigan's—with this tragic result.

'From the little I do know of her, I'd say that she probably did her best to persuade him to give up his work—though she can scarcely have expected any success with that. It is difficult to imagine a man who would be willing to give up the work of years on account of what must sound to him like a sort of gipsy's warning. So, clearly, she went there prepared to fall back on direct action, if necessary. It looks as if the police are quite right when they suppose her to have shot him deliberately; but not so right when they suppose that she burnt the place down to hide evidence of the crime. The statement makes it pretty obvious that her main intention in doing that was to wipe out Perrigan's work.'

He shook his head. 'Poor girl! There's a clear conviction of duty in her last page or two: the sort of simplified clarity that drives martyrs on, regardless of consequences. She has never denied that she did it. What she wouldn't tell the police is *why* she did it.'

He paused again, before he added: 'Anyway, thank goodness for this document. It ought at least to save her life. I should be very surprised indeed if a plea of insanity could fail, backed up by this.' He tapped the pile of manuscript with his finger. 'It's a lucky thing she put off her intention of taking it to her bank.'

Dr. Hellyer's face was lined and worried.

'I blame myself most bitterly for the whole thing,' he said. 'I ought never to have let her try the damned drug in the first place, but I thought she was over the shock of her husband's death. She was trying to keep her time fully occupied, and she was anxious to volunteer. You've met her enough to know how purposeful she can be. She saw it as a chance to contribute something to medical knowledge—which it was, of course. But I ought to have been more careful, and I ought to have seen afterwards that there was something wrong. The real responsibility for this thing runs right back to me.'

'H'm,' said the solicitor. 'Putting that forward as a main line of defence isn't going to do you a lot of good professionally, you know, Hellyer.'

'Possibly not. I can look after that when we come to it. The point is that I hold a responsibility for her as a member of my staff, if for no other reason. It can't be denied that if I had refused her offer to take part in the experiment, this would not have happened. Therefore it seems to me that we ought to be able to argue a state of temporary insanity; that the balance of her mind was disturbed by the effects of the drug which I administered.

And if we can get that as a verdict it will result in detention at a mental hospital for observation and treatment—perhaps quite a short spell of treatment.'

'I can't say. We can certainly put it up to counsel and see what he thinks of it.'

'It's valid, too,' Hellyer persisted. 'People like Jane don't do murder if they are in their right minds, not unless they're really in a corner, then they do it more cleverly. Certainly they don't murder perfect strangers. Clearly, the drug caused an hallucination sufficiently vivid to confuse her to a point where she was unable to make a proper distinction between the actual and the hypothetical. She got into a state where she believed the mirage was real, and acted accordingly.'

'Yes. Yes, I suppose one might put it that way,' agreed the solicitor. He looked down again at the pile of paper before him. 'The whole account is, of course, unreasonable,' he said, 'and yet it is pervaded throughout with such an air of reasonableness. I wonder. . . .' He paused pensively, and went on: 'This expendability of the male, Hellyer. She doesn't seem to find it so much incredible, as undesirable. That seems odd in itself to a layman who takes the natural order for granted, but would you, as a medical scientist, say it was—well, not impossible, in theory?'

Dr. Hellyer frowned.

'That's very much the kind of question one wants more notice of. It would be very rash to proclaim it *impossible*. Considering it purely as an abstract problem, I can see two or three lines of approach. . . . Of course, if an utterly improbable situation were to arise calling for intensive research—research, that is, on the sort of scale they tackled the atom—well, who can tell . . . ?' He shrugged.

The solicitor nodded again.

'That's just what I was getting at,' he observed. 'Basically it is only just such a little way off the beam; quite near enough to possibility to be faintly disturbing. Mind you, as far as the defence is concerned, her air of thorough conviction, taken in conjunction with the near-plausibility of the thing will probably help. But, for my part, it is just that nearness that is enough to make me a trifle uneasy.'

The doctor looked at him rather sharply.

'Oh, come! Really now! A hardboiled solicitor, too! Don't tell me you're going in for fantasy-building. Anyway, if you are, you'll have to conjure up another one. If Jane, poor girl, has settled one thing, it is that there's no future in this particular fantasy. Perrigan's finished with, and all his work's gone up in smoke and fire.'

'H'm,' said the solicitor, again. 'All the same, it would be more satisfactory if we knew of some way other than this'—he tapped the pile of papers—'some other way in which she is likely to have acquired some knowledge of Perrigan and his work. There is, as far as one knows, *no* other way in which he can have come into her orbit at all—unless, perhaps, she takes an interest in veterinary subjects?'

'She doesn't. I'm sure of that,' Hellyer told him, shaking his head.

'Well that, then, remains one slightly disturbing aspect. And there is another. You'll think it foolish of me, I'm sure—and no doubt time will prove you right to do so—but I have to admit I'd be feeling just a bit easier in my mind if Jane had been just a bit more thorough in her inquiries before she went into action.'

'Meaning——?' asked Dr. Hellyer, looking puzzled.

'Only that she does not seem to have found out that there is a son. But there is, you see. He appears to have taken quite a close interest in his father's work, and is determined that it shan't be wasted. In fact he has already announced that he will do his best to carry it on with the very few specimens that were saved from the fire. . . .

'Laudably filial, no doubt. All the same it does disturb me a little to find that he, also, happens to be a D.Sc., a biochemist; and that, very naturally, his name, too, is Perrigan. . . .'

AN EYE FOR A WHAT?

DAMON KNIGHT

A story of Crime and Punishment and the attempt to make the punishment fit the criminal—though the lovable and spherical Extra-Terrestrial, George, was a criminal only by the standards of his own planet.

I

On his way across the wheel one morning, Dr. Walter Alvarez detoured down to C level promenade. A few men were standing, as usual, at the view window looking out at the enormous blue-green planet below. They were dressed alike in sheen-grey overalls, a garment with detachable gauntlets and hood designed to make it convertible into a spacesuit. It was uncomfortable, but regulation: according to the books, a Survey and Propaganda Satellite might find itself under attack at any moment.

Nothing so interesting had happened to SAPS 3107A, orbiting off the seventh planet of a G-type star in Ophiuchus. They had been here for two years and a half, and most of them had not even touched ground yet.

There it was, drifting by out there, blue-green, fat and juicy—an oxygen planet, two-thirds land, mild climate, soil fairly bursting with minerals and organics.

Alvarez felt his mouth watering when he looked at it. He had 'wheel fever'; they all did. He wanted to get *down* there, to natural gravity and natural ailments.

The last month or so, there had been a feeling in the satellite that a break-through was coming. Always coming: it never arrived.

A plump orthotypist named Lola went by, and a couple of the men turned with automatic whistles. 'Listen,' said Olaf Marx conspiratorially, with a hand on Alvarez's arm, 'that reminds me, did you hear what happened at the big banquet yesterday?'

'No,' said Alvarez, irritably withdrawing his arm. 'I didn't go. Can't stand banquets. Why?'

'Well, the way I got it, the Commandant's wife was sitting right across from George——'

Alvarez's interest sharpened. 'You mean the gorgon? What did he do?'

'I'm *telling* you. See, it looked like he was watching her all through dinner. Then up comes the dessert—lemon meringue. So old George——'

The shift bell rang. Alvarez started nervously and looked at his thumbwatch. The other men were drifting away. So was Olaf, laughing like a fool. 'You'll die when you hear,' he called back. 'Boy, do I wish I'd been there myself! So long, Walt.'

Alvarez reluctantly went the other way. In B corridor, somebody called after him, 'Hey, Walt? Hear about the banquet?'

He shook his head. The other man, a baker named Pedro, grinned and waved, disappearing up the curve of the corridor. Alvarez opened the door of Xenology Section and went in.

During his absence, somebody had put a new chart on the wall. It was ten feet high and there were little rectangles all over it, each connected by lines to other rectangles. When he first saw it, Alvarez thought it was a new table of organization for the Satellite Service, and he winced: but on closer inspection, the chart was *too* complex, and besides, it had a peculiar disorganized appearance. Boxes had been white-rubbed out and other boxes drawn on top of them. Some parts were crowded illegibly together and others were spacious. The whole thing looked desperately confused; and so did Elvis Womrath, who was on a wheeled ladder erasing the entire top righthand corner. '*N* panga,' he said irritably. 'That right?'

'Yes,' a voice piped unexpectedly. Alvarez looked around, saw nobody. The voice went on, 'But he is *R* panga to his cousins and all their *N* pangas or bigger, except when——'

Alvarez leaned over and peered around the desk. There on the carpet was the owner of the voice, a pinkish-white spheroid with various appendages sprouting in all directions, like a floating mine: 'George' the gorgon.

'Oh, it's you,' said Alvarez, producing his echo sounder and humidometer. 'What's all this nonsense I hear——' He began to prod the gorgon with the test equipment, making his regular morning examination. It was the only bright moment of his day; the infirmary could wait.

'All right,' Womrath interrupted, scrubbing furiously. '*R* panga to cousins—wait a minute, now.' He turned with a scowl. 'Alvarez, I'll be through in a minute. *N* panga or bigger, except when . . .' He sketched in half a dozen boxes, labelled them and began to draw connecting lines. 'Now is *that* right?' he asked George.

'Yes, only now it is wrong panga to *mother's* cousins. Draw again, from father's cousins' *N* pangas, to mother's cousins' *O* pangas or bigger . . . Yes, and now from father's uncles' *R* pangas, to mother's uncles' pangas *cousins*——'

Womrath's hand faltered. He stared at the chart; he had drawn such a tangle of lines, he couldn't tell what box connected with which. '*You* go nuts,' he said hopelessly. He climbed down off the ladder and slapped the stylus into Alvarez's palm. He thumbed the intercom on the desk and said, 'Chief, I'm going off now. *Way* off.'

'*Did you get that chart straightened out?*' the intercom demanded.

'No, but——'

'*You're on extra duty as of now. Take a pill. Is Alvarez here?*'

'Yes,' said Womrath resignedly.

'*Both of you come in, then. Leave George outside.*'

'Hello, Doctor,' the spheroid piped. 'Are you panga to me?'

'Don't let's get into *that*,' said Womrath, twitching, and took Alvarez by the sleeve. They found the chief of the Xenology Section, Edward H. Dominick, huddled bald and bear-like behind his desk. The cigar in his hand looked chewed. 'Womrath,' he said, 'when can you give me that chart?'

'I don't know. Never, maybe.'

Dominick swivelled his gaze to Alvarez. 'Have you,' he asked, 'heard about what happened at the banquet in George's honour yesterday?'

'No, I have not,' said Alvarez. 'Will you be so kind as to tell me, or else shut up about it?'

Dominick rubbed his shaven skull, absorbing the insult. 'It was during the dessert,' he said. 'George was sitting opposite Mrs. Carver, in that little jump seat. Just as she got her fork into the pie—it was lemon meringue—George rolled up over the table and grabbed the plate away. Mrs. Carver screamed, pulled back—thought she was being attacked, I suppose—and the chair went out from under her. It—was—a—mess.'

Alvarez ended the awed silence. 'What did he do with the pie?'

'Ate it,' said Dominick glumly. 'Had a perfectly good piece of his own, that he didn't touch.' He popped a lozenge into his mouth.

Alvarez shook his head. 'Not typical. His pattern is strictly submissive. I don't like it.'

'That's what I told Carver. But he was livid. Shaking. We all sat there until he escorted his wife to her room and came back. Then we had an interrogation. All we could get out of George was, "I thought I was panga to her". '

Alvarez shifted impatiently in his chair, reaching automatically for a bunch of grapes from the bowl on the desk. He was a small, spare man, and he felt defensive about it. 'Now what is all this panga business?' he demanded.

Womrath snorted, and began to peel a banana.

'Panga,' said Dominick, 'would appear to be some kind of complicated authority-submission relationship that exists among the gorgons.' Alvarez sat up straighter. 'They never mentioned it to us, because we never asked. Now it turns out to be crucial.' Dominick sighed. 'Fourteen months, just getting a three-man base down on the planet. Seven more to get the elders' permission to bring a gorgon here experimentally. All according to the book. We picked the biggest and brightest-looking one we could find: that was George. He seemed to be coming along great. And now this.'

'Well, chief,' said Womrath carefully, 'nobody has any more admiration than I have for Mrs. Carver as a consumer—she really puts it away, but it seems to me the question is, is *George* damaged——'

Dominick was shaking his head. 'I haven't told you the rest of it. This panga thing stopped Carver cold, but not for long. He beamed down to the planethead and had Rubinson ask the elders, "Is George panga to the Commandant's wife?" '

Alvarez grinned mirthlessly and clicked his tongue.

'Sure.' Dominick nodded. 'Who knows what a question like that may have meant to them? They answered back, in effect, "Certainly not," and wanted to know the details. Carver *told* them.'

'And?' said Alvarez.

'They said George was a shocking criminal who should be appropriately punished. Not by them, you understand —by us, because we're the offended parties. Moreover— now this must make sense to their peculiar way of looking at things—if *we* don't punish George to their satisfaction, *they'll* punish Rubinson and his whole crew.'

'How?' Alvarez demanded.

'By doing,' Dominick said, 'whatever it is we should have done to George—and that could be anything.'

Womrath pursed his lips to whistle, but no sound came out. He swallowed a mouthful of banana and tried again. Still nothing.

'You get it?' said Dominick with suppressed emotion. They all looked through the open doorway at George, squatting patiently in the other room. 'There's no trouble about "punishment"—we all know what it means, we've read the books. But how do you punish an alien like that? *An eye for a what?*'

'Now let's see if we have this straight,' said Dominick, sorting through the papers in his hand. Womrath and Alvarez looked on from either side. George tried to peek, too, but his photoceptors were too short. They were all standing in the outer office, which had been stripped to the bare walls and floor. 'One. We know a gorgon changes colour according to its emotional state. When they're contented, they're a kind of rose-pink. When they're unhappy, they turn blue.'

'He's been pink ever since we've had him on the Satellite,' said Womrath, glancing down at the gorgon.

'Except at the banquet,' Dominick answered thoughtfully. 'I remember he turned bluish just before . . . If we could find out what it was that set him off—— Well, first things first.' He held down another finger. 'Two, we don't have any information at all about local systems of reward and punishment. They may cut each other into bits for spitting on the slidewalk, or they may just slap each other's —um, wrists——' he looked unhappily down at George, all his auricles and photoceptors out on stalks '—for arson, rape and mopery,' he finished. 'We don't know; we'll have to play it by ear.'

'What does George say about it?' Alvarez asked. 'Why don't you ask him?'

'We thought of that,' Womrath said glumly. 'Asked him what the elders would do to him in a case like this, and he said they'd quabble his infarcts, or something.'

'A dead end,' Dominick added. 'It would take us years. Well, number three, we've got all the furniture out of here —it's going to be damned crowded with the whole staff working in my office, but never mind . . . Number four, there's his plate with the bread and water. And number five, that door has been fixed so it latches on the outside. Let's give it a dry run.'

He led the way to the door; the others followed, including George.

'No, you stay in here,' Womrath told him. George stopped, blushing an agreeable pink.

Dominick solemnly closed the door and dropped the improvised latch into its socket. He punched the door button, found it satisfactorily closed. Through the transparent upper pane, they could see George inquisitively watching.

Dominick opened the door again. 'Now, George,' he said, 'pay attention. This is a *prison*. You're being *punished*. We're going to keep you in here, with nothing to eat but what's there, until we think you're punished enough. Understand?'

'Yes,' said George doubtfully.

'All right,' said Dominick, and closed the door. They all stood watching for a while, and George stood watching them back, but nothing else happened. 'Let's go into my office and wait,' said Dominick, with a sigh. 'Can't expect miracles, all at once.'

They trooped down the corridor to the adjoining room and ate peanuts for a while. 'He's a sociable creature,' Womrath said hopefully. 'He'll get lonesome after a while.'

'And hungry,' Alvarez said. 'He never turns down a meal.'

Half an hour later, when they looked in, George was thoughtfully chewing up the carpet.

'No, no, no, *no*, George,' said Dominick, bursting in on him. 'You're not supposed to eat anything except what we give you. This is a *prison*.'

'Good carpet,' said George, hurt.

'I don't care if it is. You don't eat it, understand?'

'Okay,' said George cheerfully. His colour was an honest rose-pink.

Four hours later, when Alvarez went off shift, George had settled down in a corner and pulled in all his appendages. He was asleep. If anything, he looked pinker than ever.

When Alvarez came on shift again, there was no doubt about it. George was sitting in the middle of the room, photoceptors out and waving rhythmically; his colour was a glowing pink, the pink of a rose pearl. Dominick kept him in there for another day, just to make sure; George seemed to lose a little weight on the austere diet, but glowed a steady pink. He liked it.

II

Goose Kelly, the games instructor, tried to keep up a good front, but he had the worst case of wheel fever on SAPS 3107A. It had got so that looking out at that fat, blue-green planet, swimming there so close, was more than he could bear. Kelly was a big man, an outdoor man by instinct; he longed for natural air in his lungs, and turf under his feet. To compensate, he strode faster, shouted louder, got redder of face and bulgier of eye, bristled more fiercely. To quiet an occasional trembling of his hands, he munched sedative pills.

'Is that it?' he asked now, disapprovingly. He had never seen the gorgon before; Semantics, Medical and Xenology Sections had been keeping him pretty much to themselves.

Dominick prodded the pinkish sphere with his toe. 'Wake up, George.'

After a moment, the gorgon's skin became lumpy at half a dozen points. The lumps grew slowly into long, segmented stems. Some of these expanded at the tips into 'feet' and 'hands'; others flowered into the intricate patterns of auricles and photoceptors—and one speech organ, which looked like a small trumpet. 'Hello,' said George cheerfully.

'He can pull them back in any time?' Kelly asked, rubbing his chin.

'Yes. Show him, George.'

'All right.' The feathery stalks became blank-tipped, then rapidly shrank, segment by segment. In less than two seconds, George was a smooth sphere again.

'Well, that makes for a little problem here,' said Kelly. 'You see what I mean? If you can't get a grip on him, how are you going to *punish* him like you say?'

'We've tried everything we could think of,' said

Dominick. 'We locked him up, kept him on short rations, didn't talk to him . . . He doesn't draw any pay, you know, so you can't fine him.'

'Or downgrade him on the promotion lists, either,' said Womrath gloomily.

'No. And it's a little late to use the Pavlov-Morganstern treatments we all had when we were children. We can't prevent a crime he's already committed. So our thought was, since you're the games instructor——'

'We thought,' Womrath said diplomatically, 'you might have noticed something that might be useful. You know, rough-housing and so on.'

Kelly thought this over. 'Well, there's low blows,' he said, 'but I mean, hell——' He gestured futilely at George, who had just decided to put his auricles out again. 'What would you——'

'No, that's out of the question,' Dominick said heavily. 'Well, I'm sorry, Kelly. It was nice of you to help out.'

'No, now, wait a minute.' said Kelly. 'I got something coming to me, maybe.' He nibbled a thumbnail, staring down at the gorgon. 'How would this be. I was thinking—sometimes the boys in the pool, they get kind of frisky, they take to ducking each other. Under the water. Now what I was thinking, he breathes air, doesn't he? You know what I mean?'

Dominick and Womrath looked at each other. 'It sounds possible,' said Dominick.

'Out of the question. We don't know what his tolerance is. Suppose Kelly should damage him severely, or even——'

'Oh,' said Dominick. 'No, you're right, we couldn't take a chance.'

'I've been a games instructor for seventy-three years—two rejuvenations——' Kelly began, bristling.

'No, it isn't that, Kelly,' said Womrath hastily. 'We're

just thinking. George isn't human. So how do we know how he'd react to a ducking?'

'On the other hand,' Dominick said, 'gorgons *do* turn blue when they're not happy—we have Rubinson's assurance for that. It seems to me George wouldn't be happy when smothering; that would be the whole point, wouldn't it? Dr. Alvarez would supervise closely, of course. Really, Alvarez, I don't see why not. Kelly, if you'll tell me what time would be most convenient for you——'

'Well,' said Kelly, looking at his thumbwatch, 'hell, the pool is empty now—it's ladies' day, but all the girls are down in Section Seven, hanging around Mrs. Carver. I hear she's still hysterical.'

Struck by a thought, Alvarez was bending over to speak to the gorgon. 'George, you breathe by spiracles, is that correct? Those little tubes all over your skin?'

'Yes,' said George.

'Well, do they work under water?'

'No.'

Dominick and Kelly were listening with interest.

'If we held you under water, would it hurt you?'

George flickered uncertainly, from rose to pale magenta. 'Don't know. Little bit.'

The three men leaned closer. 'Well, George,' said Dominick tensely, ' would that be a *punishment*?'

George flickered again, violently. 'Yes. No. Maybe. Don't know.'

They straightened again, disappointed; Dominick sighed gustily. 'He always gives us those mixed-up answers. *I* don't know. Let's try it—what else can we do?'

Kelly found himself paired off with George, following Dominick and Dr. Alvarez, and preceding Womrath and an orderly named Josling who was wheeling one of the dispensary pul-motors. The up-curving corridors were deserted. Kelly lagged a little, adjusting his pace to George's waddling steps. After a moment, he was surprised to feel something small and soft grip his fingers. He looked down; George the gorgon had put one seven-fingered 'hand' into his. The gorgon's flower-like photoceptors were turned trustfully upward.

Kelly was taken by surprise. No children were allowed on the Satellite, but Kelly had been the father of eight in a previous rejuvenation. The confiding touch stirred old memories. 'That'll be all right,' said Kelly gruffly. 'You just come along with me.'

The pool, as he had predicted, was empty. Ripples reflected the faint threads of light up the walls. 'The shallow end would be better,' said Kelly. His voice was hollow, and echoed back flatly. Pausing to peel off his coverall, he led George carefully down the steps into the pool. Half submerged, George floated. Kelly drew him gently out into deeper water.

Dominick and the others arranged themselves along the brink in interested attitudes. Kelly cleared his throat. 'Well,' he said, 'the way it generally happens, one of the boys will grab a hold of another one, like this——' He put his hands on the smooth floating globe, and hesitated.

'Go ahead now, Kelly,' called Dominick. 'Remember, you have a direct order to do this.'

'Sure,' said Kelly. 'Well——' He turned to the gorgon. 'Hold your breath now!' He pressed downward. The gorgon seemed lighter than he had expected, like an inflated ball; it was hard to force it under.

Kelly pushed harder. George went under briefly and slipped out of Kelly's hands, bobbing to the surface. The gorgon's speaking trumpet cleared itself of water with a *phonk* and said, 'Nice. Do again, Kelly.'

Kelly glanced over at Dominick, who said, 'Yes. Again.' Dr. Alvarez stroked his thin beard and said nothing.

Kelly took a deep sympathetic breath, and shoved the gorgon under. A few bubbles came to the surface; George's speaking trumpet broke water, but made no sound. Down below, Kelly could see his own pale hands gripping the gorgon's body; the water made them look bloodless; but not George; he was a clear, unblemished pink.

There was a discouraged silence when Kelly brought him back up.

'Listen,' said Dominick, 'I've got another idea. George, can you breathe through that speaking trumpet, too?'

'Yes,' said George cheerfully.

There was a chorus of disgusted 'Oh, wells.' Everybody brightened perceptibly. Josling polished his pul-motor with a rag. 'Go ahead, Kelly,' said Dominick. 'And this time, you hold him under.'

George went down for the third time. The bubbles swirled upward. The gorgon's speaking trumpet swayed toward the surface, but Kelly leaned farther over, blocking it with his forearm. After a moment, all of George's appendages began to contract. Kelly craned his neck downward anxiously. Was a hint of blue beginning to show?

'Keep him down,' said Alvarez sharply.

George was a blank sphere again. Then one or two of the limbs began to reappear; but they looked different somehow.

'Now,' said Kelly.

'Give him a second more,' said Dominick, leaning over precariously. 'It seems to me——'

Kelly's back muscles were knotted with tension. He did not like the way George's new limbs seemed to be flattening out, trailing limply—it was as if something had gone wrong in the works.

'I'm bringing him up,' he said hoarsely.

To Kelly's horror, when he lifted his hands, George stayed where he was. Kelly made a grab for him, but the gorgon slipped out from under his fingers. The new limbs stiffened and sculled vigorously; George darted away, deep under the water.

Leaning, open-mouthed, Dominick slipped and went into the pool with a majestic splash. He floundered and rose up, a moment later, streaming with water like a sea-lion. Kelly, wading anxiously towards him, stopped when he saw that Dominick was safe. Both men looked down. Between them and around them swam George, darting and drifting by turns, as much at home in the pool as a speckled trout.

'Fins!' said Dominick, stack-jawed. 'And *gills*!'

It may as well be said that Dr. Walter Alvarez was a misanthrope. He did not like people; he liked diseases. Down there on Planet Seven, once the trade mission was established, he could confidently expect enough new and startling ailments to keep him happy as a lark for years. Up here, all he got was sprained ankles, psychosomatic colds, hives and indigestion. There was one cook's helper named Samuels who kept coming back every Wednesday with the same boil on the back of his neck. It got so that in spite of himself, Alvarez spent the whole week dreading Wednesday. When he saw Samuels's earnest face coming through the door, something seemed to wind itself a little tighter inside him.

Some day, when Samuels opened his mouth to say, 'Hey, Doc'— Samuels always called him 'Doc'—the something inside him was going to break with a sound like a banjo string. What would happen then, Dr. Alvarez was unable to imagine.

When the gorgon had first been brought up to the Satellite, there had been two or three delightful little fungus infections, then nothing. A great disappointment. Alvarez had isolated and cultured almost a hundred micro-organisms found in smears he had taken from George, but they were all non-viable in human tissue. The viable bacteria, viruses, parasites that always turned up on a life-infested planet, were evidently lurking in some organism other than the gorgons. They swam, at night, across the optical field of Dr. Alvarez's dreaming mind—rod-shaped ones, lens-shaped ones, wriggly ones, leggy ones and ones with teeth.

One morning Dr. Alvarez awoke with a desperate resolve. It was a Tuesday. He went directly to the infirmary, relieved Nurse Trumble, who was on duty, and, opening a locked cabinet, filled a hypodermic from an ampoule of clear straw-coloured fluid. The trade name of this substance was Bets-off; it was a counter-inhibitant which stunned the censor areas of the forebrain chiefly affected by the Pavlov-Morgenstern treatments. (By an odd coincidence, the patentee was a Dr. Jekyll.) Alvarez injected two c.c.'s of it directly into his median basilic vein and sat down to wait.

After a few minutes his perpetual bad humour began to lift. He felt a pleasant ebullience; the colours of things around him seemed brighter and clearer. 'Ha!' said Alvarez. He got up and went to his little refrigerator, where, after some search, he found half a dozen of the cultures he had made of micro-organisms taken from gorgon smears. They were quiescent, of course—deep-frozen. Alvarez warmed them cautiously and added nutrients. All morning, while the usual succession of minor complaints paraded through the infirmary, the cultures grew and multiplied. Alvarez was jovial with his patients;

he cracked a joke or two, and handed out harmless pills all around.

By noon, four of the cultures were flourishing. Alvarez carefully concentrated them into one, and loaded another hypodermic with the resulting brew. To his liberated intelligence, the matter was clear: No organism, man or pig or gorgon, was altogether immune to the microbes it normally carried in its body. Upset the balance by injecting massive colonies of any one of them, and you were going to have a sick gorgon—*i.e.*, Alvarez thought, a punished gorgon.

The treatment might also kill the patient, but Alvarez light-heartedly dismissed this argument as a quibble. (Or quabble?) Armed with his hypo, he went forth looking for George.

He found him in the small assembly room, together with Dominick, Womrath, and a mechanic named Bob Ritner. They were all standing around a curious instrument, or object of art, built out of bar aluminium. 'It's a rack,' Ritner explained proudly. 'I saw a picture of it once in a kid's book.'

The chief feature of the 'rack' was a long, narrow table, with a windlass at one end. It looked like a crude device for stretching something.

'We thought the time had come for stern measures,' Dominick said, mopping his head.

'In the olden days,' Ritner put in, 'they used these on the prisoners when they wouldn't talk.'

'I talk,' said George unexpectedly.

'It's another punishment, George,' Dominick explained kindly. 'Well, Alvarez, before we go ahead, I suppose you want to examine your patient.'

'Yes, just so, ha ha!' said Alvarez. He knelt down and peered keenly at George, who swivelled his photoceptors interestedly around to stare back. The doctor prodded George's hide; it was firm and resilient. The gorgon's colour was a clear pink; the intricate folds of his auricles seemed crisp and alert.

Alvarez took a hand scale from his kit; it was preset for A-level gravity. 'Climb up here, George.' Obediently, the gorgon settled himself on the pan of the scale while Alvarez held it up. 'Hm,' said Alvarez. 'He's lost a good deal of weight.'

'He has?' asked Dominick hopefully.

'But he seems to be in unusually good condition—better than a week ago, I would say. Perhaps just a little sugar solution to pep him up——' Alvarez withdrew the hypo from his kit, aimed it at George's smooth skin and pressed the trigger.

Dominick sighed. 'Well, I suppose we might as well go ahead. George, just hop up there and let Ritner tie those straps on to you.'

George obediently climbed on to the table. Ritner buckled straps around four of his limbs and then began to tighten the cylinder.

'Not too much,' said George anxiously.

'I'll be careful,' Ritner assured him. He kept on winding the cylinder up. 'How does that feel?' George's 'arms' and 'legs' were half again their usual length, and still stretching.

'Tickles,' said George.

Ritner went on turning the handle. Womrath coughed nervously and was shushed. George's limbs kept on getting longer; then his body started to lengthen visibly.

'Are you all right, George?' Dominick asked.

'All right.'

Ritner gave the handle a last despairing twist. George's elongated body stretched all the way in comfort from one end of the rack to the other: there was no place else for him to go. 'Nice,' said George. 'Do again.' He was glowing a happy pink.

Ritner, who seemed about to cry, petulantly kicked his machine. Alvarez snorted and went away. In the corridor, unseen, he jumped up and clicked his heels together. He was having a wonderful time; his only regret was that it was not tomorrow. Come to think of it, why wait till Wednesday?

Commandant Charles Watson Carver, S. S., had been trained to make quick and courageous decisions. Once you began to entertain a doubt of your own rightness, you would hesitate too much, begin to second-guess yourself, fall prey to superstition and anxiety, and end up without any power of decision at all.

The trouble was, you could never be right all the time. Following the book to the letter, or improvising brilliantly, either way, you were bound to make mistakes. The thing was, to cross them off and go ahead just the same.

Carver firmed his chin and straightened his back, looking down at the sick gorgon. It was sick, all right, there was no question about that: the thing's limbs drooped and weaved slightly, dizzily. Its hide was dry and hot to the touch. 'How long has he been like this?' Carver demanded, hesitating only slightly over the 'he': aliens were 'it' to him and always had been, but it didn't do to let anybody know it.

'Twenty minutes, more or less,' said Dr. Nasalroad. 'I just got here myself—' he stifled a yawn '—about ten minutes ago.'

'What are you doing here, anyway?' Carver asked him. 'It's Alvarez's shift.'

Nasalroad looked embarrassed. 'I know. Alvarez is in the hospital, as a patient. I think he assaulted a cook's helper named Samuels—poured soup over his head. He was shouting something about boiling the boil on Samuels' neck. We had to put him under sedation; it took three of us.'

Carver set his jaw hard. 'Nasalroad, what in thunder is happening on this wheel, anyhow? First this thing attacks my wife, then Alvarez——' He glared down at George. 'Can you put him out of this, whatever it is?'

Nasalroad looked surprised. 'That would be a large order. We don't know any gorgon medicine—I was assuming you'd want to beam down and ask *them*.'

That was reasonable, of course: the only hitch was, as usual, a matter of interpretation. Was this something they had negligently allowed to happen to an important alien representative, or was it the necessary and proper punishment they had all been looking for? Carver glanced at his thumb-watch: it was just about three hours before the elders' deadline.

He asked Nasalroad, 'What colour would you say he is now? Not pink, certainly.'

'No-o. But not blue, either. I'd call it a kind of violet.'

'Hm. Well, anyhow, he's got smaller than he was, isn't that right? *Conspicuously* smaller.'

Nasalroad admitted it.

Carver made his decision. 'Do the best you can,' he said to Nasalroad. He lifted his wristcom, said briskly, 'Have you got a line-of-sight to the planethead?'

'*Yes sir*,' the operator answered.

'All right, get me Rubinson.'

A few seconds passed. '*Planethead*.'

'Rubinson, this is Carver. Tell the elders we've got a pretty unhappy gorgon here. We're not sure just what did it—might have been any one of a lot of things—but he's lost a good deal of weight, and his colour—' Carver hesitated '—it's bluish. Definitely *bluish*. Got that?'

'Yes chief. Thank goodness! I'll pass the message along right away, and call you back.'

'Right.' Carver closed the wristcom with an assertive snap. The gorgon, when he glanced down at it, looked sicker than ever, but never mind. What happened to the gorgon was its lookout; Carver was doing his duty.

III

Alvarez awoke with a horrible headache and a sense of guilt. He was not in his own cubicle, but in one of the hospital bunks, dressed in a regulation set of hospital pyjamas (with removable hood and gloves, capable of being converted into a spacesuit). He could just see the wall clock at the far end of the room. It was twenty-three hours—well into his shift. Alvarez scuttled out of bed, groaning, and looked at the chart beside it. *Mania, delusions. Sedation. Signed, Nasalroad.*

Delusions: yes, he was having one now. He imagined he could remember heaving up a big tureen of mock-turtle soup over Samuels's startled face—splash, a smoking green torrent.

Good heavens! If that was *real*—Samuels! And the gorgon!

Groaning and lurching, Alvarez darted out of the room, past the orderly, Munch, who was sitting with a story-viewer on his lap and couldn't get up fast enough. 'Dr. Alvarez! Dr. Nasalroad said——'

'Never mind Nasalroad,' he snapped, pawing in the refrigerator. He remembered those cultures being right back *there*: but now they were gone.

'—not to let you up until you acted normal again. Uh, how do you feel, Doctor?'

'I feel fine! What difference does that make? How is *he*?,

Munch looked puzzled and apprehensive. 'Samuels? Just superficial burns. We put him to bed in his own cubby because——'

'Not Samuels!' Alvarez hissed, grabbing Munch by the front of his suit. 'The gorgon!'

'Oh, well, he's been sick, too. How did you know, though, Doctor? You were snoring when it happened. Listen, let go my suit, you're making me nervous.'

'Where?' Alvarez demanded, thrusting his scrawny face close to the other's.

'Where what? Oh, you mean the *gorgon*? Up in the little assembly room, the last I——'

Alvarez was gone, out of the door and down the corridor like a small, bearded fireball. He found an anxious crowd assembled—Commandant and Mrs. Carver, Dominick and his staff, Urban and two assistants from Semantics, orderlies, porters, and Dr. Nasalroad. Nasalroad had the gaunt and bright-eyed appearance of a man who has been on wake-up pills too long. He started when he saw Alvarez.

'What's up?' Alvarez demanded, grabbing his sleeve. 'Where's the gorgon? What——'

'Be quiet,' said Nasalroad. 'George is over in that corner behind Carver. We're waiting for the delegation from planethead. Rubinson said they were coming up, three of them with some kind of a box. . . .'

A loudspeaker said suddenly, 'I have the tender locked on. Contact. Contact is made. The lock is opening; get ready, here they come.'

Alvarez couldn't see past Carver's bulk; he tried to get away, but Nasalroad stopped him. 'I want to *see*,' he said irritably.'

'Listen,' Nasalroad said. 'I know what you did. I checked the Bets-off and those cultures against inventory. The gorgon seems to be recovering nicely, no thanks to you. Now has the stuff worn off you, or not? Because if not——'

A rustle went over the group. Alvarez and Nasalroad turned in time to see the door opening. Two large, vigorous-looking gorgons waddled through; they were carrying an enamelled metal box between them. '*Foop!*' said the first one, 'Where is gorgon George?'

'I'm all right,' Alvarez muttered. 'If I wasn't, I'd have done something uncivilized to you by now, wouldn't I?'

'I guess so,' said Nasalroad. They elbowed closer as the group shifted, making a space around the three gorgons. Peering, on tiptoe, Alvarez could see George standing shakily beside the other two. 'He looks terrible. Those are big ones, those other two, aren't they?'

'Not as big as George was when we got him,' Nasalroad muttered. 'Listen, Walt, if it turns out you've ruined the whole thing, I'll take a dose of Bets-off myself, and——'

'Listen,' snarled Alvarez.

One of the gorgons was explaining, 'This is panga box. What you call? You know panga?'

'Well, uh, yes and no,' said Dominick uncomfortably. 'But what about the punishment? We understood——'

'Punishment later. You George, go in box.'

Obediently, George waddled over and squatted beside the mouth of the box. He bobbed uncertainly; he looked for all the world like a large woman trying to get into a small sports copter. There was a minor outbreak of nervous laughter, quickly suppressed.

George leaned, retracting most of his upper appendages. His round body began to be compressed into a squarish shape, wedging itself into the box.

The gorgons watched with an air of tension, photoceptors rigidly extended. A hush fell. Among the humans present there was a general air of Why-are-we-all-whispering?

George wriggled and oozed farther into the box. Momentarily he stuck. He flickered blue, then pink. His 'feet', almost retracted, scrabbled feebly at the bottom of the box. Then he was in.

One of the other gorgons solemnly closed the lid on him and fastened it to make sure, then opened it again and helped him out. All three gorgons began to make rhythmic swaying motions with their 'arms' and other appendages. George, Alvarez thought, looked smug. He felt a sudden premonitory pang. What had he done?

'What's it all about?' Nasalroad demanded. 'Are they measuring him for a coffin, or——'

Dominick, overhearing, turned and said, 'I don't think so. Now this is interesting. You remember they said a panga box. What I'm afraid of is, they may have a standard of size. You see what I mean, they're measuring George to see if he falls below the minimum standard of, uh, panga relations.'

'Oh, heavens,' said another voice. It was Urban of Semantics, who had been neglected of late; they hadn't needed him since George learned English. He was peering over Dominick's shoulder, looking dumbfounded. He said, 'But don't you know the word we've been translating 'elders' really means 'smallest ones'? Good heavens——'

'I don't see——' Dominick began, but the Commandant's voice drowned him out.

'Quiet! Quiet please!' Carver was trumpeting. He went on, 'Our friends from Seven have an announcement to make. Now, then.'

To everyone's surprise, it was George who spoke, in the lisping accents of the gorgon language. No human present understood a word of it except Urban, who turned pale under his tan and began stammering inaudibly to himself.

One of the larger gorgons began to speak when George

stopped. 'Most elder person, known to you by name George, wishes me to thank you for all kindness done to him when he was humble youth.'

('Youth,' muttered Urban. 'But it really means "ungainly one"—or "fat boy"! Oh, my *heavens*!')

'Now that he has become an elder, it will be his most pleasure to repay all kindness in agreeable legislative manner.'

('What does all this mean?' Alvarez said aggrievedly. 'Why can't he talk for himself, anyway?'

'It would be beneath his dignity now,' said Nasalroad. 'Hush!')

'—*If*,' said the gorgon, 'you will succeed in giving elder person, known by name George, proper punishment as aforesaid.'

While the others stared with dumb dismay, Carver briskly snapped open his wristcom. 'Exactly how long have we got until that gorgon deadline is up?' he demanded.

There was a pause, while ears strained to catch the tiny voice.

'*Just under half an hour.*'

'This meeting will come to order!' said Carver, banging on the table. George and the other two gorgons were sitting opposite him, with the centrepiece of nasturtiums and ferns between them. Grouped around Carver were Dominick, Urban, Womrath, Alvarez, Nasalroad, Kelly and Ritner.

'Now this is the situation,' Carver said aggressively. 'This gorgon turns out to be a member of their ruling council, I don't understand why, but never mind that now—the point is, he's friendly disposed towards us, so we've succeeded in this mission *if* we can find the proper punishment—otherwise we're in the soup. Suggestions.'

(Dominick craned his bald head towards Alvarez across the table. 'Doctor, I had a thought,' he murmured. 'Would you say—is there anything peculiar about the gorgon's body constitution, as compared say to ours?'

'Certainly,' said Alvarez, dourly. 'Any number of things. You name it, they——')

Giving them a dirty look, Carver nodded to Ritner. 'Yes?'

'Well, I was thinking. I know the rack was a washout, but there was another thing they used to use, called the Iron Virgin. It had a door, like, with spikes on it——'

('What I had in mind,' Dominick said, 'is there anything that would tend to limit their body size—any danger or disadvantage in growing large?'

Alvarez frowned and looked at Nasalroad, who hitched his chair closer.

'The pressure——?' said Nasalroad tentatively.

They rubbed their chins and looked at each other with professional glints in their eyes.

'What *about* the pressure?' Dominick prompted eagerly.)

'How long would it take you to build a thing like that?' Carver was asking Ritner.

'Well—ten, eleven hours.'

'Too long. That's out. Next!'

('They're actually a single cell—all colloidal fluid, at a considerable osmotic pressure. The bigger they get, the more pressure it takes to keep that shape. If they got too big, I rather imagine——'

Alvarez snapped his fingers, awed. 'They'd burst!')

Carver turned with an indignant glare. 'Gentlemen, if I could get a little co-operation out of you, instead of this continual distraction—— All right, Womrath?'

'Sir, I was just wondering, suppose if we let him turn into a fish, the way he did before in the pool—but then we'd net him and take him out of the water fast. That way, maybe——'

'It wouldn't work,' said Kelly. 'He changed back in about a second, the other time.'

Nobody was paying any attention to him. One of the big gorgons, who had been staring fixedly at the flowers in the middle of the table, had suddenly grabbed a handful and was stuffing them into his mouth. George said something shrill in gorgon talk, and snatched the flowers away again. The other gorgon looked abashed, but flushed pink.

George, on the other hand, was distinctly blue.

His 'hand,' clutching the mangled flowers, hesitated. Slowly, as if with an effort, he put them back in the bowl.

The other two gorgons twined their 'arms' around him. After a moment George looked more like his old self, but a hint of blue remained.

'What is it?' said Calver alertly. 'Did we do something, finally?' He snapped open his wristcom. 'There's still ten minutes before the deadline, so——'

'Did you turn blue because we punished you, George?' Womrath asked.

'No,' said George unexpectedly. 'Hard for me to be elder.' He added a few words in his own language to the other gorgons, and their 'arms' twined around him again. 'Before, they panga to *me*,' added George.

('Then that's why he took the pie away from the Commandant's wife!' said Dominick, smiting himself on the forehead.

'Of course. They——')

'What's that? What's that?' Carver turned, bristling.

'Why, this explains that pie business,' said Dominick. 'He felt protective towards your wife, you see—that's what "panga" means. They none of them have much control over their own appetites, so they guard each other. As they grow older, and get more self-control, they're expected to get smaller, not bigger. George felt confused about his panga relationships to us, but in your wife's case, he was positive one more mouthful would make her explode——'

Carver was red to the ears. 'Nonsense!' he shouted. 'Dominick, you're being insulting, insubordinate and unpatriotic!'

George, looking on interestedly, piped a few words in the gorgon language. One of the other gorgons immediately spoke up: 'Elder person says, you with smooth head are a smart man. He says, the other big one who talks too much is wrong.'

Carver's jaws worked. He looked at the gorgons, then around the table. No one said anything.

Carver set his jaw heroically. 'Well, gentlemen,' he began, 'we certainly tried, but——'

'Wait a minute!' said Alvarez. Somewhere in his narrow skull a great light had dawned. 'George, am I panga to you?'

George's auricles weaved tensely. 'Yes,' he said. 'You very small man.'

'Good,' said Alvarez, dry-washing his bony hands. 'And you still have to be punished, for that mistake you made at the banquet?'

George's speaking-tube buzzed unhappily. 'Yes,' he said.

'All right,' said Alvarez. Everybody was looking at him, with expressions varying from puzzlement to alarm. Alvarez took a deep breath. 'Then here are my orders to you,' he said. '*Do as you please!*'

There was a hiss of indrawn breath from Urban. Most of the others looked at Alvarez as if he had grown snakes for hair. 'Doctor,' said Carver, 'have you gone off your——'

The chorus of gasps stopped him. Up on the table,

flushing blue and bright pink by turns like a sky sign, George was gobbling up the flowers in the centrepiece. Next he ate the bowl. One of his flailing limbs raked in the scratch pad Urban had been doodling on. He ate that.

Next moment, he was leaping to the floor, making Ritner duck wildly as he passed. Part of Dominick's detachable hood went with him, disappearing with hoarse munching sounds. With a gulp, George swallowed it and began on the carpet. He was eating greedily, frantically. The other two gorgons hovered around him with shrill gorgon cries, but he ate on, oblivious. Now he was bright blue and bulging, but still he ate.

'Stop it,' shouted Alvarez. 'George, *stop* that!'

George rocked to a halt. Gradually his blueness faded. The other gorgons were prodding and patting him anxiously. George looked all right, but it was obvious as he stood there that he would never fit into the panga box again.

He was as big as the other two; maybe a little bigger.

'Alvarez,' said Carver wildly, 'why did you——'

'He was going to burst,' said Alvarez, twitching with excitement. 'Couldn't you tell? Another mouthful or two——'

Carver recovered himself. He straightened his coverall and thrust out his chin. 'At any rate,' he said, 'he was certainly blue that time. You all saw it—isn't that right?' He looked around triumphantly. 'And by heaven, it happened inside the time limit. So, unless I'm very much mistaken——'

One of the two attendant gorgons raised his photoceptors. It was hard to tell which was George, now, except that his colour was still a little lavender. The other gorgon spoke two brief sentences in his own language, and then all three of them waddled off together towards the exit.

'What was that? What did he say?' demanded Carver.

Urban cleared his throat; he had turned pale again. 'He said you should get the tender ready to take them back home.'

'The tender is there,' said Carver indignantly, 'they can go back any time they want. But what did he say about the punishment?'

Urban cleared his throat again, looking bemused. 'They say the punishment is good. More severe than any they ever thought of, in twenty thousand years. They say they won't have to punish Rubinson and the others, now, because you have done all the punishment necessary.'

'Well?' said Carver. 'Why are you looking that way? What's the hitch? Are they going to refuse to enter the Union, after all this?'

'No,' said Urban. 'They say we are all panga to them now. They'll do as we say—let us land and build the distribution centres, start them consuming in massive quantity. . . .'

'But that'll destroy them!' someone interjected in a horrified tone.

'Oh, yes,' said Urban.

Carver sighed. He had been in the SAPS service most his life and was proud of his record. He played it as a game; the new, virgin planets were the prizes, and he kept score with the row of tiny iridium buttons on his breast pocket. He said into his wristcom, 'Let me know when Rubinson and his crew are on the way up.'

There was a long wait. The silence grew oppressive. At length the wall screen lighted up with a view of Planet Seven, gilded along one cusp, blue-green and mysterious in the shadow. A silver spark was floating up out of the night side. '*Here they come now*,' said the voice.

Carver sighed again. 'When they make contact,' he said,

'secure the tender and then call for acceleration stations. We're leaving Seven—tell Mr. Fruman to set a first approximation for our next star of call.'

Alvarez, twitching and frowning, clutched at the front of his coverall. 'You're letting them go?' he demanded. 'Not landing on Seven—after all this work?'

Carver was staring into the view plate. 'Some things,' he said slowly and unwillingly, 'are not meant to be consumed.'

CAPTIVITY

ZENNA HENDERSON

The Francher kid seemed to be an incorrigible delinquent, but the reasons for his delinquency were out of this world and had strange consequences—not only for himself, but for most of those who had hated or loved him.

I

I suppose many lonely souls have sat at their windows many nights looking out into the flood of moonlight, sad with a sadness that knows no comfort, a sadness underlined by a beauty that is in itself a pleasant kind of sorrow—but very few ever have seen what I saw that night.

I leaned against the window frame, close enough to the inflooding light so that it washed across my bare feet and the hem of my gown and splashed whitely against the foot of my bed, but picked up none of my features to identify me as a person, separate from the night. I was enjoying hastily, briefly, the magic of the loveliness before the moon would lose itself behind the heavy grove of cottonwoods that lined the creek below the curve of the backyard garden. The first cluster of leaves had patterned itself against the edge of the moon when I saw him—the Francher kid. I felt a momentary surge of disappointment and annoyance that this perfect beauty should be marred by any person at all, let alone the Francher kid, but my annoyance passed as my interest sharpened.

What was he doing—half black and half white in the edge of the moonlight? In the higgledy-piggledy haphazardness of the town, Groman's Grocery sidled in at an angle to the backyard of Somansen's house where I boarded—not farther than twenty feet away. The tiny high-up windows under the eaves of the store blinked in the full light. The Francher kid was standing, back to the moon, staring up at the windows. I leaned closer to watch. There was a waitingness about his shoulders, a prelude to movement, a beginning of something. Then there he was —up at the windows, pushing softly against the panes, opening a dark rectangle against the white side of the store. And then he was gone. I blinked and looked again. Store. Windows. One opened blankly. No Francher kid. Little windows. High up under the eaves. One opened blankly. No Francher kid.

Then the blank opening had movement inside it and the Francher kid emerged with both hands full of something and slid down the moonlight to the ground outside.

Now looky here! I said to myself. *Hey! Lookit now!*

The Francher kid sat down on one end of a 12-by-12 timber that lay half in our garden and half behind the store. Carefully and neatly he arranged his booty along the plank. Three cokes, a box of candy bars, and a huge harmonica that had been in the store for years. He sat and studied the items, touching each one with a finger tip. Then he picked up a coke and studied the cap on it. He opened the box of candy and closed it again. He ran a finger down the harmonica and then lifted it between the pointer fingers of his two hands. Holding it away from him in the moonlight, he looked at it, his head swinging slowly down its length. And, as his head swung, faintly, faintly, I heard a musical scale run up, then down. Careful note by careful note singing softly but clearly in the quiet night.

The moon was burning holes through the cottonwood tops by now and the yard was slipping into shadow. I heard notes riff rapidly up and cascade down, gleefully, happily, and I saw the glint and chromium glitter of the harmonica, dancing from shadow to light and back again, singing untouched in the air. Then the moon reached an opening in the trees and spotlighted the Francher kid almost violently. He was sitting on the plank, looking up at the harmonica, a small smile on his usually sullen face. And the harmonica sang its quiet song to him as he watched it. His face shadowed suddenly as he looked down at the things laid out on the plank. He gathered them up abruptly and walked up the moonlight to the little window and slid through, head first. Behind him, alone, unattended the harmonica danced and played, hovering and darting like a dragon fly. Then the kid reappeared, sliding head first out the window. He sat himself cross-legged in the air beside the harmonica and watched and listened. The gay dance slowed and changed. The harmonica cried softly in the moonlight, an aching, asking cry as it spiralled up and around until it slid through the open window and lost its voice in the darkness. The window clicked shut and the Francher kid thudded to the ground. He slouched off through the shadows, his elbows swinging sharply backward as he jammed his fists in his pockets.

I let go of the curtain where my clenched fingers had cut four nail-sized holes through the age-fragile lace, and released a breath I couldn't remember holding. I stared at the empty plank and wet my lips. I took a deep breath of the mountain air that was supposed to do me so much good and turned away from the window. For the thousandth time I muttered *I won't* and groped for the bed. For the thousandth time I finally reached for my crutches and swung myself over to the edge of the bed. I dragged the unresponsive half of me up on to the bed, arranging myself for sleep. I leaned against the pillow and put my hands behind my head, my elbows fanning out on either side. I stared at the light square that was the window until it wavered and rippled before my sleepy eyes. Still my mind was only nibbling at what had happened and showed no inclination to set its teeth into any sort of explanation. I awakened with a start to find the moonlight gone, my arms asleep and my prayers unsaid.

Tucked in bed and ringed about with the familiar comfort of my prayers, I slid away from awareness to sleep, following the dance and gleam of a harmonica that cried in the moonlight.

Morning sunlight slid across the boarding-house breakfast table, casting alpine shadows behind the spilled cornflakes that lay beyond the sugar bowl. I squinted against the brightness and felt aggrieved that anything should be alive and active and so—so—hopeful so early in the morning. I leaned on my elbows over my coffee cup and contemplated a mood as black as the coffee.

'. . . Francher kid.'

I rotated my head upwards on the axis of my two supporting hands, my interest caught. *Last night*, I had remembered, *last night*——

'I give up.' Anna Semper put a third spoonful of sugar in her coffee and stirred morosely. 'Every child has a something—I mean there's *some* way to reach every child . . . all but the Francher kid. I can't reach him at all. If he'd even be aggressive or actively mean or actively *anything* maybe I could do something, but he just sits there being a vegetable. And then I get so spittin' mad when he finally *does* do something, just enough to keep him from flunking, that I could bust a gusset. I can't abide a child who can and won't.' She frowned darkly and added two more spoonfuls of sugar to her coffee. 'I'd rather have an eager moron than a won't-do genius!' She tasted the coffee and grimaced.

'Can't even get a decent cup of coffee to arm me for my struggle with the little monster.'

I laughed. 'Five spoonfuls of sugar would spoil almost anything. And don't give up hope. Have you tried music? Remember, music hath charms——'

Anna reddened to the tip of her ears. I couldn't tell if it was anger or embarrassment. 'Music!' Her spoon rattled against her saucer sharply. She groped for words. 'This is ridiculous, but I have had to send that Francher kid out of the room during musical appreciation.'

'Out of the room? Whatever for? I thought he was a vegetable.'

Anna reddened still further. 'He is,' she said stubbornly, 'but——' She fumbled with her spoon, then burst forth, 'But sometimes the record player won't work when he's in the room.'

I put my cup down slowly. 'Oh, come now!' I said. 'This coffee is awfully strong, I'll admit, but it's not *that* strong.'

'No, really!' Anna twisted her spoon between her two hands. 'When he's in the room that darned player goes too fast or too slow or even backwards. I swear it. And one time . . .' Anna looked around furtively and lowered her voice. 'One time it played a whole record and it wasn't even plugged in!'

'You ought to patent that!' I said. 'That'd be a real money-maker.'

'Go on, laugh!' Anna gulped coffee again and grimaced. 'I'm beginning to believe in poltergeists—you know, the kind that are supposed to work through or because of adolescent kids. If you had that kid to deal with in class——'

'Yes.' I fingered my cold toast. 'If only I did.'

And for a minute I hated Anna fiercely for the sympathy

on her open face and for the studied unlooking at my leaning crutches. She opened her mouth, closed it, then leaned across the table.

'Polio?' she blurted, reddening.

'No,' I said. 'Car wreck.'

'Oh.' She hesitated. 'Well, maybe some day——'

'No,' I said. 'No,' denying the faint possibility that was just enough to keep me nagged out of resignation.

'Oh,' she said. 'How long ago?'

'How long?' For a minute I was suspended in wonder at the distortion of time. How long? Recent enough to be a shock each time of immobility when I expected motion. Long enough ago that eternity was between me and the last time I moved unthinkingly.

'Almost a year,' I said, my memory aching to *this time last year I could*——

'You were a teacher?' Anna gave her watch a quick appraising look.

'Yes,' I said. I didn't automatically verify the time. The immediacy of watches had died for me. Then I smiled. 'That's why I can sympathize with you about the Francher kid. I've had them before.'

'There's always one,' sighed Anna, getting up. 'Well, it's time for my pilgrimage up the hill. I'll see you.' And the swinging door to the hall repeated her departure again and again with diminishing enthusiasm. I struggled to my feet and swung myself to the window.

'Hey!' I shouted. She turned at the gate, peering back as she rested her load of work books on the gate post.

'Yes?'

'If he gives you too much trouble, send him over here with a note for me. It'll take him off your hands for a while at least.'

'Hey, that's an idea. Thanks. That's swell! Straighten

your halo!' And she waved an elbow at me as she disappeared beyond the box elder outside the gate.

I didn't think she would, but she did.

It was only a couple of days later that I looked up from my book at the creak of the old gate. The heavy old gear that served as a weight to pull it shut thudded dully behind the Francher kid. He walked up the porch steps under my close scrutiny with none of the hesitant embarrassment that most people would feel. He mounted the three steps and wordlessly handed me an envelope. I opened it. It said:

Dust off your halo! I've reached the !! stage. Wouldn't you like to keep him permanent-like?

'Won't you sit down?' I gestured to the porch swing, wondering how I was going to handle this deal.

He looked at the swing and sank down on the top porch step.

'What's your name?'

He looked at me incuriously. 'Francher.' His voice was husky and unused-sounding.

'Is that your first name?'

'That's my name.'

'What's your other name?' I asked patiently, falling into a first-grade dialogue in spite of his age.

'They put down Clement,' he said.

'Clement Francher,' I said. 'A good-sounding name, but what do people call you?'

His eyebrows slanted subtly upwards and a tiny bitter smile lifted the corners of his mouth.

'With their eyes—juvenile delinquent, lazy trash, no-good off-scouring, potential criminal, burden——'

I winced away from the icy malice of his voice.

'But mostly they call me a whole sentence, like—"Well, what can you expect from a background like that?"'

His knuckles were white against his faded levis. Then as I watched them, the colour crept back and, without visible relaxation, the tension was gone. But his eyes were the eyes of a boy too big to cry and too young for any other comfort.

'What *is* your background?' I asked quietly, as though I had the right to ask. He answered as simply as though he owed me an answer.

'We were with the carnival. We went to all the fairs around the country. Mother——' His words nearly died. 'Mother had a mind-reading act. She was good. She was better than anyone knew—better than she wanted to be. It hurt and scared her sometimes to walk through people's minds. Sometimes she would come back to the trailer and cry and cry and take a long, long shower and wash herself until her hands were all water-soaked and her hair hung in dripping strings. They curled at the end. She couldn't get all the fear and hate and—and tired dirt off even that way. Only if she could find a Good to read, or a dark church with tall candles.'

'And where is she now?' I asked, holding a small warm picture in my mind of narrow, fragile shoulders, thin and defenceless under a flimsy moist robe, with one wet strand of hair dampening one shoulder of it.

'Gone.' His eyes were over my head but empty of the vision of the weather-worn siding of the house. 'She died. Three years ago. This is a foster home. To try to make a decent citizen of me.'

There was no inflection in his words. They lay as flat as paper between us in our silence.

'You like music,' I said, curling Anna's note around my forefinger, remembering what I had seen the other night.

'Yes.' His eyes were on the note. 'Miss Semper doesn't think so, though. I hate that scratchy wrapped-up music.'

'You sing?'

'No. I make music.'

'You mean you play an instrument?'

He frowned a little impatiently. 'No. I make music with instruments.'

'Oh,' I said. 'There's a difference?'

'Yes.' He turned his head away. I had disappointed him or failed him in some way.

'Wait,' I said. 'I want to show you something.' I struggled to my feet. Oh, deftly and quickly enough under the circumstances, I suppose, but it seemed an endless, aching effort in front of the Francher kid's eyes. But finally I was up and swinging in through the front door. When I got back with my key chain, the kid was still staring at my empty chair and I had to struggle myself back into it under his unwavering eyes.

'Can't you stand alone?' he asked, as though he had a right to.

'Very little, very briefly,' I answered, as though I owed him an answer.

'You don't walk without those braces?' he said.

'I can't walk without those braces,' I said. 'Here.' I held out my key chain. There was a charm on it: a harmonica with four notes, so small that I had never managed to blow one by itself. The four together made a tiny breathy chord, like a small hesitant wind.

He took the chain between his fingers and swung the charm back and forth, his head bent so that the sunlight flickered across its tousledness. The chain stilled. For a long moment there wasn't a sound. Then, clearly, sharply, came the musical notes, one after another. There was a slight pause and then four notes poured their separateness together to make a clear, sweet chord.

'You make music,' I said, barely audibly.

'Yes.' He gave me back my key chain and stood up. 'I guess she's cooled down now. I'll go on back.'

'To work?'

'To work.' He smiled wryly. 'For a while, anyway.' He started down the walk.

'What if I tell?' I called after him.

'I told once,' he called back over his shoulder. 'Try it if you want to.'

I sat for a long time on the porch after he left. My fingers were closed over the harmonica as I watched the sun creep up my skirts and into my lap. Finally I turned Anna's envelope over. The seal was still secure. The end was jagged where I had torn it. The paper was opaque. I blew a tiny breathy chord on the harmonica. Then I shivered as cold crept across my shoulders. The chill was chased away by a tiny hot wave of excitement. So his mother could walk through the minds of others. So he knew what was in a sealed letter—or had he got his knowledge from Anna before the letter? So he could make music with harmonicas. So the Francher kid was—— My hurried thoughts caught and came to a full stop. What *was* the Francher kid?

II

After school that day, Anna toiled up the four front steps and rested against the railing, half sitting and half leaning. 'I'm too tired to sit down,' she said. 'I'm wound up like a clock and I'm going to strike something pretty darned quick.' She half laughed and grimaced a little. 'Probably my laundry. I'm fresh out of clothes.' She caught a long ragged breath. 'You must have built a fire under that Francher kid,' she said. 'He came back and piled into his math book and did the whole week's assignments that he hadn't bothered with before. Did them in less than an hour, too. Makes me mad, though——' She grimaced again and pressed her hand to her chest. 'Darn that chalk dust, anyway. Thanks a million for your assist. I wish I were optimistic enough to believe it would last.' She leaned and breathed, her eyes closing with the effort. 'Awful shortage of air around here.' Her hands fretted with her collar. 'Anyway the Francher kid said you'd substitute for me until my pneumonia is over.' She laughed, a little soundless laugh. 'He doesn't know that it's just chalk dust and that I'm never sick.' She buried her face in her two hands and burst into tears. 'I'm not sick, am I? It's only that darn Francher kid!'

She was still blaming him when Mrs. Somansen came out and led her into her bedroom and when the doctor arrived to shake his head over her chest.

So that's how it was that the first-floor First Grade was hastily moved upstairs and the Junior High was hastily moved downstairs and I once more found myself facing the challenge of a class, telling myself that the Francher kid needed no special substitute. After all, I liked Anna, I was the only substitute available, and besides, any slight—substitute's pay!—addition to the exchequer was most welcome. You *can* live on those monthly cheques, but it's pleasant to have a couple of extra coins to clink together.

By mid-morning I knew a little of what Anna was sweating over. His absolutely dead-weight presence in the room was a drag on everything we did. Recitations paused, limped and halted when they came to him. Activities swirled around his inactivity, creating distracting eddies. It wasn't only a negative sort of non-participation on his part but an aggressively positive not-doingness. It wasn't just a hindrance, but an active opposition—without any overt action or any sort of proof of his attitude. This, coupled with my disappointment in not having the same comfortable rapport with him that I'd had before, and the bone-weariness of having to be vertical all day instead of collapsing horizontally at intervals, and the strain of getting back into harness, cold, with a roomful of teeners and sub-teeners, had worn me down to a frazzle by early afternoon.

So I fell back on the perennial refuge of teachers and opened a discussion of 'What I want to be when I grow up.' We had gone through the usual nurses and airplane hostesses and pilots and bridge builders and the usual unexpected ballet dancer until the discussion frothed like a breaking wave against the Francher kid and stilled there.

He was lounging down in his seat, his weight supported by the back of his neck and the remote end of his spine. The class sighed collectively though inaudibly and waited for his contribution.

'And you, Clement?' I prompted, shifting vainly, trying to ease the taut cry of aching muscles.

'An outlaw,' he said huskily, not bothering to straighten up. 'I'm going to keep a list and break every law there is—and get away with it, too.'

'Whatever for?' I asked, trying to reassure the sick pang inside me. 'An outlaw is no use at all to society.'

'Who wants to be of use?' he asked. 'I'll use society—and I can do it.'

'Perhaps,' I said, knowing full well it was so. 'But that's not the way to happiness.'

'Who's happy?' he asked. 'The bad are unhappy because they are bad. The good are unhappy because they're afraid to be bad——'

'Clement,' I said gently, 'I think you are——'

'I think he's crazy,' said Rigo, his black eyes flashing. 'Don't pay him no never mind, Miss Carolle. He's a screwball. He's all the time saying crazy things.'

I saw the heavy world globe on the top shelf of the bookcase behind Rigo shift and slide towards the edge. I saw it lift clear off the shelf and I cried out, 'Clement!' The whole class started at the loud urgency of my voice, the Francher kid included, and Rigo moved just far enough out of line for the falling globe to miss him and crack itself apart at his feet.

Someone screamed and several gasped and a babble of voices broke out. I caught the Francher kid's eyes and he flushed hotly and ducked his head. Then he straightened up proudly and defiantly returned my look. He wet his forefinger in his mouth and drew an invisible tally mark in the air before him. I shook my head at him, slowly, regretfully. What could I do with a child like this?

Well, I had to do something, so I told him to stay in after school, though the kids wondered why. He slouched against the door, defiance in every awkward angle of his body and in the hooking of his thumbs into his front pockets. I let the parting noises fade and die, the last hurried clang of lunch pail, the last flurry of feet, the last reverberant slam of the outside door. The Francher kid shifted several times, easing the tension of his shoulders as he waited. Finally, I said 'Sit down.'

'No.' His word was flat and uncompromising. I looked at him, the gaunt young planes of his face, the unhappy mouth, thinned to stubbornness, the eyes that blinded themselves with dogged defiance. I leaned across my desk, my hands clasped, and wondered what I could say. Argument would do no good. A kid of that age has an answer for everything.

'We all have violences,' I said, tightening my hands, 'but we can't always let them out. Think what a mess things would be if we did.' I smiled wryly into his unresponsive face. 'If we gave in to every violent impulse, I'd probably have slapped you with an encyclopedia before now.' His eyelids flicked, startled, and he looked straight at me for the first time.

'Sometimes we can just hold our breath until the violence swirls away from us. Other times it's too big and it swells inside us like a balloon until it chokes our lungs and aches our jaw hinges.' His lids flickered down over his watching eyes. 'But it can be put to use. Then's when we stir up a cake by hand or chop wood or kick cans across the back yard or'—I faltered—'or run until our knees bend both ways from tiredness.'

There was a small silence while I held my breath until my violent rebellion against unresponsive knees swirled away from me.

'There are bigger violences, I guess,' I went on. 'From them come assault and murder, vandalism and war, but even those can be used. If you want to smash things, there are worthless things that need to be smashed, and things that ought to be destroyed, ripped apart and ruined. But you have no way of knowing what those things are, yet. You must keep your violences small until you learn how to tell the difference.'

'I can smash.' His voice was thick.

'Yes,' I said. 'But smash to build. You have no right to hurt other people with your own hurt.'

'People!' The word was profanity.

I drew a long breath. If he were younger. . . . You can melt stiff rebellious arms and legs with warm hugs or a hand across a wind-ruffled head or a long look that flickers into a smile, but what can you do with a creature that's neither adult nor child, but puzzlingly both? I leaned forward.

'Francher,' I said softly. 'If your mother could walk through your mind now——'

He reddened, then paled. His mouth opened. He swallowed tightly. Then he jerked himself upright in the doorway.

'Leave my mother alone.' His voice was shaken and muffled. 'You leave her alone. She's dead.'

I listened to his footsteps and the crashing slam of the outside door. For some sudden reason I felt my heart follow him down the hill to town. I sighed, almost with exasperation. So this was to be My Child. We teacher-types sometimes find them. They aren't our pets—often they aren't even in our classes. But they are the children who move unasked into our hearts and make claims upon them over-and-above-the-call-of-duty. And this My Child I had to reach. Somehow I had to keep him from sliding on over the borderline to lawlessness as he so surely was doing—this My Child, even more than the usual My Child, was different.

I put my head down on the desk and let weariness ripple up over me. After a minute I began to straighten up my papers. I made the desk-top tidy and took my purse out of the bottom drawer. I struggled to my feet and glared at my crutches. Then I grinned weakly.

'Come, friends,' I said. 'Let us help one another depart.'

Anna was out for a week. After she returned, I was surprised at my reluctance to let go of the class. The sniff of chalk dust was in my nostrils and I ached to be busy again. So I started helping out with the school programmes and teen-age dances, which led naturally to the day my committee and I stood in the town recreation hall and looked about us despairingly.

'How long have those decorations been up?' I craned my neck to get a better view of the wilderness of sooty cobwebby crepe-paper that clotted the whole of the high ceiling and the upper reaches of the walls of the ramshackle old hall that leaned wearily against the back of the saloon. Twyla stopped chewing the end of one of her heavy braids of hair. 'About four years, I guess. At least the newest. Pea-Green put it all up.'

'Pea-Green?'

'Yeah. He was a screwball. He used up every piece of crepe-paper in town and used nails to put the stuff up—big nails. He's gone now. He got silicosis and went down to Hot Springs.'

'Well, nails or no nails, we can't have a Hallowe'en dance with that stuff up.'

'Going to miss the old junk. How're we going to get it down?' asked Janniset.

'Pea-Green used an extension ladder he borrowed from a power crew that was stringing some wires up to the Bluebell mine,' said Rigo. 'But we'll have to find some other way to get it down, now.'

I felt a flick of something at my elbow. It might have been the Francher kid shifting from one foot to the other, or it might have been just a thought slipping by. I glanced sideways, but caught only the lean line of his cheek and the shaggy back of his neck.

'I think I can get a ladder.' Rigo snapped his thumbnail loudly with his white front teeth. 'It won't reach clear up, but it'll help.'

'We could take rakes and just drag it down,' suggested Twyla.

We all laughed until I sobered us all with, 'It might come to that yet, bless the buttons of whoever thought up twenty-foot ceilings. Well, tomorrow's Saturday. Everybody be here about nine and we'll get with it.'

'Can't.' The Francher kid cast anchor unequivocally, snagging all our willingness up short.

'Oh?' I shifted my crutches and, as usual, his eyes fastened on them, almost hypnotically. 'That's too bad.'

'How come?' Rigo was belligerent. 'If the rest of us can, you oughta be able to. Ever'body's s'posed to do this together. Ever'body does the dirty work and ever'body has the fun. You're nobody special. You're on this committee, aren't you?'

I restrained myself from a sudden impulse to clap my hand over Rigo's mouth midway in his protest. I didn't like the quietness of the Francher kid's hands, but he only looked slantwise up at Rigo and said, 'I got volunteered on this committee. I didn't ask to. And to fix this joint up today. I gotta work tomorrow.'

'Work? Where?' Rigo frankly disbelieved.

'Sorting ore at the Absolom.'

Rigo snapped his thumbnail again derisively. 'That penny-picking stuff? They pay peanuts.'

'Yes.' And the Francher kid slouched off around the corner of the building without a glance or a goodbye.

'Well, he's working!' Twyla thoughtfully spat out a stray hair and pointed the wet end of her braid with her fingers. 'The Francher kid's doing something. I wonder how come?'

'Trying to figure that dopy dilldock out?' asked Janniset. Don't waste your time. I bet he's just goofing off.'

'You kids run on,' I said. 'We can't do anything tonight. I'll lock up. See you in the morning.'

I waited inside the dusty, echoing hall until the sound of their going died down the rocky alley that edged around the rim of the railroad cut and dissolved into the streets of the town. I still couldn't reconcile myself to slowing their steps to match my uncertain feet. Maybe someday I would be able to accept my braces as others accept glasses; but not yet—oh, not yet!

I left the hall and snapped the dime-store padlock shut. I struggled precariously along through the sliding shale and loose rocks until suddenly one piece of shale shattered under the pressure of one of my crutches and I stumbled off balance. I saw with shake-making clarity in the accelerated speed of the moment that the only place my groping crutch could reach was the smooth curving of a small boulder, and, in that same instant, I visualized myself sprawling helplessly, hopelessly in the clutter of the alley, a useless, non-functioning piece of humanity, a drag and a hindrance on everyone again. And then, at the last possible instant, the smooth boulder slid aside and my crutch caught and steadied on the solid damp hollow beneath it. I caught my breath with relief and unclenched my spasmed hands a little—Lucky!

Then all at once there was the Francher kid at my elbow again, quietly waiting.

'Oh!' I hoped he hadn't seen me floundering in my awkwardness. 'Hi! I thought you'd gone.'

'I really will be working.' His voice had lost its flatness. 'I'm not making much, but I'm saving to buy me a musical instrument.'

'Well, good!' I said, smiling into the unusualness of his straightforward look. 'What kind of instrument?'

'I don't know,' he said. 'Something that will sing like this——'

And there on the rocky trail with the long light slanting through the trees for late afternoon, I heard soft, tentative notes that stumbled at first and then began to sing: *Oh Danny Boy, the pipes, the pipes are calling* . . . Each note of this, my favourite, was like a white flower opening inside me in ascending order like steps—steps that I could climb freely, lightly——

'What kind of instrument am I saving for?' The

Francher kid's voice pulled me back down to earth.

'You'll have to settle for less.' My voice shook a little. 'There isn't one like that.'

'But I've heard it——' He was bewildered.

'Maybe you have,' I said. 'But was anyone playing it?'

'Why yes—no,' he said. 'I used to hear it from Mom. She thought it to me.'

'Where did your mom come from?' I asked impulsively.

'From Terror and from Panic Places. From Hunger and from Hiding—to live midway between Madness and The Dream——' He looked at me, his mouth drooping a little. 'She promised me I'd understand some day but this is some day and she's gone.'

'Yes,' I sighed, remembering how once I had dreamed that someday I'd run again. 'But there are other somedays ahead—for you.'

'Yes,' he said. 'And time hasn't stopped for you, either.' And he was gone.

I looked after him. 'Doggone!' I thought. 'There I go again, talking to him as though he made sense!' I poked the end of my crutch in the damp earth three times, making interlacing circles. Then with quickened interest, I poked the boulder that had rolled *up* out of the slight hollow before the crutch tip had landed there.

'Son-a-gun!' I cried aloud. 'Well, son-a-gun!'

Next morning at five to nine the kids were waiting for me at the door to the hall, huddled against the October chill that the milky sun hadn't had time to disperse yet. Rigo had a shaky old ladder with two broken rungs and splashes of old paint gumming it liberally.

'That looks awfully rickety,' I said. 'We don't want any blood spilled on our dance floor. It's bad for the wax.'

Rigo grinned. 'It'll hold me up,' he said. 'I used it last

night to pick apples. You just have to be kinda careful.'

'Well, be so then,' I smiled, unlocking the door. 'Better safe than——' My words faltered and died as I gaped in at the open door. The others pushed in around me, round-eyed and momentarily silenced. My first wild impression was that the ceiling had fallen in.

'My gosh!' gasped Janniset. 'What hit this place?'

'Just look at it!' shrilled Twyla. 'Hey! Just look at it!'

We looked as we scuffled forward. Every single piece of paper was gone from the ceiling and walls. Every scrap of paper was on the floor, in tiny twisted confetti-sized pieces like a tattered, faded snowfall, all over the floor. There must have been an incredible amount of paper tangled in the decorations, because we waded wonderingly almost ankle-deep through it.

'Looky here!' Rigo was staring at the front of the bandstand. Lined up neatly across the front stood all the nails that had been pulled out of the decorations, each balanced precisely on its head.

Twyla frowned and bit her lip. 'It scares me,' she said. 'It doesn't feel right. It looks like somebody was mad or crazy—like they tore up the paper wishing they was killing something. And then to put all those nails so—so even and careful, like they had been put down gently—that looks madder than the paper.' She reached over and swept her finger sideways, wincing as though she expected a shock. A section of the nails toppled with faint pings on the bare boards of the stand. In a sudden flurry, Twyla swept all the nails over. 'There!' she said, wiping her finger on her dress. 'Now it's all crazy.'

'Well,' I said, 'crazy or not, somebody's saved us a lot of trouble. Rigo, we won't need your ladder. Get the brooms and let's get this mess swept out.'

While they were gone for the brooms, I picked up two

nails and clicked them together in a metrical cadence: '*Oh Danny Boy, the pipes, the pipes are calling . . .*

By noon we had the place scrubbed out and fairly glistening through its shabby paint. By evening we had the crisp new orange-and-black decorations up, low down and with thumb tacks, and all sighed with tired satisfaction at how good the place looked. As we locked up Twyla suddenly said in a small voice, 'What if it happens again before the dance Friday? All our work——'

'It won't,' I promised. 'It won't.'

In spite of my hanging back and trying the lock a couple of times, Twyla was still waiting when I turned away from the door. She was examining the end of her braid carefully as she said, 'It was him, wasn't it?'

'Yes, I suppose so,' I said.

'How did he do it?' she asked.

'You've known him longer than I have,' I said. 'How did he do it?'

'Nobody knows the Francher kid,' she said. Then softly, 'He looked at me once, really looked at me. He's funny—but not to laugh,' she hastened. 'When he looked at me it——' Her hand tightened on her braid until her head tilted and she glanced up slantingly at me. 'It made music in me. 'You know,' she said quickly into the echo of her unorthodox words, 'you're kinda like him. He makes me think things and believe things I wouldn't ever by myself. You make me say things I wouldn't ever by myself—no, that's not quite right. You *let* me say things I wouldn't dare to say to anyone else.'

'Thank you,' I said. 'Thank you, Twyla.'

III

I had forgotten the trembling glamour of a teen-age

dance. I had forgotten the cautious stilted gait of high heels on loafer-type feet. I had forgotten how the look of maturity could be put on with a tie and sports jacket and how—how *people-like* teen-agers could look when divorced for a while from levis and flannel shirts. Janniset could hardly contain himself for his own splendour and turned not a hair of his incredibly polished head when I smiled my 'Good evening, Mr. Janniset.' But in his pleased satisfaction at my formality, he forgot himself as he turned away and hoisted up his sharply creased trousers as though they were his old levis.

Rigo was stunning in his Latin handsomeness and he and Angie so drowned in one another's dark eyes that I could see why our Mexican youngsters usually marry so young. And Angie! Well, she didn't look like any eighth grader—her strapless gown, her dangly earrings, her laughing flirtatious eyes—but taken out of the context and custom and tradition, she was breathtakingly lovely. Of course it was on her 'unsuitable for her age' dress and jewellery and make-up that the long line of mothers and aunts and grandmothers fixed disapproving eyes, but I'd be willing to bet that there were plenty who wished their own child could look as lovely.

In this small community, the girls always dressed up to the hilt at the least provocation, and the Hallowe'en dance was usually the first event in the Fall that could serve as an excuse. Crinolined skirts belled like blossoms across the floor above the glitter of high heels, but it was only a matter of a few minutes before the shoes were kicked off, to toe in together forlornly under a chair or dangle from some motherly forefinger while unprotected toes braved the brogans of the boys.

Twyla was bright-cheeked and laughing, dance after dance, until the first intermission. She and Janniset brought me punch where I sat among the other spectators, then Janniset skidded off across the floor, balancing his paper cup precariously as he went to take another look at Marty who, at school, was only a girl, but here, all dressed up, was the dawn of woman-wonder for him. Twyla gulped her punch hastily and then licked the corners of her mouth.

'He isn't here,' she said huskily.

'I'm sorry,' I said. 'I wanted him to have fun with the rest of you. Maybe he'll come yet.'

'Maybe.' She twisted her cup slowly, then hastily shoved it under the chair as it threatened to drip on her dress.

'That's a beautiful dress,' I said. 'I love the way your petticoat shows red against the blue when you whirl.'

'Thank you.' She smoothed the billowing of her skirt. 'I feel funny with sleeves. None of the others have them. That's why he didn't come, I bet. Not having any dress-up clothes like the others, I mean. Nothing but levis.'

'Oh, that's a shame,' I said. 'If I had known——'

'No,' she said. 'Mrs. McVey is supposed to buy his clothes. She gets money for them. All she does is sit around and talk about how much she sacrifices to take care of the Francher kid and she doesn't take care of him at all. It's her fault——'

'Let's not be too critical of others,' I said. 'There may be circumstances we know nothing of—and besides'—I nodded my head—'he's here now.'

Almost I could see the leap of her heart under the close-fitting blue as she turned to look.

The Francher kid was lounging against the door, his face closed and impassive. I noted with a flame of anger at Mrs. McVey that he was dressed in his levis, faded almost white from many washings, and a flannel shirt, the plaid of which was nearly indistinguishable except along the seams. It wasn't fair to keep him from being like the other kids even in this minor way—or maybe especially in this way because clothes can't be hidden the way a mind or soul can.

I tried to catch his eye and beckon him in, but he looked only at the bandstand where the band members were preparing to resume playing. It was almost tragic that the Francher kid had only this handful of inexpertly played instruments to feed his hunger on. He winced back into the darkness at their first blare and I felt Twyla's tenseness as she turned to me.

'He won't come in,' she half-shouted against the take-a-melody-tear-it-to-pieces-stick-it-back-together-bleeding type of music that was going on.

I shook my head regretfully. 'I guess not,' I mouthed and then was drawn into a half-audible, completely incomprehensible conversation with Mrs. Frisney. It wasn't until the next dance started and she was towed away by Grampa Griggs that I could turn back to Twyla. She was gone. I glanced around the room. Nowhere the swirl of blue echoing the heavy brown-gold swing of her pony tail.

There was no reason for me to feel apprehensive. There were any number of places she might have gone and quite legitimately, but I suddenly felt an overwhelming need for fresh air, and swung myself past the romping dancers and out into the gasping chill of the night. I huddled closer inside my jacket, wishing it were on right instead of merely flung around my shoulders. But the air tasted clean and fresh. I don't know what we'd been breathing in the dance hall, but it wasn't air. By the time I'd got the whatever-it-was out of my lungs and filled them with the freshness of the night, I found myself halfway down the path over the edge of the railroad cut. There hadn't been a train over the single track since nineteen-o-something and just across it was a thicket of willows and cottonwoods and a few scraggly piñon trees. As I moved into the shadow of the trees, I glanced up at the sky ablaze with a billion stars that dissolved into light near the lopsided moon and perforated the darker horizon with brilliance. I was startled out of my absorption by the sound of movement and music. I took an uncertain step into the dark. A few yards away, I saw the flick of skirts and started to call out to Twyla. But instead I rounded the brush in front of me and saw what she was intent upon.

The Francher kid was dancing—dancing all alone in the quiet night. No, not alone, because a column of yellow leaves had swirled up from the ground around him and danced with him to a melody so exactly their movement that I couldn't be sure there was music. Fascinated, I watched the drift and sway, the swirl and turn, the treetop-high rise and the hesitant drifting fall of the Francher kid and the autumn leaves. But somehow I couldn't see the kid as a separate levi'd, flannel-shirted entity. He and the leaves blended so together that the sudden sharp definition of a hand or of a turning head was startling. The kid was just a larger leaf borne among the smaller in the chilly winds of fall. On a final mirror glissade of the music, the Francher kid slid to the ground.

He stood for a moment, head bent, crumbling a crisp leaf in his fingers, then he turned swiftly defensive to the rustle of movement. Twyla stepped out into the clearing. For a moment they stood looking at each other without a word. Then Twyla's voice came so softly I could barely hear it.

'I would have danced with you.'

'With me like this?' He gestured at his clothes.

'Sure,' she said. 'It doesn't matter.'

'In front of everyone?'

'If you wanted to,' she said. 'I wouldn't mind.'

'Not there,' he said. 'It's too tight and hard.'

'Then here,' she said, holding out her hands.

'The music——' but his hands were reaching for hers.

'The music,' she said.

'My mother's music,' he corrected.

And the music began, a haunting, lilting waltztime melody. As lightly as the leaves that stirred at their feet, the two circled the clearing.

I have the picture yet, but when I return to it, my heart is emptied of adjectives because there are none for such enchantment. The music quickened and swelled, softly, richly full—the lost music that a mother bequeathed to a child.

Twyla was so completely engrossed in the magic of the moment that I'm sure she didn't even know when their feet no longer rustled in the fallen leaves. She couldn't have known when the treetops brushed their shoes—when the long turning of the tune brought them back, spiralling down into the clearing. Her scarlet petticoat caught on a branch as they passed and left a bright shred to trail the wind, but even that did not distract her.

Before my heart completely broke with wonder, the music faded softly away and left the two standing on the ragged grass. After a breathless pause, Twyla's hand went softly, wonderingly, to Francher's cheek. The kid turned his face to her palm. Then they turned and left each other, without a word.

Twyla passed so close to me that her skirts brushed mine. I let her cross the tracks back to the dance before I followed. I got there just in time to catch the whisper on apparently the second round: '. . . alone out there with the

Francher kid!' and the gleefully malicious shock of '. . . and her petticoat is torn——'

It was like pigsty muck clotting an Easter dress.

IV

Anna said 'Hi!' and flung herself into my one armchair. As the front leg collapsed, she caught herself with the dexterity of long practice, tilted the chair, re-inserted the leg and then eased herself back into its dusty depths.

'From the vagaries of the small town, good Lord deliver me!' she moaned.

'What now?' I asked, shifting gears on my crotchet hook as I finished another row of my rug.

'You mean you haven't heard the latest scandal?' Her eyes widened in mock horror and her voice sank conspiratorially. 'They were out there in the dark—alone—doing Nobody Knows What. Imagine!' Her voice shook with avid outrage. 'With the Francher kid! Honestly!' Her voice returned to normal. 'You'd think the Francher kid was leprosy or something. What a to-do about a little nocturnal smooching. I'd give you the odds that most of the other kids are being shocked to ease their own consciences of the same kind of carrying-on. But just because it is the Francher kid——'

'They weren't alone,' I said casually, holding a tight rein on my indignation. 'I was there.'

'You were?' Anna's eyebrows bumped her crisp bangs. 'Well, well. This complexions things different. What did happen? Not,' she hastened, 'that I credit those wild tales about, my golly, Twyla, but what did happen?'

'They danced,' I said. 'The Francher kid was ashamed of his clothes and wouldn't come in the hall. So they danced down in the clearing.'

'Without music?'

'The Francher kid . . . hummed,' I said, my eyes intent on my work.

There was a brief silence. 'Well,' said Anna. 'That's interesting, especially that vacant spot I feel in there. But you *were* there?'

'Yes,' I said.

'And they just danced?'

'Yes.' I apologized mentally for making so pedestrian the magic I had seen. 'And Twyla caught her petticoat on a branch and it tore before she knew it.'

'Hmmm.' Anna was suddenly sober. 'You ought to take your rug up to the Sew-Sew Club.'

'But I——' I was bewildered.

'They're serving nice heaping portions of Twyla's reputation for refreshments and Mrs. McVey is contributing the dessert—the unplumbed depravity of foster children.'

I stuffed my rug back into its bag. 'Is my face on?' I asked.

Well, I got back to the Somansons' that evening considerably wider of eye than I had left it. Anna took my things from me at the door.

'How did it go?' she asked.

'My gorsh!' I said, easing myself into a chair. 'If they ever got started on me, what would I have left?'

'Bare bones,' said Anna promptly. 'With plenty of tooth marks on them. Well, did you get them told?'

'Yes,' I said, 'but they didn't want to believe me. It was too tame. And of course Mrs. McVey didn't like being pushed out on a limb about the Francher kid's clothes. Her delicate hint about the high cost of clothes didn't impress Mrs. Holmes much, not with her six boys. I guess I've got me an enemy for life. She got a good-sized look at herself through my eyes and she didn't like it at all, but I'll bet the Francher kid won't turn up levi'd for a dance again.'

'Heaven send he'll never do anything worse,' Anna intoned piously.

That's what I hoped fervently for a while, but lightning hit Willow Creek anyway, a subtle slow lightning—a calculated, angry lightning. I held my breath as report after report came in. Turbow's old shed exploded without a sound on the stroke of nine o'clock, Tuesday night, and scattered itself as kindling wood over the whole barnyard. Of course Turbow had talked for years of tearing the shaky old thing down but—— I began to wonder how you went about bailing a juvenile out of the clink.

Then the last sound timber on the old railroad bridge below Thurman's house shuddered and dissolved loudly into sawdust at eleven o'clock, Tuesday night. The rails, deprived of their support, trembled briefly, then curled tightly *up* into two absurd rosettes. The bridge being gone meant an hour's brisk walk to town for Thurman instead of a fifteen-minute stroll. It also meant safety for the toddlers too young to understand why the rotting timbers weren't a wonderful kind of jungle-gym.

Wednesday evening at five, all the water in Holmes's pond geysered up and crashed down again, reducing to pulp the few catfish that were still left in it and breaking a spillway over into the creek, thereby draining the stagnant old mosquito-bearing spot with a conclusive slurp. As the neighbours had nagged at Holmes to do for years—but . . .

I was awestruck at this simple, literal translation of my words, and searched my memory with wary apprehensiveness. Almost I could have relaxed by now if I could have drawn a line through the last two names on my mental roll of the club.

But Thursday night there was a crash and a roar and I huddled in my bed praying a wordless prayer against I didn't know what and Friday morning I listened to the shrill wide-eyed recitals at the breakfast table.

'—since the devil was an imp and now there it is——'

'—right in the middle, big as life and twice as natural——'

'What is?' I asked, braving the battery of eyes that pinned me like a moth in a covey of searchlights.

There was a stir around the table. Everyone was aching to speak, but there's always a certain rough protocol to be observed, even in a boarding-house.

Ol' Charlie cleared his throat, took a huge mouthful of coffee and sloshed it thoughtfully around his teeth before swallowing it.

'Balance rock,' he choked, spraying his vicinity finely, 'came plumb unbalanced last night. Came a-crashing down, bouncing like a dang ping-pong ball, an'nen it hopped over half a dozen fences, an'nen *whammo!* it lit on a couple of Scudder's pigs, an'nen tore out a section of Leland's stone fence and now it's settin' there in the middle of their alfalfa field as big as a house. He'll have a helk of a time mowing that field now.' He slurped his coffee noisily.

'Strange things going on around here.' Blue Nor's porchy eyebrows rose and fell portentously. 'Never heard of a balance rock falling before. And all them other funny things. The Devil's walking our land, sure enough!'

I left on the wave of a violent argument between proponents of the devil theory and the atom bomb testing theory as the prime cause. Now I could draw another line through the list. But what of the last name? What of it?

That afternoon the Francher kid materialized on the bottom step at the boarding-house, his eyes intent on my braces. We sat there in silence for a while, mostly I suppose because I could think of nothing rational to say. Finally I decided to be irrational.

'What about Mrs. McVey?'

He shrugged. 'She feeds me,' he said.

'And what about the Scudders' pigs?'

Colour rose blotchily to his cheeks. 'I goofed,' he said. 'I was aiming for the fence and let it go too soon.

'I told all those ladies the truth Monday,' I said. 'They knew they had been wrong about you and Twyla. There was no need——'

'No need!' His eyes flashed and I blinked away from the impact of his straight, indignant glare. 'They're dern lucky I didn't smash them all flat.'

'I know,' I said hastily. 'I know how you feel, but I can't congratulate you on your restraint because, however little you did compared to what you might have done, it was still more than you had a right to do. Especially the pigs and the wall.'

'I didn't mean the pigs,' he muttered as he fingered a patch on his knee. 'Old man Scudder's a pretty right guy.'

'Yes,' I said. 'So what are you going to do about it?'

'I don't know,' he said. 'I could swipe some pigs from somewhere else for him, but I suppose that wouldn't fix things.'

'No, it wouldn't,' I said. 'You should buy—do you have any money?'

'Not for pigs!' He flared. 'All I have is what I'm saving for my musical instrument and not one penny of that'll ever go for pigs!'

'All right, all right,' I said. 'You figure out something.'

He ducked his head again, fingering the patch, and I watched the late sun run across the curve of his cheek, thinking what an odd conversation this was.

'Francher,' I said, leaning forward impulsively. 'Do you ever wonder how come you can do the things you do?'

His eyes were quick on my face. 'Do you ever wonder why you *can't* do the things you can't do?'

I flushed and shifted my crutches. 'I *know* why,' I said.

'No you don't,' he said. 'You only know when your Can't began. You don't know the real why. Even you doctors don't know all of it. Well, I don't know the why of my Cans. I don't even know the beginning of them, only that sometimes I feel a wave of something inside me that hollers to get out of all the Can'ts that are around me like you can't do this, you can't do that, and then I *remember* that I can.'

He flicked his fingers and my crutches stirred. They lifted and thudded softly down the steps and then up again to lean back in their accustomed place.

'Crutches *can't* walk,' said the Francher kid. 'But you—— Something besides your body musta got smashed in that wreck.'

'Everything got smashed,' I said bitterly, the cold horror of that night and all that followed choking my chest. 'Everything ended—everything.'

'There aren't any endings,' said the Francher kid. 'Only new beginnings. When you going to get started?' Then he slouched away, his hands in his pockets, his head bent as he kicked a rock along the path. Bleakly I watched him go, trying to keep alive my flame of anger at him.

Well, Leland's wall had to be rebuilt and it was the Francher kid that got the job. He toiled mightily, lifting the heavy stones and cracking his hands with the dehydrating effect of the mortar he used. Maybe the fence wasn't as straight as it had been, but it was repaired and perhaps, I hoped, a stone had been set strongly somewhere in the Francher kid by this act of atonement. That he received pay for it didn't detract too much from the act itself—especially considering the amount of pay, and the fact that it all went in on the other reparation.

The appearance of two strange pigs in Scudder's east field created quite a stir, but the wonder of it was dulled by all the odd events preceding it. Mr. Scudder made inquiries but nothing ever came of them so he kept the pigs, and I made no inquiries but relaxed for a while about the Francher kid.

V

It was along about this time that a Dr. Curtis came to town briefly. Well, came to town is a euphemism. His car broke down on his way up into the hills and he had to accept our hospitality until Bill Thurman could get around to finding a necessary part. He stayed at Somansons' in a room opposite mine after Mrs. Somanson had frantically cleared it out, mostly by the simple expedient of shoving all the boxes and crates and odds and ends to the end of the hall and draping a cover over them. Then she splashed water over the barely settled dust and mopped out the resultant mud, put a brick under one corner of the bed, made it up with two army surplus mattresses, one sheet edged with crocheted lace, and one of heavy unbleached muslin. She unearthed a pillow that fluffed beautifully but sighed itself to a wafer-thin odour of damp feathers at a touch, and topped the splendid whole with two hand-pieced, hand-quilted quilts and a chenille spread with a technicolor peacock flamboyantly dominating it.

'There,' she sighed, using her apron to dust the edge of the dresser where it showed along the edge of the dresser runner, 'I guess that'll hold him.'

'I should hope so,' I smiled. 'It's probably the quickest room he's ever had.'

'He's lucky to have this at such short notice,' she said, turning the rag rug over so the burned place wouldn't show. 'If it wasn't that I had my eye on that new winter coat——'

Dr. Curtis was a very relaxing, comfortable sort of fellow and it seemed so good to have someone to talk to who cared to use words of more than two syllables. It wasn't that the people in Willow Creek were ignorant, they just didn't usually care to discuss three-syllable matters. I guess, besides the conversation, I was drawn to Dr. Curtis because he neither looked at my crutches nor not looked at them. It was pleasant except for the twinge of here's-someone-who-has-never-known-me-without them.

After supper that night, we all sat around the massive oil burner in the front room and talked against the monotone background of the radio turned low. Of course the late shake-making events in the area were brought up. Dr. Curtis was most interested—especially in the rails that curled up into rosettes. Because he was a doctor and a stranger, the group expected an explanation of these goings-on from him, or at least an educated guess.

'What do I think?' He leaned forward in the old rocker and rested his arms on his knees. 'I think a lot of things happen that can't be explained by our usual thought patterns, and once we get accustomed to certain patterns we find it very uncomfortable to break over into others. So maybe it's just as well not to want an explanation.'

'Hmmm.' Ol' Charlie knocked the ashes out of his pipe into his hand and looked around for the waste basket. 'Neat way of saying you don't know either. Think I'll remember that. It might come in handy sometime. Well, g'night all.' He glanced around hastily, dumped the ashes in the geranium pot, and left, sucking on his empty pipe.

His departure was a signal for the others to drift off to bed at the wise hour of ten, but I was in no mood for wisdom, not of the early-to-bed type, anyway.

'Then there *is* room in this life for inexplicables.' I pleated my skirt between my fingers and straightened it out again.

'It would be a poor, lack-lustre sort of world if there weren't,' the doctor said. 'I used to rule out anything that I couldn't explain, but I got cured of that good one time.' He smiled reminiscently. 'Sometimes I wish I hadn't. As I said, it can be mighty uncomfortable.'

'Yes,' I said impulsively. 'Like hearing impossible music and sliding down moonbeams——' I felt my heart sink at the sudden blankness of his face. Oh, gee! Goofed again. He could talk glibly of inexplicables, but he didn't really believe in them. 'And crutches that walk by themselves,' I rushed on rashly, 'and autumn leaves that dance in the windless clearing——' I grasped my crutches and started blindly for the door. 'And maybe some day if I'm a good girl and disbelieve enough, I'll walk again——'

' "And disbelieve enough?" ' His words followed me. 'Don't you mean believe enough?'

'Don't strain your pattern,' I called back. 'It's "disbelieve".'

Of course I felt silly the next morning at the breakfast table, but Dr. Curtis didn't refer to the conversation so I didn't either. He was discussing renting a jeep for his hunting trip and leaving his car to be fixed.

'Tell Bill you'll be back a week before you plan to,' said Ol' Charlie. 'Then your car will be ready when you do get back.'

The Francher kid was in the group of people who gathered to watch Bill transfer Dr. Curtis's gear from the car to the jeep. As usual he was a little removed from the rest, lounging against a tree. Dr. Curtis finally came out, his 30-06 under one arm and his heavy hunting jacket under the other. Anna and I leaned over our side fence watching the whole procedure.

I saw the Francher kid straighten slowly, his hands leaving his pockets as he stared at Dr. Curtis. One hand went out tentatively and then faltered. Dr. Curtis inserted himself in the seat of the jeep and fumbled at the knobs on the dashboard. 'Which one's the radio?' he asked Bill.

'Radio? In this jeep?' Bill laughed.

'But the music——' Dr. Curtis paused for a split second, then turned on the ignition. 'Have to make my own, I guess,' he laughed.

The jeep roared into life and the small group scattered as he wheeled it in reverse across the yard. In the pause as he shifted gears, he glanced sideways at me and our eyes met. It was a very brief encounter, but he asked questions and I answered with my un-knowing and he exploded in a kind of wonderment—all in the moment between reverse and low.

We watched the dust boil up behind the jeep as it growled its way down to the highway.

'Well,' said Anna, 'a-hunting we do go indeed!'

'Who's he?' The Francher kid's hands were tight on the top of the fence, a blind sort of look on his face.

'I don't know,' I said. 'His name is Dr. Curtis.'

'He's heard music before.'

'I should hope so,' said Anna.

'*That* music?' I asked the Francher kid.

'Yes,' he nearly sobbed. 'Yes!'

'He'll be back,' I said. 'He has to get his car.'

'Well,' sighed Anna. 'The words are the words of English, but the sense is the sense of confusion. Coffee, anybody?'

That afternoon the Francher kid joined me, wordlessly,

as I struggled up the rise above the boarding-house for a little wideness of horizon to counteract the day's shut-in-ness. I would rather have walked alone, partly because of a need for silence and partly because he just couldn't ever keep his—accusing?—eyes off my crutches. But he didn't trespass upon my attention as so many people would have, so I didn't mind too much. I leaned, panting, against a grey granite boulder and let the fresh-from-distant-snow breeze lift my hair as I caught my breath. Then I huddled down into my coat, warming my ears. The Francher kid had a handful of pebbles and was lobbing them at the scattered rusty tin cans that dotted the hillside. After one pebble turned a square corner to hit a can, he spoke.

'If he knows the name of the instrument, then——' He lost his words.

'What is the name?' I asked, rubbing my nose where my coat collar had tickled it.

'It really isn't a word,' he said. 'It's just two sounds it makes.'

'Well, then, make me a word,' I said. ' "Musical instrument" is mighty unmusical and unhandy.'

The Francher kid listened, his head tilted, his lips moving. 'I suppose you call it a *rappoor*,' he said, softening the *a*. 'But it isn't that.'

'*Rappoor*,' I said. 'Of course you know by now we don't have any such instrument.' I was intrigued at having been drawn into another Francher-type conversation. I was developing quite a taste for them. 'It's probably just something your mother dreamed up for you.'

'And for that doctor?' he asked.

'Ummm.' My mental wheels spun, tractionless. 'What do you think?'

'I almost know,' he said, 'that there are some more like Mother. Some who know "the Madness and the Dream" too.'

'Dr. Curtis?' I asked.

'No,' he said slowly, rubbing his hand along the boulder. 'No. I could feel a far-away, strange-to-me feeling with him. He's like you. He—he knows someone who knows, but he doesn't know.'

'Well, thanks,' I said. 'He's a nice bird to be a feather of. Then it's all very simple. When he comes back, you ask him who he knows.'

'Yes . . .' The Francher kid drew a tremendous breath. 'Yes!'

We eased down the hillside, talking money and music. The Francher kid had enough saved up to buy a good instrument of some kind . . . but what kind? He was immersed in tones and timbres and ranges and keys and the possibility of sometime finding a something that would sound like a *rappoor*.

We paused at the foot of the hill. Impulsively I spoke. 'Francher, why do you talk with me?' I wished the words back before I finished them. Words have a ghastly way of shattering delicate situations and snapping tenuous bonds.

He lobbed a couple more stones against the bank and turned away, hands in his pockets. His words came back to me after I had given them up.

'You don't hate me—yet.'

I was jarred. I suppose I had imagined all the people around the Francher kid were getting acquainted with him as I was, but his words made me realize differently. After that I caught at every conversation that included the Francher kid, and alerted at every mention of his name. It shook me to find that to practically everyone he was still juvenile delinquent, lazy trash, no-good, off-scouring, potential criminal, burden. By some devious means it had been decided that he was responsible for all the odd happenings in town. I asked a number of people how the kid could possibly have done it. The only answer I got was 'The Francher kid can do anything—bad.'

Even Anna still found him an unwelcome burden in her classroom despite the fact that he was finally functioning on a fairly acceptable level academically.

Here I'd been thinking—Heaven knows why!—that he was establishing himself in the community. Instead he was doing well to hold his own. I reviewed to myself all that had happened since I first met him and found hardly a thing that would be positive in the eyes of the general public.

'Why,' I thought to myself, 'I'm darned lucky he's kept out of the hands of the law!' And my stomach knotted coldly at what might happen if the Francher kid ever did step over into out-and-out lawlessness. There's something insidiously sweet to the adolescent in flouting authority and I wanted no such appetite for any My Child of mine.

Well, the next few days after Dr. Curtis left were typical hunting weather days. Minutes of sunshine and shouting autumn colours—hours of cloud and rain and near snow and raw, aching winds. Reports came of heavy snow across Mingus Mountain, and Dogietown was snowed in for the winter, a trifle earlier than usual. We watched our own first flakes idle down, then whip themselves to tears against the huddled houses. It looked as though all excitement and activity were about to be squeezed out of Willow Springs by the drab greyness of winter.

Then the unexpected, which sometimes splashes our greyness with scarlet, happened. The big dude-ranch school, the Half Circle Star, that occupied the choicest of the range land in our area, invited all the school kids out to a musical splurge. They had imported an orchestra that played concerts as well as being a very good dance band, and they planned a gala weekend with a concert Friday evening followed by a dance for the teeners Saturday night. The ranch students were usually kept aloof from the town kids, poor little tikes. They were mostly unwanted or maladjusted children whose parents could afford to get rid of them with a flourish under the guise of giving them the advantage of growing up in healthful surroundings.

Of course the whole town was flung into a tizzy. There were the children of millionaires out there and famous people's kids too, but about the only glimpse we ever got of them was as they swept grandly through the town in the ranch station wagons. On such occasions, we collectively blinked our eyes at the chromium glitter, and sighed—though perhaps for different reasons. I sighed for thin, unhappy faces pressed to windows and sad eyes yearning back at houses where families lived who wanted *their* kids.

Anyway, the consensus of opinion was that it would be worth suffering through a 'music concert' to get to go to a dance with a real orchestra—because only those who attended the concert were eligible for the dance.

There was much discussion and much heart-burning over what to wear to the two so divergent affairs. The boys were complacent after they found out that their one good outfit was right for both. The girls discussed endlessly, and embarked upon a wild lend-borrow spree when they found that fathers positively refused to spend largely even for this so special occasion.

I was very pleased for the Francher kid. Now he'd have a chance to hear live music—a considerable cut above what snarled in on our staticky wavelengths from the available radio stations. Now maybe he'd hear a faint echo of his *rappoor* and in style too, because Mrs. McVey had finally broken down and bought him a new suit, a really nice one by the local standards. I was as anxious as Twyla to see how the Francher kid would look in such splendour.

So it was with a distinct shock that I saw the kid at the concert, lounging, thumbs in his pockets, against the door of the room where the crowd gathered. His face was shut and dark and his patched, faded levis made a blotch in the dimness of the room.

'Look!' whispered Twyla. 'He's in levis!'

'How come?' I breathed. 'Where's his new suit?'

'I don't know,' she answered. 'And those levis aren't even clean!' And she hunched down in her seat, feeling the accusing eyes of the whole world searing her through the Francher kid.

The concert was splendid. Even our rockin'est rollers were caught up in the wonderful web of music. EvenI lost myself for long, lovely moments in the bright melodic trails that led me out of the grey lanes of familiarity. But I also felt the bite of tears behind my eyes. Music is made to be moved to and my unresponsive feet wouldn't even tap a tempo. I let the brasses and drums smash my rebellion into bearable-sized pieces again and joined joyfully in the enthusiastic applause.

'Hey!' said Rigo behind me as the departing stir of the crowd began. 'I didn't know anything could sound like that. Man! Did you hear that horn! I'd like to get me one of them things and blow it!'

'You'd sound like a sick cow,' said Janniset. 'Them's hard to play.'

Their discussion moved on down the aisle.

'He's gone.' Twyla's voice was a breath in my ear.

'Yes,' I said. 'But we'll probably see him out at the bus.'

But we didn't. He wasn't at the bus. He hadn't come out on the bus. No one knew how he got out to the ranch or where he had gone.

Anna and Twyla and I piled into Anna's car and headed back for Willow Creek, my heart thudding with apprehension, my thoughts busy. When we pulled up at Somansons', there was a car parked in front.

'The McVey!' Anna sizzled in my ear. 'Ah ha! Methinks I smell trouble.'

I didn't even have time to take my coat off in the smothery warmth of the front room before I was confronted by the monumental violence of Mrs. McVey's wrath.

'Dress him!' she hissed, her chin thrust out as she lunged forward in the chair. 'Dress him so's he'll feel equal to the others!' Her hands flashed out and I dodged instinctively and blinked as a bunch of white rags fluttered to my feet. 'His new shirt!' she half-screamed. Another shower of tatters—dark ones this time. 'His new suit! Not a piece in it as big as your hand!' There was a spatter like muffled hail. 'His shoes!' Her voice caught on the edge of her violence and she repeated raggedly, 'His *shoes*!' Fear was battling with anger now. 'Look at those pieces—as big as stamps—*shoes*!' Her voice broke. 'Anybody who can tear up *shoes*!'

She sank back in her chair, spent and breathless, fishing for a crumpled Kleenex to wipe the spittle from her chin. I eased into a chair after Anna helped me shrug off my coat. Twyla huddled, frightened, near the door, her eyes big with fascinated terror.

'Let him be like the others,' the McVey half-whispered. 'That limb of Satan ever be like anyone decent?'

'But why?' My voice sounded thin and high in the calm after the hurricane.

'For no reason at all,' she gasped, pressing her hand to her panting ribs. 'I gave all them brand-new clothes to him to try on, thinking he'd be pleased. Thinking'—her voice slipped to a whining tremolo—'thinking he'd see how I had his best interest at heart.' She paused and sniffed lugubriously. No ready sympathy for her poured into the hiatus so she went on angrily aggrieved. 'And he took them and went into his room and came out with them like that!' Her finger jabbed at the pile of rags. 'He—he *threw* them at me! You and your big ideas about him wanting to be like other kids!' Her lips curled away from the venomous spate of words. 'He don't want to be like nobody 'cepting hisself. And he's a devil!' Her voice sank to a whisper and her breath drew in on the last word, her eyes wide.

'But why did he do it?' I asked. 'He must have said *something*.'

Mrs. McVey folded her hands across her ample middle and pinched her lips together. 'There are some things a lady don't repeat,' she said prissily, tossing her head.

'Oh, cut it out!' I was suddenly dreadfully weary of trying to be polite to the McVeys of this world. 'Stop trying on that kind of act. You could teach a stevedore——' I bit my lips and swallowed hard. 'I'm sorry, Mrs. McVey, but this is no time to hold back. What did he say? What excuse did he give?'

'He didn't give any excuse,' she snapped. 'He just—just——' Her heavy cheeks mottled with colour. 'He called names.'

'Oh.' Anna and I exchanged glances.

'But what on earth got into him?' I asked. 'There must be some reason——'

'Well,' Anna squirmed a little. 'After all, what can you expect——'

'From a background like that?' I snapped. 'Well, Anna, I certainly expected something different from a background like yours!'

Anna's face hardened and she gathered up her things. 'I've known him longer than you have,' she said quietly.

'Longer,' I admitted, 'but not better, Anna', I pleaded,

leaning towards her. 'Don't condemn him unheard.'

'Condemn?' She looked up brightly. 'I didn't know he was on trial.'

'Oh, Anna.' I sank back in my chair 'The poor kid's been on trial, presumed guilty of anything and everything ever since he's arrived in town and you know it.'

'I don't want to quarrel with you,' Anna said. 'I'd better say good night.'

The door clicked to behind her. Mrs. McVey and I measured each other with our eyes. I had opened my mouth to say something when I felt a whisper of a motion at my elbow. Twyla stood under the naked flood of the overhead light, her hands clasped in front of her, her eyes shadowed by the droop of her lashes as she narrowed her glance against the glare.

'What did you buy his clothes with?' Her voice was very quiet.

'None of your business, young lady,' snapped Mrs. McVey, reddening.

'This is almost the end of the month,' said Twyla. 'Your cheque doesn't come till the first. Where did you get the money?'

'*Well!*' Mrs. McVey began to hoist her bulk out of the chair. 'I don't have to stay here and have a sassy snip like this——'

Twyla swept in closer—so close that Mrs. McVey shrank back, her hands gripping the dusty, overstuffed arms of the chair.

'You never have any of the cheque left after the first week,' said Twyla. 'And you have bought a purple nylon nightgown this month. It took a week's pay——'

Mrs. McVey lunged forward again, her mouth agape with horrified outrage.

'You took *his* money,' said Twyla, her eyes steely in her

tight young face. 'You stole the money he was saving!' She whirled away from the chair, her skirts and hair flaring. 'Some day,' she said with clenched teeth, 'some day I'll probably be old and fat and ugly, but heaven save me from being old and fat and ugly and a *thief*!'

'Twyla!' I warned, truly afraid that Mrs. McVey would have a stroke then and there.

'Well, she *is* a thief! cried Twyla. 'The Francher kid has been working and saving almost a year to buy——' She faltered, palpably feeling the thin ice of betraying a confidence. 'To buy something. And he had almost enough. And she must have gone snooping around——'

'Twyla!' I had to stop her.

'It's true! It's true!' Her hands clenched rebelliously.

'Twyla.' My voice was quiet, but it silenced her.

'Goodbye, Mrs. McVey,' I said. 'I'm sorry this happened.'

'Sorry!' she snorted, rearing up out of her chair. 'Sour old maids with never a chick or child of their own sticking their noses into decent people's affairs——' She waddled hastily to the door. She reached for the doorknob, her eyes narrow and venomous over her shoulder. 'I got connections,' she said. 'I'll get even with you.' The door shuddered as it emphasized her departure.

I let the McVey sweep out of my mind.

'Twyla.' I took her cold hands in mine. 'You'd better go on home. I've got to figure out how to find the Francher kid.'

The swift movement of her hands protested. 'But I want——'

'I'm sorry, Twyla,' I said. 'I think it'd be better.'

'OK.' Her shoulders relaxed in acquiescence.

Just as she left, Mrs. Somanson bustled in. 'Y' better come on out to the table and have a cup of coffee,' she said. I straightened wearily.

'That McVey! She'd drive the devil to drink,' she said cheerfully. 'Well, I guess people are like that. I've had more teachers over the years say that it wasn't the kids they minded, but the parents.' She shooed me through the door and went to the kitchen for the percolator. 'Now, I was always one to believe that the teacher was right—right or wrong——' Her voice faded out in a long familiar story that proved just the opposite of what she'd said, as I stared into my cup of coffee, wondering despairingly where in all this world I could find the Francher kid. After the episode of the gossip, I had my fears. Still, often people who react violently to comparatively minor troubles, were seemingly unshaken by really serious ones—a sort of being at a loss for a proportionate emotional reaction.

But what would he do? Music—music—he'd planned to buy the means for music and he had lost the wherewithal. Now he had nothing to make music with. What would he do first? Revenge—or find his music elsewhere? Run away? To where? Steal the money? Steal the music? —*Steal?*

I snapped to awareness, my abrupt movement slopping my cold coffee over into the saucer. Mrs. Somanson was gone. The house was quiet with the twilight pause—the indefinable transitional phase from day to night.

This time it wouldn't be only a harmonica! I groped for my crutches, my mind scrabbling for some means of transportation. I was reaching for the doorknob when the door flew open and nearly bowled me over.

'Coffee! Coffee!' croaked Dr. Curtis, to my complete bewilderment. He staggered over, all bundled in his hunting outfit, his face ragged with whiskers, his clothes odorous of campfires and all out-of-doors, to the table and clutched the coffee pot. It was very obviously cold.

'Oh, well,' he said in a conversational tone. 'I guess I can survive without coffee.'

'Survive what?' I asked.

He looked at me a moment, smiling, then he said, 'Well, if I'm going to say anything about it to anyone it might as well be you, though I hope that I've got sense enough not to go around babbling indiscriminately. Of course, it might be a slight visual hangover from this hunting trip—you should hunt with these friends of mine sometime—but it kinda shook me.'

'Shook you?' I repeated stupidly, my mind racing around the idea of asking him for help in finding the Francher kid.

'Somewhat,' he admitted. 'After all, there I was, riding along, minding my own business, singing, lustily, if not musically, 'A Life On The Ocean Wave', when there they were, marching sedately across the road.'

'They?' This story dragged in my impatient ears.

'The trombone and the big bass drum,' he explained.

VI

'The what!' I had the sensation of running unexpectedly into a mad tangle of briars.

'The trombone and the big bass drum,' Dr Curtis repeated. 'Keeping perfect time and no doubt in perfect step, though you couldn't thump your feet convincingly six feet off the ground. Supposing, of course, you were a trombone with feet which this wasn't.'

'Dr. Curtis.' I grabbed the corner of his hunting coat. 'Please, *please*! what happened? Tell me! I've got to know.'

He looked at me and sobered. 'You are taking this seriously, aren't you?' he said wonderingly.

I gulped and nodded.

'Well, it was about five miles above the Half Circle Ranch, where the heavy pine growth begins. And so help me, a trombone and a bass drum marched in the air across the road, the bass drum marking the time—though come to think of it, the drum sticks just lay on the top. I stopped the jeep and ran over to where they had disappeared. I couldn't see anything in the heavy growth there, but I swear I heard a faint cheer from the trombone. I have no doubt that the two of them were hiding behind a tree, snickering at me.' He rubbed his hand across his fuzzy chin. 'Maybe I'd better drink that coffee, cold or not.'

'Dr. Curtis,' I said urgently. 'Can you help me? Without waiting for questions? Can you take me out there? Right now?'

I reached for my coat. Wordlessly, he helped me on with it and opened the door for me. The day was gone and the sky was clear around the horizon, shading into rose where the sun had dropped behind the hills. It was only a matter of minutes before we were roaring up the hill to the junction. I shouted over the jolting rattle.

'It's the Francher kid,' I yelled. 'I've got to find him and make him put them back before they find out.'

'Put who back where?' shouted Dr. Curtis into the sudden diminution of noise as we topped the rise, much to the astonishment of Mrs. Frisney who was pattering across the intersection with her black umbrella protecting her from the early starshine.

'It's too long to explain,' I screamed as we accelerated down the highway. 'But he must be stealing the whole orchestra because Mrs. McVey bought him a new suit, and I've got to make him take them back or they'll arrest him, then Heaven help us all.'

'You mean the Francher kid had that bass drum and trombone?' he yelled.

'Yes!' My chest was aching from the tension of speech. 'And probably all the rest.'

I caught myself with barked knuckles as Dr. Curtis braked to a sudden stop.

'Now look,' he said. 'Let's get this straight. You're talking wilder than I am. Do you mean to say that that kid is swiping a whole orchestra?'

'Yes,' I said, 'Don't ask me how. I don't know how, but he can do it——' I grabbed his sleeve. 'But he said you knew! The day you left on your trip, I mean, he said you knew someone who would know. We were waiting for you!'

'Well, I'll be blowed!' he said in slow wonder. 'Well, dang me!' He ran his hand over his face. 'So now it's *my* turn!' He reached for the ignition key. 'Gangway, Jemmy!' he shouted. 'Here I come with Another! Yours or mine, Jemmy? Yours or mine?'

It was as though his outlandish words had tripped a trigger. Suddenly all this strangeness, this out-of-stepness became a mad foolishness. Despairingly I wished I'd never seen Willow Creek or the Francher kid or a harmonica that danced alone or Twyla's tilted side-glance, or Dr. Curtis or the white road dimming in the rapid coming of night. I huddled down in my coat, my eyes stinging with weary, hopeless tears, and the only comfort I could find was in visualizing me twisting my hated braces into rigid confetti and spattering the road with it.

I roused as Dr. Curtis braked the jeep to a stop.

'It was about there,' he said, peering through the dusk. 'It's mighty deserted up here—the raw end of isolation. The kid's probably scared by now and plenty willing to come home.'

'Not the Francher kid,' I said. 'He's not the run-of-the mill type kid.'

'Oh, so!' said Dr. Curtis. 'I'd forgotten.'

Then there it was. At first I thought it the evening wind in the pines, but it deepened and swelled and grew into a thunderous, magnificent, shaking chord—a whole orchestra giving tongue. Then, one by one, the instruments soloed, running their scales, displaying their intervals, parading their possibilities. Somewhere between the strings and woodwinds, I eased out of the jeep.

'You stay here,' I half-whispered. 'I'll go find him. You wait.'

It was like walking through a rainstorm, the notes spattering all around me, the shrill lightning of the piccolos and the muttering thunder of the drums. There was no melody, only a child running gleefully through a candy store, snatching greedily at everything, gathering delight by the handful and throwing it away for the sheer pleasure of having enough to be able to throw it.

I struggled up the rise above the road, forgetting in my preoccupation to be wary of unfamiliar territory in the half dark. There they were—in the sand hollow beyond the rise—all the instruments arranged in orderly precise rows as though at the recital, each one wrapped in a sudden, shadowy silence, broken only by the shivery giggle of the cymbals which hastily stilled themselves against the sand.

'Who's there?' He was a rigid figure, poised atop a boulder, arms half lifted.

'Francher,' I said.

'Oh.' He slid through the air to me. 'I'm not hiding any more,' he said. 'I'm going to be me all the time now.'

'Francher,' I said bluntly, 'you're a thief.'

He jerked in protest. 'I'm not either——'

'If this is being you,' I said, 'you're a thief. You stole these instruments.'

He groped for words then burst out. 'They stole my money! They stole all my music.'

'They?' I asked. 'Francher, you can't lump people together and call them "*they*". Did I steal your money? Or Twyla—or Mrs. Frisney—or Rigo?'

'Maybe you didn't put your hands on it,' said the Francher kid. 'But you stood around and let McVey take it.'

'That's a guilt humanity has shared since the beginning,' I said. 'Standing around and letting wrong things happen. But even Mrs. McVey felt she was helping you. She didn't sit down and decide to rob you. Some people have the idea that children don't have any exclusive possessions, but what they have belongs to the adults who care for them. Mrs. McVey thinks that way. Which is quite a different thing from deliberately stealing from strangers. What about the owners of all these instruments? What have they done to deserve your ill-will?'

'They're people,' he said stubbornly. 'And I'm not going to be people any more.' Slowly he lifted himself into the air and turned himself upside down. 'See,' he said, hanging above the hillside. 'People can't do things like this.'

'No,' I said. 'But apparently whatever kind of creature you have decided to be can't keep their shirt tails in either.'

Hastily he scrabbled his shirt back over his bare midriff and righted himself. There was an awkward silence in the shadowy hollow; then I asked:

'What are you going to do about the instruments?'

'Oh, they can have them back when I'm through with them—if they can find them,' he said contemptuously. 'I'm going to play them to pieces tonight.'

The trumpet jabbed brightly through the dusk and the violins shimmered a silver obbligato.

'And every downbeat will say "*thief*", I said. 'And every roll of the drums will growl "*stolen*".'

'I don't care, I don't care!' he almost yelled. ' "*Thief*" and "*stolen*" are words for people, and I'm not going to be people any more, I told you!'

'What are you going to be?' I asked, leaning wearily against a tree trunk. 'An animal?'

'No sir.' He was having trouble deciding what to do with his hands. 'I'm going to be *more* than just a human.'

'Well, for a more-than-human, this kind of behaviour doesn't show very many smarts,' I said. 'If you're going to be more than human, you have to be thoroughly a human first. If you're going to be better than a human, you have to be the best a human can be, first—then go on from there. Being entirely different is no way to make a big impression on people. You have to be able to outdo them at their own game first and then go beyond them. It won't matter to them that you can fly like a bird unless you can walk straight like a man, first. To most people "different" is "wrong". Oh, they'd probably say, "My goodness! How wonderful!" when you first pulled some fancy trick, but—' I hesitated, wondering if I were being wise—'but they'd forget you pretty quick, just as they would any cheap carnival attraction.'

He jerked at my words, his fists clenched.

'You're as bad as the rest.' His words were tight and bitter. 'You think I'm just a freak——'

'I think you're an unhappy person,' I said, 'because you're not sure who you are or what you are, but you'll have a much worse time trying to make an identity for yourself if you tangle with the law.'

'The law doesn't apply to me,' he said coldly. 'Because I know who I am——'

'Do you, Francher?' I asked softly. 'Where did your mother come from? Why could she walk through the minds of others? Who are you, Francher? Are you going to cut yourself off from people before you even try to find out just what wonders you are capable of? Not these little sideshow deals, but maybe miracles that really count.' I swallowed hard as I looked at his averted face, shadowy in the dusk. My own face was congealing from the cold wind that had risen, but he didn't even shiver in its iciness though he had no jacket on. My lips moved stiffly. 'Both of us know you could get away with this lawlessness, but you know as well as I do that if you take this first step, you won't ever be able to untake it. And, how do we know, it might make it impossible for you to be accepted by your own kind—if you're right in saying there are others. Surely they're above common theft. And Dr. Curtis is due back from his hunting trip. So close to knowing—maybe——

'I didn't know your mother, Francher, but I do know this is not The Dream she had for you. This is not why she endured Hunger and Hiding, Terror and Panic Places——'

I turned and stumbled away from him, making my way back to the road. It was dark—horribly dark around me and in me as I wailed soundlessly for this My Child. Somewhere before I got back, Dr. Curtis was helping me. He got me back into the jeep and pried my frozen fingers from my crutches and warmed my hands between his broad-gloved palms.

'He *isn't* of this world, you know,' he said. 'At least his parents or grandparents weren't. There are others like him. I've been hunting with some of them. He doesn't know, evidently, nor did his mother, but he *can* find his people. I wanted to tell you to help you persuade him——'

I started to reach for my crutches, peering through the dark, then I relaxed. 'No,' I said with tingling lips. 'It wouldn't be any good if he only responded to bribes. He has to decide now, with the scales weighted against him.

He's got to *push* into this new world. He just can't slide in limply. You kill a chick if you help it hatch.'

I dabbed all the way home at tears for a My Child, lost in a wilderness I couldn't chart, bound in a captivity from which I couldn't free him.

Dr. Curtis saw me to the door of my room. He lifted my averted face and wiped it.

'Don't worry,' he said. 'I promise you the Francher kid will be taken care of.'

'Yes,' I said, closing my eyes against the nearness of his. 'By the Sheriff if they catch him. They'll discover the loss of the orchestra any minute now, if they haven't already.'

'You made him think,' he said. 'He wouldn't have stood still for all that time if you hadn't.'

'Too late,' I said. 'A thought too late.'

Alone in my room I huddled on my bed, trying not to think of anything. I lay there until I was stiff with the cold, then I crept into my night clothes and buttoned my warm woolly robe up to my chin. I sat in the darkness there by the window, looking out at the lacy ghosts of the cottonwood trees, in the dim moonlight. How long would it be before some kindly soul would come blundering in to regale me with the latest about the Francher kid?

I put my elbows on the window sill and leaned my face on my hands, the heels of my palms pressing against my eyes. *Oh Francher, My Child, My lonely lost Child . . .*

'I'm not lost.'

I lifted a startled face. The voice was so soft. Maybe I had imagined——

'No, I'm here.' The Francher kid stepped out into the milky glow of the moon, moving with a strange new strength and assurance, quite divorced from his usual teenage gangling.

'Oh, Francher——' I couldn't let myself sob, but my voice caught on the last of his name.

'It's O.K.,' he said. 'I took them all back.'

My shoulders ached as the tension ran out of them.

'I didn't have time to get them all back in the hall, but I stacked them carefully on the front porch.' A glimmer of a smile crossed his face. 'I guess they'll wonder how they got out there.'

'I'm so sorry about your money,' I said awkwardly.

He looked at me soberly. 'I can save again. I'll get it yet. Someday I'll have my music. It doesn't *have* to be now.'

Suddenly a warm bubble seemed to be pressing up against my lungs. I felt excitement tingle clear out to my fingertips. I leaned across the sill. 'Francher,' I cried softly. 'You *have* your music. Now. Remember the harmonica? Remember when you danced with Twyla? Oh Francher! All sound is vibration. You can vibrate the air without an instrument. Remember the chord you played with the orchestra? Play it again, Francher!'

He looked at me blankly and then it was as if a candle had been lighted behind his face. 'Yes!' he cried. 'Yes!'

Softly—oh, softly—because miracles come that way, I heard the chord begin. It swelled richly, fully, softly until the whole backyard vibrated to it—a whole orchestra crying out in a whisper in the pale moonlight.

'But the tunes!' he cried, taking this miracle at one stride and leaping beyond it. 'I don't know any of the tunes for an orchestra!'

'There are books,' I said. 'Whole books of scores for symphonies and operas and——'

'And when I know the instruments better!' Here was the eager, alive voice of the-Francher-kid-who-should-be. 'Anything I hear——' The backyard ripped raucously to a couple of bars of the latest rock'n'roll, then blossomed softly to an 'Adoramus Te' and skipped to 'The Farmer In The Dell.' 'Then some day I'll make my own——' Tremulously a *rappoor* threaded through a melodic phrase and stilled itself.

In the silence that followed, the Francher kid looked at me—not at my face, but deep inside me somewhere.

'Miss Carolle!' I felt my eyes tingle to tears at his voice. 'You've given me my music!' I could hear him swallow. 'I want to give you something.' My hand moved in protest, but he went on quickly, 'Please come outside.'

'Like this?' I asked. 'I'm in my robe and slippers.'

'They're warm enough,' he said. 'Here, I'll help you through the window.'

And before I knew it, I was over the low sill and clinging dizzily to it from the outside.

'My braces,' I said, loathing the words with a horrible loathing. 'My crutches.'

'No,' said the Francher kid. 'You don't need them. Walk across the yard, Miss Carolle, all alone.'

'I can't!' I cried through my shock. 'Oh, Francher, don't tease me!'

'Yes, you can,' he said. 'That's what I'm giving you. I can't mend you, but I can give you that much. Walk.'

I clung frantically to the sill. Then I saw again Francher and Twyla spiralling down from the tree-tops, Francher upside down in the air with his midriff showing, Francher bouncing Balance Rock from field to field.

I let go of the sill. I took a step. And another, and another. I held my hands far out from my sides. Glorious freedom from clenched hands and aching elbows! Across the yard I went, every step in the milky moonlight a paean of praise. I turned at the fence and looked back. The Francher kid was crouched by the window in a tight huddle of concentration. I rose on tiptoe and half-skipped, half-ran back to the window, feeling the wind of my going lift my hair back from my cheeks. Oh, it was like a drink after thirst! Like food after famine! Like gates swinging open!

I fell forward and caught at the window-sill. And cried out inarticulately as I felt the old bonds clamp down again, the old half-death seize hold of me, I crumpled to the ground beside the Francher kid. His tormented eyes looked into mine, his face pale and haggard. His forearm went up to wipe his sweat-drenched face. 'I'm sorry,' he panted. 'That's all I can do now.'

My hands reached for him. There was a sudden movement, so quick and so close that I drew my foot back out of the way. I looked up, startled. Dr. Curtis and a shadowy someone else were standing over us. But the surprise of their being there was drowned in the sudden up-surge of wonderment.

'It moved!' I cried. 'My foot moved. Look! Look! It moved!' And I concentrated on it again—hard, hard! After laborious seconds, my left big toe wiggled.

My hysterical laugh was half a shout. 'One toe is better than none!' I sobbed. 'Isn't it, Dr. Curtis? Doesn't that mean that some day—that maybe——'

He had dropped to his knees and he gathered my frantic hands into his two big quiet ones.

'It might well be,' he said. 'Jemmy will help us find out.'

The other figure knelt beside Dr. Curtis. There was a curious, waiting kind of silence—but it wasn't me he was looking at. It wasn't my hands he reached for. It wasn't my voice that cried out softly.

But it was the Francher kid that suddenly launched himself into the arms of the stranger and began to wail, the wild, noisy crying of a child—a child who could be brave as long as he was completely lost, but who had to dissolve into tears when rescue came.

The stranger looked over the Francher kid's head at Dr. Curtis. 'He's mine,' he said. 'But she's almost one of yours.'

It could all have been a dream—or a mad explosion of imagination of some sort; but they don't come any less imaginative than Mrs. McVey, and I know she will never forget the Francher kid. She has another foster-child now, a placid, plump little girl who loves to sit and listen to women talk—but the Francher kid is indelible in the McVey memory. Unborn generations will probably hear of him and his shoes.

And Twyla . . . she will carry his magic to her grave, unless (and I know she sometimes hopes prayerfully) unless Francher some day comes back for her. Because he's gone.

Jemmy, the stranger, took him to Cougar Canyon up in the hills where the others of his kind are gathered—star children, children of The People, the People who came last century to Earth, refugees from a shattered world, scattered over ours by their near-disastrous arrival here. And there at Cougar Canyon they are helping the Francher kid sort out all his many gifts and capabilities—some of which are unique to him—so that he will be able, finally, to fit into his most effective slot in their scheme of things which is so wonderfully, brightly above ours. They tell me that there are those of this world who are developing even now in the footsteps of The People. That's what Jemmy meant when he told Dr. Curtis I was almost one of his.

And I shall walk again. Dr. Curtis brought Bethie, a Sensitive of The People. She only touched me softly with her hands and Read me to Dr. Curtis. And I *had* to accept it then—that it was mostly myself that stood in my own way. That my doctor had been right: that time, patience and believing will make me whole again.

The more I think about The People, about Jemmy and Bethie and the Francher kid, the more I think that those three words are the key to them and to what they hope to do on our earth.

Time, patience and believing—and the greatest of these is believing.

O'MARA'S ORPHAN

JAMES WHITE

It would have been bad enough in any case, on the top of a criminal charge, to be landed with the care of a sick baby, but a sick baby weighing half a ton presented a problem. Could O'Mara solve it?

I

The alien occupying O'Mara's sleeping-compartment weighed roughly half a ton, possessed six short, thick appendages which served both as arms and legs and had a hide like flexible armour-plate. Coming as it did from Hudlar, a four-G world with an atmospheric pressure nearly seven times Earth normal, such ruggedness of physique was to be expected. But despite its enormous strength the being was helpless, O'Mara knew, because it was barely six months old, it had just seen its parents die in a construction accident, and its brain was sufficiently well developed for the sight to have frightened it badly.

'I've b-b-brought the kid,' Waring, one of the section's tractor-beam operators, had said. He hated O'Mara, and with good reason, but he was trying not to gloat. 'C-C-Caxton sent me. He says your leg makes you unfit for normal duty, so you can look after the young one until somebody arrives from its home planet. He's on his way over n-now. . . .'

Waring trailed off. He began checking the seals of his spacesuit, obviously in a hurry to get out before O'Mara could mention the accident. 'I brought some of its food with me,' he ended quickly. 'It's in the airlock.'

O'Mara nodded without speaking. He was a young man cursed with the kind of physique which ensured his winning every fight he had ever been in, and there had been a great many of them recently, as well as a face as square, heavy and roughly formed as his over-muscled body. He knew that if he allowed himself to show how much that accident had affected him, Waring would think that he was simply putting on an act. Men who were put together as he was, O'Mara had long ago discovered, were not supposed to have any of the softer emotions.

Immediately Waring left, O'Mara went to the air-lock for the glorified paint-sprayer with which Hudlarians away from their home planet were fed. While checking the gadget and its spare food tanks he tried to go over the story he would have to tell Caxton when the section chief arrived. Staring moodily through the airlock port at the bits and pieces of the gigantic jigsaw puzzle spread across fifty cubic miles of space outside, he tried to think. But his mind kept ducking away from the accident and slipping instead into generalities and events which were in the far past or future.

The vast structure which was slowly taking shape in Galactic Sector Twelve, midway between the rim of the parent galaxy and the densely populated systems of the Greater Magellanic Cloud, was to be a hospital—a hospital to end all hospitals. Hundreds of different environments would be accurately reproduced here, any extreme of heat, cold, pressure, gravity, radiation or atmosphere necessary for the patients and staff it would contain. Such a tremendous and complex structure was far beyond the resources of any one planet, so that hundreds of worlds had each fabricated sections of it and transported them to the assembly point.

But fitting the jigsaw together was no easy job.

Each of the worlds concerned had their copies of the master plan. But errors occurred despite this—probably through the plan having to be translated into so many different languages and systems of measurement. Sections which should have fitted snugly together very often had to be modified to make them join properly, and this necessitated moving the sections together and apart several times with massed tractor and pressor beams. This was very tricky work for the beam operators, because while the weight of the sections out in space was nil, their mass and inertia was tremendous.

And anyone unlucky enough to be caught between the joining faces of two sections in the process of being fitted together became, no matter how tough a life-form, an almost perfect representation of a two-dimensional body.

The beings who had died did belong to a tough species, physiological classification FROB to be exact. Adult Hudlarians weighed in the region of two Earth tons, and possessed an incredibly hard but flexible tegument which, as well as protecting them from their own native and external pressures, allowed them to live and work comfortably in any atmosphere of lesser pressure down to and including the vacuum of space. In addition they had the highest radiation-tolerance level known, which made them invaluable during power pile assembly.

The loss of two such valuable beings from his section would, in any case, have made Caxton mad, quite apart from other considerations. O'Mara sighed heavily, decided that his nervous system demanded a more positive release than that, and swore. Then he picked up the feeder and returned to the bedroom.

Normally the Hudlarians absorbed food directly through their skin from the thick, soupy atmosphere of their planet, but on any other world or in space a concentrated food compound had to be sprayed on to the absorbent hides at certain intervals. The young e-t was showing large bare patches and in other places the previous food coating had worn very thin. Definitely, thought O'Mara, the infant was due for another feed. He moved as close as seemed safe and began to spray carefully.

The process of being painted with food seemed to be a pleasant one for the young FROB. It ceased to cower in the corner and began blundering excitedly about the small bedroom. For O'Mara it became a matter of trying to hit a rapidly moving object while practising violent evasive manœuvres himself, which set his injured leg throbbing more painfully than ever. His furniture suffered, too.

As well as the exterior of the now-quiescent young alien, practically the whole interior surface of O'Mara's sleeping compartment was covered with the sticky, sharp-smelling food compound when Caxton arrived.

'What's going on?' said the Section Chief.

Space construction men as a class were simple, uncomplicated personalities whose reactions were easily predictable. Caxton was the type who always asked what was going on, and especially when such unnecessary questions were meant simply to needle somebody.

O'Mara answered the question without showing the anger he felt, and ended, '. . . After this I think I'll keep the kid in space, and feed it there. . . .'

'You will not!' Caxton snapped. 'You'll keep it here with you, all the time. But more about that later. At the moment I want to know about the accident. Your side of it, that is.'

His expression said that he was prepared to listen, but that he already doubted every word O'Mara would say.

'Before you go any farther,' Caxton broke in after O'Mara had completed two sentences, 'you know that this project is under Monitor Corps jurisdiction. This case involves extra-terrestrials and they'll have to be brought in on it. There'll be an investigation.' He tapped the small, flat box hanging from his chest. 'It's only fair to warn you that I'm taping everything you say.'

O'Mara nodded and began giving his account of the accident in a low monotone. It was a weak story, he knew. Finally Caxton said:

'But did anyone *see* you doing these things? Or even see the two e-ts moving about in the danger area while the warning lights were burning? You have a neat little story to explain this madness on their part—which, incidentally, makes you quite a hero—but it could be that you switched on the lights *after* the accident, that it was your negligence regarding the lights which caused it, and that all this about the straying youngster is a pack of lies designed to get you out of a very serious charge——'

'Waring saw me,' O'Mara cut in.

Caxton stared at him intently, his expression changing from suppressed anger to one of utter disgust and scorn. Despite himself O'Mara felt his face heating up.

'Waring, eh?' said the section chief tonelessly. 'You know, and we all know, that you have been riding Waring constantly, needling him to such an extent that he must hate you like poison. Even if he did see you, the court would expect him to keep quiet about it. And if he did not see you, they would think that he had and was keeping quiet about it anyway. O'Mara, you make me sick.'

Caxton wheeled and stamped towards the airlock. With one foot through the inner seal he turned again.

'You're nothing but a trouble-maker, O'Mara,' he said angrily, 'a surly, quarrelsome lump of bone and muscle with just enough skill to make you worth keeping. You may think that it was technical ability which got you these quarters on your own. It wasn't! You're good but not that good! The truth is that nobody else in my section would share accommodation with you. . . .'

The section chief's hand moved to the cut-off switch on his recorder. His voice, as he ended, became quiet and deadly.

'. . . And, O'Mara, if you let any harm come to that youngster, if anything happens to it at all, the Monitors won't even get the chance to try you.'

As the section chief left, O'Mara thought angrily that he was sentenced to live with this organic half-ton tank for a period that would feel like eternity, no matter how short it was. Everybody knew that exposing Hudlarians to space was like putting a dog out for the night—there were no harmful effects at all. But what some people knew and what they felt were two vastly different things and O'Mara was dealing here with the personalities of simple, uncomplicated, over-sentimental and very angry construction men.

When he had joined the project, O'Mara had found that he was doomed again to a job which, while important, gave him no satisfaction. Since school his life had been a series of such frustrations. Personnel officers could not believe that a young man with such square features and shoulders so huge that his head looked small by comparison could be interested in *subtle* subjects like psychology or electronics. Despite constant efforts during interviews to impress people with his quite considerable knowledge, his applications were invariably stamped 'Approved Suitable for Heavy, Sustained Labour.'

On joining this project he had decided to make the best

of what promised to be another boring job—he decided to become an unpopular character. Now he was wishing that he had not been so successful at making himself disliked.

What he needed most at this moments was friends, and he hadn't a single one.

O'Mara's mind was dragged back from these dismal thoughts by the sharp all-pervading odour of the Hudlarian's food compound. Something would have to be done about that, and quickly. He hurriedly got into his lightweight suit and went through the lock.

II

His living quarters were in a tiny sub-asssembly which would one day form the theatre, surgical ward and adjoining storage compartments of the hospital's low-gravity MSVK section. Two small rooms with a connecting section of corridor had been pressurized and fitted with artificial gravity grids for O'Mara's benefit, the rest of the structure remaining both airless and weightless. Outside he drifted along unfinished corridors whose ends were open to space, staring into bare, angular compartments, all full of plumbing and half-built machinery. But all the compartments were either too small to hold the alien or they were open in one direction to space. O'Mara swore with great feeling, pushed himself out to one of the ragged edges of his tiny domain and glared around him.

Above, below and all around him out to a distance of ten miles floated pieces of hospital, invisible except for the bright blue lights scattered over them as a warning to ship traffic in the area. O'Mara thought it was rather beautiful if you were in a mood to appreciate it. He wasn't, because on most of those floating sub-assemblies there were pressor-beam men on watch, placed there to fend off sections which threatened to collide. These men would see and report it if O'Mara took his baby alien outside even for feeding.

The only answer apparently, he told himself disgustedly as he retraced his way, was nose-plugs.

Inside the lock he was greeted by a noise like a tinny foghorn. It blared out in long, discordant blasts with just enough interval in between to make him dread the arrival of the next one. Investigation revealed bare patches of hide showing through the last coat of food, so presumably his little darling was hungry again. O'Mara went for the sprayer.

When he had about three square yards covered, there was an interruption. Dr. Pelling arrived.

The project doctor took off his helmet and gauntlets only, flexed the stiffness out of his fingers and growled, 'I believe you hurt your leg. Let's have a look.'

Pelling could not have been more gentle as he explored O'Mara's injured leg, but what he was doing was plainly a duty rather than an act of friendship. His voice was reserved as he said, 'Severe bruising and a couple of pulled tendons—you were lucky. Rest. I'll give you some stuff to rub on it. Have you been redecorating?'

'What . . . ?' began O'Mara, then saw where the doctor was looking. 'That's food compound. The little so-and-so kept moving while I was spraying it. But speaking of the youngster, can you tell me——'

'No, I can't,' said Pelling. 'My brain is overloaded enough with the ills and remedies of my own species without my trying to stuff it with FROB physiology tapes. Besides, they're tough—nothing *can* happen to them!' He sniffed loudly and made a face. 'Why don't you keep it outside?'

'Certain people are too soft-hearted,' O'Mara replied

bitterly. 'They are horrified by such apparent cruelties as lifting kittens by the scruff of the neck. . . .'

'Humph,' said the doctor, looking almost sympathetic. 'Well, that's your problem. See you in a couple of weeks.'

'Wait!' O'Mara called urgently, hobbling after the doctor with one empty trouser-leg flapping. 'What if something does happen? There must be simple rules about the care and feeding of these things. You can't just leave me to . . . to. . . .'

'I see what you mean,' said Pelling. He looked thoughtful for a moment, then went on, 'There's a book kicking around my place somewhere, a sort of Hudlarian first aid handbook. But it's printed in Universal. . . .'

'I read Universal,' said O'Mara.

Pelling looked surprised. 'Bright boy. All right, I'll send it over.' He nodded curtly and left.

O'Mara closed the bedroom door in the hope that this might cut down the intensity of the food smell, then lowered himself carefully into the living-room couch for what he told himself was a well-deserved rest. He settled his leg so that it ached almost comfortably and began trying to talk himself into an acceptance of the situation. The best he could achieve was a seething, philosophical calm.

But he was so weary that even the effort of feeling angry became too much for him. His eyelids dropped and a warm deadness began creeping up from his hands and feet. O'Mara sighed and prepared to sleep. . . .

The sound which blasted him out of his couch had the strident, authoritative urgency of an alarm siren and a volume which threatened to blow the bedroom door off. O'Mara reached instinctively for his spacesuit, dropped it with a curse as he realized what was happening, then went for the sprayer.

Junior was hungry again . . . !

During the eighteen hours which followed it was brought home to O'Mara how much he did not know about infant Hudlarians. He had spoken many times to its parents via a Translator, and the baby had been mentioned often, but they had not spoken of the important things. Sleep, for instance.

Judging from recent observation and experience, infant FROBs did not sleep. In the short intervals between feeds they blundered around the bedroom, smashing all items of furniture which were not metal and bolted down—and these they bent beyond recognition or usefulness—or they huddled in a corner knotting and unknotting their tentacles. Probably this sight of a baby doing the equivalent of playing with its fingers would have brought coos of delight from an adult Hudlarian, but it made O'Mara cross-eyed.

And every two hours, plus or minus a few minutes, he had to feed the brute. If he was lucky it lay quiet, but more often he had to chase it around with the sprayer. Normally FROBs of this age were too weak to move about—but that was under Hudlar's crushing gravity-pull and pressure. Here in conditions which were to it less than one quarter-G, the infant Hudlarian could move. And it was having fun.

O'Mara wasn't: his body felt like sponge saturated with fatigue. After each feed he dropped on to the couch and let his bone-weary body dive into unconsciousness. He was so utterly and completely spent, he told himself after every spraying, that he could not possibly hear the brute the next time it complained—he would be too deeply out. But always that blaring, discordant foghorn jerked him at least half awake and sent him staggering through the motions which would end that horrible, mind-wrecking din.

After nearly thirty hours of it O'Mara knew he couldn't

take much more. Whether the infant was collected in two days or two months the result as far as he was concerned would be the same; he would be a raving lunatic. Pelling would never have allowed him to be subjected to this sort of punishment, he knew, but the doctor was an ignoramus where the FROB life-form was concerned. And Caxton was the simple, direct type who delighted in this sort of violent practical joke, when he considered that the victim deserved everything he got.

But just suppose the section chief was a more complex character than O'Mara had suspected? Suppose he knew exactly what he was sentencing him to by leaving the infant Hudlarian in his charge? O'Mara cursed.

Caxton wasn't going to get away with it.

O'Mara knew he himself was the strongest man on the whole project. All this fatigue and nervous twitching was simply in his mind, he told himself insistently, and a couple of days with practically no sleep meant nothing to his tremendous physique. And anyway, the present situation with the infant couldn't get any worse, so it must improve. He would beat them yet, he swore. Caxton would not drive him mad, or even to the point of calling for help.

This was a challenge. Up to now he had bemoaned the fact that no job had fully exploited his capabilities. Well, this was a problem which would tax both his physical stamina and deductive processes to the limit. An infant had been placed in his charge and he intended taking care of it whether it was here for two weeks or two months. What was more, he was going to see that the kid was a credit to him when its foster parents arrived. . . .

After the fifty-seventh hour since he had had a good sleep, there came a change in what O'Mara had accepted as the order of things. The FROB after complaining, was fed, and refused to shut up!

O'Mara's first reaction was a feeling of hurt surprise; this was against the *rules*. They cried, you fed them, they stopped crying. This was so unfair that it left him shocked and helpless.

The noise was bedlam. Long, discordant blasts of sound beat over him. Sometimes the pitch and volume varied in an insanely arbitrary manner and at others it had a grinding, staccato quality as if broken glass had got into its vocal gears. There were intervals of quiet, varying between two seconds and half a minute, during which O'Mara cringed, waiting for the next blast. He stuck it out for as long as he could—a matter of ten minutes or so—then he dragged his leaden body off the couch again.

'What the blazes is *wrong* with you?' he roared against the din. The FROB was thoroughly covered by food compound so it couldn't be hungry.

Now that the infant had seen him the volume and urgency of its cries increased. The external, bellows-like flap of muscle on the infant's back—used for sound production only, the FROBs being non-breathers—continued swelling and deflating rapidly. O'Mara jammed the palms of his hands against his ears, an action which did no good at all, and yelled '*Shut up!*'

He knew that the recently orphaned Hudlarian must still be feeling confused and frightened, that the process of feeding it could not possibly fulfil all of its emotional needs—he knew all this and felt a deep pity for the being. But these feelings were in some quiet, sane and civilized portion of his mind and divorced from all the pain and weariness and frightful onslaughts of sound currently torturing his body.

'*Shut up!* SHUT UP!' screamed O'Mara, and started swinging with his fists and feet.

Miraculously, after about ten minutes of being hit, the Hudlarian stopped crying.

O'Mara returned to the couch shaking. For ten minutes he had been in the grip of a murderous, uncontrollable rage. He had punched and kicked savagely until the pain from his hands and injured leg forced him to stop using those members, but he had gone on kicking and screeching invective with the only other weapons left to him, his good leg and tongue. The viciousness of what he had done shocked him.

It was no good telling himself that the Hudlarian was tough and might not have felt the beating. This was a baby and babies had weak spots.

When O'Mara's utterly exhausted body plunged into sleep, his last coherent thought was that he was the dirtiest, lowest louse that had ever been born.

Sixteen hours later he awoke. It was a slow, natural process which brought him barely above the level of unconsciousness. He had a brief feeling of wonder at the fact that the infant was not responsible for waking him before he drifted back to sleep again. The next time he wakened was five hours later to the sound of Waring coming through the airlock.

'Dr. P-Pelling asked me to bring this,' he said, tossing O'Mara a small book. 'And I'm not doing you a favour, understand—it's just that he said it was for the good of the youngster. How is it doing?'

'Sleeping,' said O'Mara.

Waring moistened his lips. 'I'm-I'm supposed to check. C-C-Caxton says so.'

'Ca-Ca-Caxton would,' mimicked O'Mara.

He watched the other silently as Waring's face grew a deeper red. Waring was a thin young man, sensitive, not very strong, and the stuff of which heroes were made. On his arrival O'Mara had been overwhelmed with stories about this tractor-beam operator. There had been an accident during the fitting of a power pile and Waring had been trapped in a section which was inadequately shielded. But he had kept his head and, following instructions radioed to him from an engineer outside, had managed to avert a slow atomic explosion which nevertheless would have taken the lives of everyone in his section. He had done this while all the time fully convinced that the level of radiation in which he worked would, in a few hours time, certainly cause his death.

But the shielding had been more effective than had been thought and Waring did not die. The accident had left its mark on him, however, they told O'Mara. He had blackouts, he stuttered, his nervous system had been subtly affected, they said, and there were other things which O'Mara himself would see and was urged to ignore. Waring had saved their lives and deserved special treatment. They made way for him wherever he went, let him win all fights, arguments and games of skill or chance, and generally kept him wrapped in a swathe of sentimental cotton-wool.

And that was why Waring was a spoiled insufferable, simpering brat.

Watching his white-lipped face and clenched fists, O'Mara smiled. He had never let Waring win at anything if he could possibly help it.

'Go in and have a look,' said O'Mara. 'Do what Ca-Ca-Caxton says.'

They went in, observed the gently twitching infant briefly and came out. Stammering, Waring said that he had to go and headed for the airlock. He didn't often stutter these days, O'Mara knew; probably he was scared the subject of the accident would be brought up.

'Just a minute,' said O'Mara. 'I'm running out of food compound, will you bring——'

'G-get it yourself!'

O'Mara stared at him until Waring looked away, then he said quietly, 'Caxton can't have it both ways. If this infant has to be cared for so thoroughly that I'm not allowed either to feed or keep it in airless conditions, it would be negligence on my part to go away and leave it for a couple of hours to get food. I've been made responsible for this infant's welfare so I insist. . . .'

'B-b-but it won't——'

'It only means an hour or so of your rest period every second or third day,' said O'Mara sharply. 'Cut the bellyaching.'

Waring's teeth came together with a click. He took a deep, shuddering breath; then, with his jaws still clenched furiously together, he exhaled. The sound was like an airlock valve being cracked. He said:

'It . . . will . . . take . . . all of . . . my next two rest periods. The FROB quarters . . . where the food is kept . . . are being fitted to the main assembly the day after tomorrow. The food compound will have to be transferred before then.'

'See how easy it is to speak normally when you try,' said O'Mara, grinning. 'By the way, when you're stacking the food tanks outside the airlock will you try not to make too much noise in case you wake the baby?'

III

After Waring left, O'Mara thought about the dismantling of the Hudlarian's quarters. With gravity grids set to four-Gs and what few other amenities they required, the

FROBs had been living in one of the key sections. If it was about to be fitted to the main assembly, then the completion of the hospital structure itself could only be five or six weeks off. The final stages would be exciting: tractor men at their safe positions—depressions on the joining faces—tossing thousand-ton loads about the sky, bringing them together gently while fitters prepared the slowly closing faces for joining. Many of them would disregard the warning lights until the last possible moment, and take the most hair-raising risks, just to save the time and trouble of having their sections pulled apart and rejoined again for a possible re-fitting.

O'Mara would have liked to be in on the finish, instead of baby-sitting!

Thought of the infant brought back the worry he had been concealing from Waring. It had never slept this long before—it must be twenty hours since it had gone to sleep, or he had kicked it to sleep. FROBs were tough, of course, but wasn't it possible that the infant was not simply asleep but unconscious through concussion . . . ?

O'Mara reached for the book which Pelling had sent and began to read.

It was slow, heavy going but at the end of two hours he knew a little about the handling of Hudlarian babies, and the knowledge brought both relief and despair. Apparently his fit of temper and subsequent kicking had been a good thing—FROB babies need constant petting, and a quick calculation of the amount of force used by an adult of the species administering a gentle pat to its offspring showed that O'Mara's furious attack had been a very weak pat indeed. But the book warned against the dangers of over-feeding, and O'Mara was definitely guilty on this count. Seemingly the proper thing to do was to feed it every five or six hours during its waking period and use physical methods of soothing—patting, that was—if it appeared restless or still hungry. Also it appeared that FROB infants required, at fairly frequent intervals, a bath.

On the home planet this involved something like a major sand-blasting operation, but O'Mara thought that this was probably due to the pressure and stickiness of the atmosphere. Another problem which he would have to solve was how to administer a hard enough consoling pat. He doubted if he could fly into a temper every time the baby needed its equivalent of a nursing.

But at least he would have plenty of time to work out something, because one of the things he had found out about them was that they were wakeful for two days at a stretch, and slept for five.

During the first five-day period of sleep O'Mara was able to devise methods of petting and bathing his charge, and even had a couple of days free to relax and gather his strength for the two days of hard labour when the infant woke up. It would have been a killing routine for a man of ordinary strength, but O'Mara discovered that after the first two weeks of it he seemed to make the necessary physical and mental adjustment. And at the end of four weeks the pain and stiffness had gone out of his leg and he had no worries regarding the baby at all.

Outside, the project neared completion. The vast, three-dimensional jigsaw puzzle was almost finished. A Monitor Corps investigator had arrived and was asking questions —of everybody, apparently, except O'Mara.

He couldn't help wondering if Waring had been questioned yet, and if he had, what he had said. The investigator was a psychologist, unlike the mere Engineer officers already on the project, and very likely no fool.

It was the beginning of the sixth week of O'Mara's enforced guardianship of the infant, while he was reading up on some of the diseases to which baby FROBs were prone, that his airlock telltale indicated a visitor. He got off the couch quickly and faced the opening seal, trying hard to look as if he hadn't a worry in the world.

But it was only Caxton.

'I was expecting the Monitor,' said O'Mara.

Caxton grunted. 'Hasn't seen you yet, eh? Maybe he figures it would be a waste of time, after what we've told him. He'll have handcuffs with him when he comes.'

O'Mara just looked at him.

'My reason for coming,' said Caxton harshly, 'is to find out about the water. Stores Department tells me you've been requisitioning treble the amount of water that you could conceivably use. You starting an aquarium?'

Deliberately O'Mara avoided giving a direct answer. He said, 'It's time for the baby's bath. Would you like to watch?'

He bent down, deftly removed a section of floor plating and reached inside.

'What are you doing?' Caxton burst out. 'Those are the gravity grids, you're not allowed to touch——'

Suddenly the floor took on a thirty degree list. Caxton staggered against a wall, swearing. O'Mara straightened up, opened the inner seal of the airlock, then started up what was now a stiff gradient towards the bedroom. Still insisting loudly that O'Mara was neither allowed nor qualified to alter the artificial gravity settings, Caxton followed.

Inside, O'Mara said, 'This is the spare food sprayer with the nozzle modified to project a high pressure jet of water.' He pointed the instrument and began to demonstrate, playing the jet against a small area of the infant's hide. The subject of the demonstration was engaged in pushing what was left of one of O'Mara's chairs into even more unrecognizable shapes, and ignored them.

'You can see,' O'Mara went on, 'the area of skin where the food compound has hardened. This has to be washed at intervals because it clogs the being's absorption mechanism in those areas, causing the food intake to drop. This makes a young Hudlarian very unhappy and, ah, noisy. . . '

O'Mara trailed off into silence. Caxton wasn't looking at the infant but was watching the water which rebounded from its hide streaming along the now steeply slanted bedroom floor, across the living room and into the open airlock. This was just as well, because O'Mara's sprayer had uncovered a patch of the youngster's hide which had a texture and colour he had never seen before. Probably there was nothing to worry about, but it was better not to have Caxton see it and ask questions.

'What's that up there?' said Caxton, pointing towards the bedroom ceiling.

In order to give the infant the petting it deserved, O'Mara had had to knock together a system of levers, pulleys and counterweights and suspend the whole ungainly mass from the ceiling. He was rather proud of the gadget; it enabled him to administer a good, solid pat—a blow which would instantly have killed a human being—anywhere on that half-ton carcass. But he doubted if Caxton would appreciate the gadget. Probably the section chief would swear that he was torturing the baby and forbid its use.

Over his shoulder O'Mara said casually, 'Just lifting tackle.'

He dried up the wet patches of floor with a cloth which he threw into the now partly waterfilled airlock. His sandals and coveralls were wet so he threw them in also, then he closed the inner seal and opened the outer. While the water was boiling off into the vacuum outside, he readjusted the gravity grids so that the floor was flat and the walls vertical again, then he retrieved his sandals, coveralls and cloth which were now bone-dry.

'You seem to have everything well organized,' said Caxton grudgingly as he fastened his helmet. 'At least you're looking after the youngster better than you did its parents. The Monitor will be along to see you at hour nine tomorrow,' he added, and left.

O'Mara returned quickly to the bedroom for a closer look at the coloured patch. It was a pale bluish-grey and in that area the smooth, almost steel-hard surface of the skin had taken on a sort of crackle finish. O'Mara rubbed the patch gently and the FROB wriggled and gave a blast of sound that was vaguely interrogatory.

'You and me both,' said O'Mara absently. He couldn't remember reading about anything like this, but then he had not read all the book yet. The sooner he did so the better.

The chief method of communicating between beings of different species was by means of a Translator, which electronically sorted and classified all sense-bearing sounds and reproduced them in the native language of its user. Another method, used when large amounts of accurate data of a more subjective nature had to be passed on, was the Educator tape system. This transferred bodily all the sensory impressions, knowledge and personality of one being into the mind of another. Coming a long way third in popularity and accuracy was the written language which was somewhat extravagantly called Universal.

Universal was of use only to beings who possessed brains linked to optical receptors capable of abstracting knowledge from patterns of markings on a flat surface—in short, the printed page. While there were many species with this ability, the response to colour in each species was very rarely matched. What appeared to be a bluish-grey patch to O'Mara might look like anything from yellow-grey to dirty purple to another being, and the trouble was that the other being might have been the author of the book.

One of the appendices gave a rough colour-equivalent chart, but it was a tedious, time-consuming job checking back on it, and his knowledge of Universal was not perfect anyway.

Five hours later he was still no nearer diagnosing the FROB's ailment, and the single blue-grey patch on its hide had grown to twice its original size and been joined by three more. He fed the infant, wondering anxiously whether that was the right thing to do in a case like this, then returned quickly to his studies.

According to the handbook there were literally hundreds of mild, short-lived diseases to which young Hudlarians were subject. This youngster had escaped them solely because it had been fed on tanked food compound and had avoided the air-borne bacteria so prevalent on its home planet. Probably this disease was nothing worse than the Hudlarian equivalent of a dose of measles, O'Mara told himself reassuringly, but it *looked* serious. At the next feeding the number of patches had grown to seven and they were a deeper, angrier blue; also the baby was continually slapping itself with its appendages. Obviously the coloured patches itched badly. Armed with this new datum O'Mara returned to the book.

And suddenly he found it. The symptoms were given as rough, discoloured patches on the tegument with severe itching due to unabsorbed food particles. Treatment was to cleanse the irritated patches after each feed so as to kill the itching and let nature take care of the rest. The disease was a very rare one on Hudlar these days, the symptoms appeared with dramatic suddenness and it ran its course and disappeared equally quickly. Provided ordinary care was taken of the patient, the book stated, the disease was not dangerous.

O'Mara began converting the figures into his own time and size scale. As accurately as he could come to it the coloured patches should grow to about eighteen inches across and he could expect anything up to twelve of them before they began to fade. This would occur, calculating from the time he had noticed the first spot, in approximately six hours.

He hadn't a thing to worry about.

IV

At the conclusion of the next feeding O'Mara carefully sprayed the blue patches clean, but still the young FROB kept slapping furiously at itself and quivering ponderously. Like a kneeling elephant with six angrily waving trunks, he thought. O'Mara had another look at the book, but it still maintained that under ordinary conditions the disease was mild and short-lived, and that the only palliative treatment possible was rest and seeing that the affected areas were kept clean.

Kids, thought O'Mara distractedly, *were a blasted worrisome thing . . . !*

All that quivering and slapping looked wrong, commonsense told him, and should be stopped. Maybe the infant was scratching through sheer force of habit, though the violence of the process made this seem doubtful, and a distraction of some kind would make it stop. Quickly O'Mara chose a fifty-pound weight and used his lifting tackle to swing it to the ceiling. He began raising and dropping it rhythmically over the spot which he had discovered gave the infant the most pleasure—an area two feet back of the hard, transparent membrane which protected its eyes. Fifty pounds dropping from a height of eight feet was a nice gentle pat to a Hudlarian.

Under the patting the FROB grew less violent in its movements. But as soon as O'Mara stopped it began lashing at itself worse than ever, and even running full tilt into walls and what was left of the furniture. During one frenzied charge it nearly escaped into the living room, and the only thing which stopped it was the fact that it was too big to go through the door. Up to that moment O'Mara did not realize how much weight the FROB had put on in five weeks.

Finally sheer fatigue made him give up. He left the FROB threshing and blundering about in the bedroom and threw himself on to the couch outside to try to think.

According to the book it was now time for the blue patches to begin to fade. But they weren't fading—they had reached the maximum number of twelve, and instead of being eighteen or less inches across they were nearly double that size. They were so large that at the next feeding the absorption area of the infant would have shrunk by a half, which meant that it would be further weakened by not getting enough food. And everyone knew that itchy spots should not be scratched if the condition was not to spread and become more serious. . . .

A raucous foghorn note interrupted his thoughts. O'Mara had experience enough to know by the sound that the infant was badly frightened, and by the relative decrease in volume that it was growing weak as well.

He needed help badly, but O'Mara doubted very much if

there was anyone available who could furnish it. Telling Caxton about it would be useless—the section chief would only call in Pelling and Pelling was much less informed on the subject of Hudlarian children than was O'Mara, who had been specializing in the subject for the past five weeks. That course would only waste time and not help the kid at all, and there was a strong possibility that—despite the presence of a Monitor investigator—Caxton would see to it that something pretty violent happened to O'Mara for allowing the infant to take sick, for that was the way the section chief would look at it.

Caxton didn't like O'Mara. Nobody liked O'Mara.

If he had been well liked on the project nobody would have thought of blaming him for the infant's sickness, or immediately and unanimously assuming that he was the one responsible for the death of its parents. But he had made the decision to appear a pretty lousy character, and he had been too damned successful.

Maybe he was really a despicable person and that was why the role had come so easy to him. Perhaps the constant frustration of never having the chance really to use the brain which was buried in his ugly, muscle-bound body had gradually soured him, and the part he thought he was playing was the real O'Mara.

If only he had stayed clear of the Waring business. That was what had them really mad at him.

But this sort of thinking was getting him nowhere. The solution of his own problems lay—in part, at least—in showing that he was responsible, patient, kind and possessed the various other attributes which his fellow men looked on with respect. To do that he must first show that he could be trusted with the care of a baby.

He wondered suddenly if the Monitor could help. Not personally; a Corps psychologist officer could hardly be expected to know about obscure diseases of Hudlar children, but through his organization. As the galaxy's police, maid-of-all-work and supreme authority generally, the Monitor Corps would be able to find at short notice a being who would know the necessary answers. But again, that being would almost certainly be found on Hudlar itself, and the authorities there already knew of the orphaned infant's position and help had probably been on the way for weeks. It would certainly arrive sooner than the Monitor could bring it. Help might arrive in time to save the infant. But again maybe it might not.

The problem was still O'Mara's.

About as serious as a dose of measles.

But measles, in a human baby, could be very serious if the patient was kept in a cold room or in some other environment which, although not deadly in itself, could become lethal to an organism whose resistance was lowered by disease or lack of food. The handbook had prescribed rest, cleansing and nothing else. Or had it? There might be a large and well hidden assumption there. The trouble was that the patient under discussion was residing on its home world at the time of the illness. Under ordinary conditions like that the disease probably was mild and short-lived.

But O'Mara's bedroom was not, for a Hudlarian baby with the disease, anything like normal conditions.

With that thought came the answer, if only he wasn't too late to apply it. Abruptly O'Mara pushed himself out of the couch and hurried to the spacesuit locker. He was climbing into the heavy duty model when the communicator beeped at him.

'O'Mara,' Caxton's voice brayed at him when he had acknowledged, 'the Monitor wants to talk to you. It wasn't supposed to be until tomorrow but——'

'Thank you, Mr. Caxton,' broke in a quiet, firmer voice. There was a pause, then: 'My name is Craythorne, Mr. O'Mara. I had planned to see you tomorrow as you know, but I managed to clear up some other work which left me time for a preliminary chat. . . .'

What a damned awkward time you had to pick, thought O'Mara fulminatingly. He finished putting on the suit but left the gauntlets and helmet off, then began tearing into the panel which covered the air-supply controls.

'. . . To tell you the truth,' the quiet voice of the Monitor went on, 'your case is incidental to my main work here. My job is to arrange accommodation and so on for the various life-forms who will shortly be arriving to staff this hospital, and to do everything possible to avoid friction developing between them when they do come. There are a lot of finicky details to attend to, but at the moment I'm free. And I'm curious about you, O'Mara. I'd like to ask some questions.'

This is one smooth operator, thought one half of O'Mara's mind. The other half noted that the air-supply controls were set to suit the conditions he had in mind. He left the panel hanging loose and began pulling up a floor section to get at the artificial gravity grid underneath. A little absently he said, 'You'll have to excuse me if I work while we talk. Caxton will explain——'

'I've told him about the kid,' Caxton broke in, 'and if you think you're fooling him by pretending to be the harassed mother type . . . !'

'I understand,' said the Monitor. 'I'd also like to say that forcing you to live with a FROB infant when such a course was unnecessary comes under the heading of cruel and unusual punishment, and that about ten years should be knocked off your sentence for what you've taken this past five weeks—that is, of course, if you're found guilty. And now, I always think it's better to see who one is talking to. Can we have vision, please?'

The suddenness with which the artificial gravity grids switched from one to two-Gs caught O'Mara by surprise. His arms folded under him and his chest thumped the floor. A frightened bawl from his patient in the next room must have disguised the noise he made from his listeners because they didn't mention it. He heaved himself to his knees.

He fought to keep from gasping. 'Sorry, my vision transmitter is on the blink.'

The Monitor was silent just long enough to let O'Mara know that he knew he was lying, and that he would disregard the lie for the moment. He said finally, 'Well, at least you can see me,' and O'Mara's vision plate lit up.

It showed a youngish man with close-cropped hair whose eyes seemed twenty years older than the rest of his features. The shoulder-tabs of a Major were visible on the trim, dark-green tunic and the collar-bone bore a caduceus. O'Mara thought that in different circumstances he would have liked this man.

'I've something to do in the next room,' O'Mara lied again. 'Be with you in a minute.'

He began the job of setting the anti-gravity belt on his suit to two-Gs repulsion, which would counteract the floor's present attraction and allow him to increase the pull to four-Gs without too much discomfort to himself. He would then re-set the belt for three-Gs, and that would give him back a normal gravity apparent of one-G.

At least that was what should have happened.

Instead the G-belt or the floor grids or both started producing half-G fluctuations, and the room went mad. It was like being in an express elevator which was constantly being started and stopped. The frequency of the surges built up rapidly until O'Mara was being shaken up and down so hard his teeth rattled. Before he could react to this, a new and more devastating complication occurred. Apart from the variations in gravity strength, the floor grids were no longer acting at right angles to their surface, but yawed erratically from ten to thirty degrees from the vertical. No storm-tossed ship had ever pitched and rolled as viciously as this. O'Mara staggered, grabbed frantically for the couch, missed and was flung heavily against the wall. The next surge sent him skidding against the opposite wall before he was able to switch off the G-belt.

The room settled down to a steady gravity-pull of two-Gs again.

'Will this take long?' asked the Monitor suddenly.

O'Mara had almost forgotten the Major during the past hectic seconds. He did his best to make his voice sound both natural and as if it was coming from the next room as he replied, 'It might. Could you call back later?'

'I'll wait,' said the Monitor.

For the next few minutes O'Mara tried to forget the bruising he had received despite the protection given him by the heavy spacesuit, and to concentrate on thinking his way out of this latest mess. He was beginning to see what must have happened.

When two anti-gravity generators of the same power and frequency were used close together, a pattern of interference was set up which affected the stability of both. The grids in O'Mara's quarters were a temporary job and powered by a generator similar to the one used in his suit, though normally a difference in frequency was built in against the chance of such instability occurring. But O'Mara had been fiddling with the grid settings constantly for the past five weeks—every time the infant had a bath, to be exact—so that he must have unknowingly altered the frequency.

He didn't know what he had done wrong and there wasn't enough time to try fixing it if he had known. Gingerly, he switched on his G-belt again and slowly began increasing power.

V

O'Mara closed his helmet quickly, then strung a cable from his suit mike to the communicator so that he would be able to talk without Caxton or the Monitor realizing that he was sealed inside his suit. If he was to have time to complete the treatment they must not suspect that there was anything out of the ordinary going on here. He made some final adjustments to the air-pressure regulator and gravity grids.

Inside two minutes the atmospheric pressure in the two rooms had multiplied six times and the gravity apparent was four-Gs—the nearest, in fact, that O'Mara could get to 'ordinary conditions' for a Hudlarian. With shoulder muscles straining and cracking with the effort—for his under-powered G-belt took only three-quarters of a gravity off the four-G pull in the room—he withdrew the incredibly awkward and ponderous thing which his arm had become from the grid servicing space and rolled heavily on to his back.

He felt as if his baby was sitting on his chest. He could see a section of ceiling and, at a crazy angle, the vision panel. The face in it was becoming impatient.

'I'm back, Major,' gasped O'Mara. He fought to control his breathing so that the words would not be squeezed out too fast. 'I suppose you want to hear my side of the accident?'

'No,' said the Monitor. 'I've heard the tape Caxton made. What I'm curious about is your background before coming here. There is something which doesn't quite fit . . .'

A thunderous interruption of noise blasted into the conversation. O'Mara recognized the signal for what it was; the FROB was angry and hungry.

With a mighty effort O'Mara rolled on to his side, but he found that his arms and legs were swelling and felt as if they would burst from the pressure of blood piling up in them. Gasping, he eased himself down flat on to his chest. Immediately the blood rushed to the front of his body and his vision began to red out.

O'Mara struggled on to his side again and rolled back, but this time with his elbows propping him up. Even so the strain of holding up part of his three times heavier than normal body made his heart pound.

However, inching along on his elbows, bottom and feet, O'Mara progressed snail-like towards the bedroom. It took him fifteen minutes to reach the food sprayer in the bedroom, and during practically every second of the way the baby kept up its ear-splitting racket. With the increased pressure the noise was tremendously loud and deep.

'I'm trying to talk to you!' the Monitor yelled during a lull. 'Can't you keep that blasted kid shut up!'

'It's hungry,' said O'Mara. 'It'll quiet down when it's fed. . . .'

The food sprayer was mounted on a trolley and O'Mara had fitted a pedal control so as to leave both hands free for aiming. Now that his patient was immobilized by four gravities he was able to nudge the trolley into position with his shoulders and depress the pedal with his elbow. The high-pressure jet tended to bend floorwards owing to the extra gravity but he did finally manage to cover the infant with food. But cleaning the affected areas was another matter. The water jet, handled awkwardly from floor level, had no accuracy at all, and the best he could manage was to wash down the wide, vivid blue patch—formed from three separate patches which had grown together—which covered nearly one-quarter of its total skin area.

The baby stopped crying.

'What I was about to say,' said the Monitor heavily when the silence looked like lasting for a few minutes, 'was that your record on previous jobs does not fit what I find here. Previously you were, as you are now, a restless, discontented type, but you were invariably popular with your colleagues and only a little less so with your superiors—this last being because your superiors were sometimes wrong and you never were. . . .'

'I was every bit as smart as they were,' said O'Mara wearily, 'but I didn't *look* intelligent. I had mucker written all over me!'

It was strange, O'Mara thought, but he felt almost uninterested in his own personal trouble now. He couldn't take his eyes off the angry blue patch on the infant's side. The colour had deepened and the centre of the patch seemed to have swelled. It was as if the super-hard tegument had softened and the FROB's enormous internal pressure had produced a swelling. Increasing the gravity and pressure to the Hudlarian normal should, he hoped, halt that particular development—if it wasn't a symptom of something else entirely.

'. . . Nevertheless,' the Monitor was saying, 'if a similar accident had happened on one of your previous jobs, your story would have been believed. Even if it had been your fault, they would have rallied round to defend you from outsiders like myself. What caused you to change from a friendly, likeable type of personality to *this* . . . ?'

'I was bored,' said O'Mara shortly.

There had been no sound from the infant yet, but he had seen the characteristic movements of the FROB's appendages which foretold an outburst shortly to come. And it came. For the next ten minutes speech was impossible.

O'Mara heaved himself on to his side and rolled back on to his now raw and bleeding elbows. He knew what was wrong; the infant had missed its usual after-feed nursing. O'Mara humped his way slowly across to the two counter-weight ropes of the gadget he had devised for petting the infant. The ends of the ropes hung four feet above the floor.

Lying propped by one elbow he strained to raise the dead weight of his other arm. Sweat poured off his face and body with the intensity of the effort and slowly, trembling and wobbling, he reached up and grabbed hold. Still gripping it tightly he lowered himself gently back, bringing the rope with him.

The gadget operated on a system of counterweights. A heavy weight dropped neatly on to the infant's back, administering a reassuring pat. O'Mara rested for a few minutes, then struggled up to repeat the process with the other rope, the pull on which would also wind up the first weight ready for use again.

After about the eighth pat he found that he couldn't see the end of the rope he was reaching for. His head was being kept too high above the level of the rest of his body and he was constantly on the point of blacking out. The diminished flow of blood to his brain was having other effects, too . . .

'. . . There, there,' O'Mara heard himself saying in a

definitely maudlin voice. 'You're all right now. Pappy will take care of you. There now, shush . . .'

The funny thing about it was that he really did feel a responsibility and a sort of angry concern for the infant. He had saved it once only to let *this* happen! Maybe the three-Gs which jammed him against the floor, making every breath a day's work and the smallest movement an operation which called for all the reserves of strength he possessed, was bringing back the memory of another kind of pressure—the slow, inexorable movement together of two large, inanimate and uncaring masses of metal.

The accident!

As fitter-in-charge of that particular shift O'Mara had just switched on the warning lights when he had seen the two adult Hudlarians chasing after their offspring on one of the faces being joined. He had called them through his translator, urging them to get to safety and leave him to chase the youngster clear—as it was much smaller than its parents, the slowly closing faces would take longer to reach it, and during those extra few minutes O'Mara would have been able to herd it out of danger. But either their translators were switched off or they were reluctant to trust the safety of their child to a diminutive human being. They remained between the faces until it was too late. O'Mara had to watch helplessly as they were trapped and crushed by the joining structures.

The sight of the young one, still unharmed because of its smaller girth, floundering about between the bodies of its parents sent O'Mara into action. He was able to chase it out of danger before the sections became close enough to trap it, and just barely made it himself. For a few heart-stopping seconds O'Mara had thought he would have to leave a leg behind.

This was no place for kids anyway, he told himself.

People shouldn't be allowed to bring kids out here, even tough people like the Hudlarians.

But Major Craythorne was speaking again.

'... Judging by what I hear going on over there,' said the Monitor acidly, 'you're taking very good care of your charge. Keeping the youngster happy and healthy will definitely be a point in your favour ...'

Happy and healthy, thought O'Mara as he reached towards the rope yet again. *Healthy ... !*

'... But there are other considerations,' the quiet voice went on. 'Were you guilty of negligence in not switching on the warning lights until after the accident occurred? And your previous record notwithstanding, here you have been a surly, quarrelsome bully and your behaviour towards Waring especially ... !'

The Monitor broke off, looked faintly disapproving, then went on, 'A few minutes ago you said that you did all these things because you were bored. Explain that.'

'Wait a minute, Major,' Caxton broke in, his face appearing suddenly behind Craythorne's on the screen. 'He's stalling for some reason, I'm sure of it. All those interruptions, this gasping voice he's using, and this shush-a-bye-baby stuff is just an act to show what a great little nursemaid he is. I think I'll go over and bring him back here to answer you face to face——'

'That won't be necessary,' said O'Mara quickly. 'I'll answer any questions you want, right now.'

He had a horrible picture of Caxton's reaction if the other saw the infant in its present state; the sight of it made O'Mara feel queasy and he was used to it now. Caxton wouldn't stop to think, or wait for explanations, or ask himself if it was fair to place an e-t in the care of a human who was completely ignorant of its physiology or weaknesses. He would just react. Violently.

And as for the Monitor . . .

O'Mara thought that he might get out of the accident part, but if the kid died as well he hadn't a hope. The infant had had a mild though uncommon disease which should have responded to treatment days ago, and instead had become progressively worse, so it would die if O'Mara's last desperate try at reproducing its home planet's conditions did not come off. What he needed now was time.

Suddenly the futility of it all hit him. The infant's condition had not improved—it heaved and twitched and generally looked to be the most desperately ill and pitiable creature that had ever been born. O'Mara swore helplessly. What he was trying to do now should have been tried days ago, his baby was as good as dead, and continuing this treatment for another five or six hours would probably kill or cripple him for life. And it would serve him right!

VI

The infant's appendages curled in the way O'Mara knew meant that it was going to cry again, and grimly he began pushing himself on to his elbows for another patting session. That was the very least he could do. And even though he was convinced that going on was useless, the kid had to be given the chance. O'Mara had to have time to finish the treatment without interruptions, and to insure that he would have to answer this Monitor's questions in a full and satisfactory manner. If the kid started crying again he wouldn't be able to do that.

'. . . for your kind co-operation,' the Major was saying drily. 'First off, I want an explanation for your sudden change of personality.'

'I was bored,' said O'Mara. 'The main reason for setting

out to be a lousy character was that there was a job I could do here which could not be done by a nice guy. I've studied a lot and think of myself as a pretty good rule-of-thumb psychologist. . . .'

Suddenly came disaster. O'Mara's supporting elbow slipped as he was reaching for the counterweight rope and he crashed back to the floor from a distance of two-and-a-half feet. At three-Gs this was equivalent to a fall of seven feet. Luckily he was in a heavy duty suit with a padded helmet so he did not lose consciousness. But he did cry out, and instinctively held on to the rope as he fell.

That was his mistake.

One weight dropped, the other swung up too far. It hit the ceiling with a crash and loosened the bracket which supported the light metal girder which carried it. The whole structure began to sag, and slip, then was suddenly yanked floorwards by four-Gs on to the infant below. In his dazed state O'Mara could not guess at the amount of force expended on the infant—whether it was the equivalent of a sharp smack on the bottom, or something very much more serious. The baby was very quiet afterwards, which worried him.

'. . . For the third time,' shouted the Monitor, 'what the blazes is going on in there?'

Caxton joined in.

'There's something fishy going on, and I bet it involves the kid! I'm going over to see——'

'No, wait!' said O'Mara desperately. 'Give me six hours . . .'

'I'll see you,' said Caxton, 'in ten minutes.'

'Caxton,' O'Mara shouted, 'if you come through my airlock you'll kill me! I'll have the inner seal jammed open and if you open the outer one you'll evacuate the place. Then the Major will lose his prisoner.'

There was a sudden silence, then:

'What,' asked the Monitor quietly, 'do you want the six hours for?'

O'Mara tried to shake his head to clear it. What *did* he want the six hours for? Looking around him he began to wonder, because both the food sprayer and its connecting water tank had been wrecked by the fall of tackle from the ceiling. He could neither feed nor wash his patient, so all he could do for six hours was watch and wait for a miracle.

'I'm going over,' said Caxton doggedly.

'You're not,' said the Major, still polite but with a no-nonsense tone. 'I want to get to the bottom of this. You'll wait outside until I've spoken with O'Mara alone. Now O'Mara, *what . . . is . . . happening?*'

Flat on his back again O'Mara fought to gain enough breath to carry on an extended conversation. He had decided that the best thing to do would be to tell the Monitor the exact truth, and then appeal to him to back him up in the only way possible which might save the infant—by leaving him alone for six hours. But O'Mara was feeling very low as he talked, and his vision was so poor that he couldn't tell sometimes whether his eyelids were open or shut. He did see someone hand the Major a note, but Major Craythorne didn't read it until O'Mara had finished speaking.

'You are in a mess,' Craythorne said finally. 'Ordinarily I should be forced to do as you suggest and give you that six hours. After all, you have the book and so you know more than we do. But the situation has changed. I've just had word that two Hudlarians have arrived, one of them a doctor. You had better step down, O'Mara. You tried, but it's time now for some skilled help.'

It was three hours later. Caxton, Waring and O'Mara were facing the Major across the Monitor's desk.

Craythorne said briskly, 'We'll get this business settled quickly. First, the accident. O'Mara, your case depends entirely on Waring's corroboration for your story. I've already heard Waring's evidence, but to satisfy my own curiosity I'd like to know what *you* think he said?'

'He backed up my story,' said O'Mara wearily. 'He had no choice.'

He looked down at his hands, still thinking about the desperately sick infant he had left in his quarters. He told himself again that he wasn't responsible for what had happened, but deep inside he felt that if he had shown more flexibility of mind and had started the pressure treatment sooner, the kid would have been all right now. The result of the accident inquiry didn't seem to matter now, one way or the other, and neither did the Waring business.

'*Why* do you think he had no choice?' prodded the Monitor sharply.

Caxton had his mouth open, looking confused. Waring would not meet O'Mara's eyes and he was beginning to blush.

'To understand that you have to go a bit farther back,' O'Mara said dully. 'Because of that power pile accident all the men of this section were very much in Waring's debt—you've probably heard the details. Waring himself was a mess. Physically he was below par—had to get shots to keep his blood-count up, was just about strong enough to work his control console, and was fairly wallowing in self-pity. Psychologically he was a wreck. Despite all the doctor's assurances that the shots would only be necessary for a few more months, he was convinced that he had pernicious anaemia. He also believed that he had been made sterile, again despite everything the doctor told him.

That sort of thing is pathological and there wasn't anything like that wrong with him. When I saw how things were I started to ridicule him every chance I got. I hounded him unmercifully.'

'I begin to see the light,' said the Major. 'Go on.'

'The men around him were very much in his debt,' O'Mara continued. 'But instead of giving him a good talking to, they smothered him with sympathy. They let him win all fights, card-games or whatever. I did none of these things. Whenever he lisped or stuttered or was awkward about anything, whether it was due to one of his mental and self-inflicted disabilities or a physical one which he honestly couldn't help, I jumped on him hard. Maybe I was too hard sometimes, but remember that I was one man trying to undo the harm that was being done by fifty. He hated my guts, but he always knew exactly where he was with me. On the few occasions when he was able to get the better of me, he knew that he had won despite everything I could do to stop him—unlike his friends who let him beat them and in so doing made his winning meaningless. What he needed was somebody to treat him as an equal and make no allowances. So when this trouble came,' O'Mara ended, 'I was pretty sure he would begin to see what I'd been doing for him and that simple gratitude plus the fact that basically he is a decent type would keep him from withholding the evidence which would clear me. Was I right?'

'You were,' said the Major. He paused to quell Caxton who had jumped to his feet, protesting, then continued, 'Which brings us to the FROB infant.

'Apparently your baby caught one of the mild but rare diseases which can only be treated successfully on the home planet,' Craythorne went on. He smiled suddenly. 'At least, that was what they thought until a few hours ago.

Now our Hudlarian friends state that the proper treatment has already been begun by you and that all they have to do is wait for a couple of days and the infant will be as good as new. But they're very annoyed with you, O'Mara,' the Monitor continued. 'They say that you've rigged special equipment for petting and soothing the kid and that you've done this much more often than is desirable. The baby has been overfed and spoiled shamelessly, they say.'

Suddenly Caxton banged the desk. 'You're not going to let him away with this,' he shouted, red-faced. 'Waring doesn't know what he's saying sometimes . . .'

'Mr. Caxton,' said the Monitor sharply, 'all the evidence available proves that Mr. O'Mara is blameless, both at the time of the accident and while he was looking after the infant later. However, I am not quite finished with him so perhaps you two would be good enough to leave . . .'

Caxton stormed out, followed more slowly by Waring. At the door Waring paused, addressed one printable and three unprintable words to O'Mara, grinned suddenly and left.

'O'Mara,' the Major said. 'While I don't as a rule give unasked-for advice, I would like to remind you that in a few weeks' time the staff and maintenance engineers for this hospital will be arriving and will be composed of practically every known species in the galaxy. My job is to settle them in and keep friction from developing, so that eventually they will work together as a team. No text-book rules have been written to cover this sort of thing yet, but my superiors said that it would require a good rule-of-thumb psychologist with common sense who was not afraid to take calculated risks. I think it goes without saying that two such psychologists would be even better . . .'

O'Mara was listening, but he was thinking of that grin he'd got from Waring. Both the infant and Waring were going to be all right now, and in his present happy state of mind he could refuse nothing to anybody. But apparently the Major had mistaken his abstraction for something else.

'... Dammit I'm offering you a job! This is a hospital, man, and you've cured our first patient ... !'

NUMBER TEN Q STREET

HELEN McCLOY

The craving which drove people to this sinister address might seem normal to us. It was not so in this nightmare world of the future, as Ella found to her cost. Which of us would have been law-abiding?

When Tom began to snore, Ella switched off the TV and moved quietly towards the hall closet. He had drunk six cans of neo-beer, one right after another. That was usually enough to put him out for a good hour, and one hour should be enough.

She pulled open the door of the closet. The hinges didn't squeak. She had oiled them this morning when Tom was out at the bowling alley. Or was it the poolroom? She could never remember which were Tom's bowling days and which were his pool days.

She slid her arms into the sleeves of her coat and buttoned the collar high under her chin. She reached for her handbag and—oh, God!—the car keys fell on the floor with a loud jangle.

Tom stirred, without opening his eyes, and muttered, 'Ella?'

'Yes, dear?'

'Whereya goin'?'

'Nowhere, dear. Just out for a breath of fresh air.'

'Ge'me packa cigs, willya?'

'Yes, dear.'

'An' leave on Chann'l twenny-four.'

Ella switched on the TV. A crash of canned laughter

filled the room. Tom began to snore again, but this time she left the TV on. Perhaps it would function as a lullaby, keeping him quiet until she got back.

She closed the door softly behind her and walked towards the automatic elevator. When it was first installed, she had used the fire-stairs, even though she lived on the tenth floor. Others, who shared her phobia, did the same until the management found out. Now all the doors to the fire-stairs were locked.

'Suppose there's a fire?' Ella had asked the man in charge of maintenance.

'I'll come round with the keys.'

'Suppose there isn't time?'

'Can't be helped. Can't have you folks sabotaging General Elevators.'

'Not using one elevator is sabotaging General Elevators?'

'That's for sure. If everybody went back to using stairs, General Elevators would go out of business and where would our economy be then?'

So she had to use the unmanned elevator in which she firmly believed that anything could happen. She could be stuck between floors, alone, sealed inside a mechanism she didn't understand. Or she could be attacked and beaten by some of the bored and idle boys who were always drifting in and out of the building. Not for money. Just for fun. Automatic elevators were a favourite place for such beatings. No one really blamed the boys. What could anyone expect when there were no schools beyond third grade for those who lacked engineering aptitude? The only skill most people needed was ad-literacy and that could be acquired in three years.

Tonight the elevator was empty. The lobby, too. As she stepped into the street, a bitter blast of winter wind snatched her breath away. She bent her head as if she were diving and moved into the harsh current of air. She didn't dare take the car. Someone might notice the licence number. Pedestrians were subject to many rules and regulations these days, but, at least, they didn't have licence numbers—not yet. . . .

The cold wind had swept the street clean of people. Now and then a car glided past, but there was no real traffic. Would there be more when she got to Q Street? She had never been to this particular place before.

She had not risked writing the address down, but it was fixed in her mind: *Number Ten Q Street*. Easy to remember. She had only to think of Queer Street.

But every time she thought of it, she had a searing sense of shame. Why couldn't she be like other people?

But she wasn't. That was all there was to it. She could go for weeks, for months even, without satisfying her abnormal craving and then . . . the Desire became so overpowering that nothing else mattered. Once she had been forced to put a sleeping-pill into Tom's neo-beer after dinner in order to get away. She wasn't really that sort of person. Or . . . was she becoming a different sort of person, now?

She shivered, not from cold. What would Tom do if he ever guessed the truth about her? He was so simple, so normal. He had no morbid desires. He could never be made to understand a person who did. . . .

Her flying feet brought her to a squalid neighbourhood. The moon had risen. Its cold light was pitiless to the diseased buildings. Peeling, eczematic paint. Scabrous, suppurating brick. Cramped, arthritic fire-escapes. Filth everywhere—on grimy windowpanes, in trash cans and gutters, on worn steps before dark doorways. She looked up at a sign: Q Street.

She thought she saw darkness move in one of the doorways. Now she was really afraid. This was like stepping into the elevator alone and hearing a step behind her and then turning to see a tall, strong boy with a bicycle chain in his hand.

But she couldn't go back. She had come so far and she didn't know when she would have the chance again.

Once more the darkness moved. And this time she saw the gleam of a knife.

'Oh, no! Please . . .' Ella could barely speak.

And then, faintly, it came—that sweet, memorable, enticing fragrance.

Her fear melted.

'Oh, please let me go in! I must, I must!'

The boy was young, surely under twenty, but he was looking at her with the ancient contempt of panderers for the vices they live on. 'You goin' in Number Ten? What's the word?'

Her voice quavered over the word a friend had whispered to her weeks ago—a word salvaged out of the faraway past. 'Speakeasy,' Ella whispered.

'Okay.' His thumb jerked towards the last house in the row behind him. Silently he slid back into his doorway. A guard. Of course. They would have to take such a precaution.

Outwardly, Number Ten was just another dingy tenement—street door open, doorbells and letter boxes in a vestibule, inner door locked. She had been told to ring the bell marked 3A. A wheezing mechanism, one of the earliest forms of automation, opened the inner door.

She drew her coat away from the greasy walls as she climbed the stairs. If Tom could see her now . . .

There were no bells on the third floor. She knocked on the door marked 3A—three short knocks and two long. It opened on a chain. A bloodshot eye looked at her through the slit.

'Yeah?'

She stammered a little as she gave the second countersign. 'J-joe sent me.'

The door swung open. She darted inside. In an instant the door had slammed behind her.

The room was large and relatively clean. Waiters moved among small tables covered with red-and-white checked cloths. At the far end was a long counter where people sat on stools. It would be cheaper at the counter, so she found a vacant stool.

The counterman wiped a place in front of her. 'Kind of young to be here, aren't you, lady?'

'I'm of voting age.'

'Yeah?' He was sadly sceptical. 'What'll it be?'

She moistened dry lips with her tongue. 'If you please—if you could let me have . . . ' It was hard to say the words. But now the fragrance came again, stronger, more enervating, but irresistible. She threw shame to the winds.

'I want a slice of real bread!'

The sadness in his face deepened. 'And I suppose you want real butter, too? Butter made from cream that comes from cows. Filthy, smelly, old cows covered with mud and straw and dung and flies.'

'Yes—yes, I want real butter.'

'Are you sure? Don't you ever read ads? Even if you can't read, you must listen to commercials! Wouldn't you rather have Low-price Spread, test-tube fresh, synthesized in General Nourishment's fully automated laboratories? A spread that's not just clean, but sterilized. It can be kept fresh forever because no mould or bacteria can grow in it. Not enough nourishment for a single bacterium. Yet it will fill your stomach and keep you from feeling hunger.'

She lowered her head. She couldn't meet his eyes. 'But I want *real* butter. And *real* jam, made with fruit and sugar and nothing else, not even a preservative.'

'That's going to cost you plenty.'

'How much?'

'One hundred dollars for the bread. Twenty-five for a pat of butter. Thirty for two ounces of jam.'

'I have cash.' She clawed open her purse, counted out $155 in small bills, and tossed them on the counter. 'I've been saving for months.'

He scooped up the money, then paused as he noticed her wedding ring. 'I don't often try to help the girls who come here, but you're married and—you're so young. You do know what you ought to do, don't you? Pick up that money and walk right out of here as fast as you can before it's too late. Go straight home to your husband and heat up one of those delicious frozen Tasteegood Teevee Dinners manufactured by General Nourishment. Nylon meat; chlorinated, aerated cotton bread; dehydrated, homogenized potatoes; synthetic, chlorophyll vegetables. Will you do it?'

'No.' Ella's voice was firm.

The counterman sighed. 'Do you know what's in this bread you're asking for? Flour. Real flour. And that's made by taking two dirty old stones and grinding up the fruit of a weed called "wheat" that grows in soil—rightly named —soil, mud, earth—the earth that both human beings and animals walk on. Have you ever tasted the stuff? Or is this your first——'

He faltered as his gaze went beyond Ella. She turned. Another man was standing behind her—a short, fat man with a smooth face and slitted eyes.

'Preaching again, Marvin? That's not what I pay you for! Take the little lady's money and give her whatever she wants. If I catch you trying to reform my customers again——'

He patted Ella's shoulder. She shrank from him, but a moment later all that was forgotten. There, right in front of her, was a slice of real bread, still warm from the oven, crusty and munchy between her teeth, tasting of ripe grain and sunshine and rain from heaven. And running with real butter, golden, melting, scented with clover. And the jam was made of real blackcurrants and real sugar, sweet and tart.

She didn't care what the commercials said. Jam synthesized from carefully selected peanut-shells and old shoe-soles did not taste like this. Any more than what the Kremokup people put in their Instantkaff tasted like real cream in real coffee—any more than the orange powder which General Nourishment had christened Tango-Seville tasted like juice from real Seville oranges.

Recklessly Ella ordered another slice of bread.

A man sat down on the stool beside her. 'A steak, please,' he said brazenly. 'A real steak, cut from a steer, and broiled rare.'

'Anything with it, sir?'

'Yes, real potatoes, French fried, and hearts of lettuce with chives and Roquefort dressing.'

'You know what that will cost you? Two thousand dollars.'

'Okay.'

Ella was impressed. This man was no member of the consuming classes. They didn't have that kind of money. She stole a glance at him and knew, instantly, that she had seen him somewhere before.

But where? He couldn't be a friend of Tom's. All Tom's friends, like Tom himself, were simple consumers. Could she have met this man at one of her mother's big parties? Her mother had a great-uncle who owned some stock in

General Transportation. Now and then a few stockholders and scientists turned up at her mother's parties. But if this man had met Ella at her mother's, he might recognize her now. He might tell her mother he had seen her here. Good God, he might even tell Tom——

She ought to leave now, at once, before the man noticed her. But she couldn't, not until she finished eating that second slice of bread and butter.

She risked another glance at the stranger. He looked important. A lean, craggy face. Dark eyes sunk deeply under black brows. Even his clothes . . . She had never seen real wool, but the suit he was wearing didn't look like any synthetic she knew. He even wore a ring on the little finger of one hand, a massive ring that didn't seem a bit like the 'Jooljunk for He-Men' advertised on TV. Could it be real gold?

Her second piece of bread was served at the same time as his steak. She had never smelled a real steak before. She could feel saliva gather on her tongue.

The man was looking at her. 'Like a bite?'

Never, never talk to strange men in a dive, but . . .

'Could I? Just one little bit?'

'Why not?' Even his smile was tantalizingly familiar. Still she couldn't place him.

She chewed the morsel of steak, closing her eyes in ecstasy.

He was still smiling when she opened her eyes. 'Why didn't you order steak yourself?'

'I don't have two thousand dollars.'

'Then we must share this.'

'That wouldn't be fair to you.'

'Oh, come on! You're a pretty girl. I like you.' His voice was almost a drawl, lazy, reassuring. Ella hesitated. Then he, too, noticed her wedding ring. 'Married?'

'Yes. To a good man. He's never been in a speakeasy in his life.'

'Unemployed?'

'Of course. He has no scientific aptitude and machine-minding jobs are so scarce. He's been on the waiting list for years. But he'll never get one. It doesn't bother him any more—not since we went on Full Automation; he gets paid a full salary for consuming instead of working.'

'How does he spend his time when he isn't consuming?'

'He bowls and plays pool on alternate days. Then he comes home and drinks neo-beer with his Tastegood Teevee dinner, and watches commercials and goes to sleep. He believes everything he sees and hears on commercials.'

'But you don't?'

'No. I think they're bunk.' The steak and bread and butter together had gone to her head. She had forgotten the old adage: Never mix foods.

'Tom consumes everything that is advertised on TV,' she went on. 'Everything from underarm deodorants for football players to the kind of cigs mountain climbers smoke on cliff tops. And as for food! Tom loves everything synthetic that General Nourishment puts out—even the laboratory-tested, artificial eggs with the chemical formula stamped on the edible, plastic shell. He consumes about five thousand calories a day and then, when he gets overweight, he goes on General Nourishment's Reducto Wafers to get himself back into shape for consuming again.'

'How is he on clothes?'

'The best consumer that General Garments ever had! You should see his sports shirts. When they vaporize themselves at the end of three months, he goes right out and buys more. After all, as he says, "That's what I'm paid my salary for—for consuming." '

'I suppose most people are like Tom,' mused the stranger. 'Perfectly willing to consume anything they are told to so long as everybody else is doing the same thing. People like you and me are deviates, sports of nature. Lucky there are so few of us.'

'Why?'

He looked at her surprised, almost shocked. 'Surely you realize that an Expanding Economy Under Full Automation will collapse unless everyone consumes as much of the same things as possible; and these things must be the cheapest things possible—which means they must be synthetics. We should do everything we can to support General Nourishment, General Transportation, General Buildings, General Communications, General Entertainment—all the General Organizations. They've brought plenty to everyone.'

'Plenty of what?'

'Food, cars, houses, TV sets—everything that makes life worth living.'

'But all synthetic,' said Ella. 'All mass-produced and all exactly alike.'

'They have to be. Otherwise there wouldn't be enough to go round and still make a profit under Full Automation. Can you imagine how wasteful and downright wicked it was in the old days? Think of the human labour and time, the capital and raw materials invested in just one pot roast made of real meat and real vegetables. Absolutely uneconomic and inefficient! Today General Nourishment's automated food laboratories can turn out in less than three minutes as many as five hundred thousand synthetic pot roasts, frozen and imperishable, at a cost of less than one-tenth of one cent each.'

'I suppose so, but . . .' Ella frowned. 'Once you've tasted real food, you just can't enjoy synthetics. Why don't we do as the English do? Let addicts buy a little real food once in a while on a doctor's prescription? Then there wouldn't be all this bootlegging and crime.'

'You'll be saying next that you approve of the French system—medically inspected, government-licensed restaurants where real food is sold openly.'

'You think that's bad?'

'I know it is. For one thing, the medical inspectors are underpaid and careless. The indigestion rate in France is appalling, and it increases every year.'

'It's hard to realize that in our great-grandparents' day everybody ate real food and no one thought of it as a crime.'

'Their death rate was higher than ours.'

'But they had more fun while they were alive.'

He grinned. 'You really are subversive, aren't you?'

'I don't see why something that was normal for our great-grandparents has to be abnormal for us.'

'A few hundred thousand years ago primitive man thought sexual promiscuity was normal, but for us it would——'

His voice was drowned by the shriek of an alarm bell.

'*RAID!*' shouted the counterman.

The fat man with the smooth face made his voice carry without shouting. 'Keep your seats, everybody! Be calm—we'll handle this!'

The stranger's face was grim. 'I mustn't be found here.'

Ella's lips tightened. 'Maybe—if we could phone a lawyer——'

'You forget the telephone's on full automation, too. Besides, we'd never have time to dial the complete area-code number.'

The waiters moved like lightning. In a few moments every trace of food had vanished from the room and Ella could hear the grinding noise of an old-fashioned garbage disposal unit in the kitchen. Roulette wheels were placed on some of the tables, dice and cards on others. And just in time. Only a few moments later an axe crashed through the door and a dozen uniformed policemen poured into the room.

One officer turned to a man in a resplendent uniform. 'Must have been a false tip, Chief. Nothing going on here —nothing but a little gambling.'

'Wait.' The Chief of Police held up his hand. 'Do I, or don't I, smell freshly baked bread?'

The fat man moved forward, a smile on his smooth face. 'Not a crumb of bread in the place, Chief. Take my word for it.' As he spoke his hand went out. Ella thought she saw something pass from one man to the other. She was almost sure that the Chief of Police put his hand in his pocket immediately afterward. He was smiling now. 'Guess it was a phoney tip at that. Carry on, folks! If I wasn't on duty, I'd join in the blackjack game.'

'He didn't even look in the kitchen,' whispered Ella.

'He was paid off. Didn't you notice?'

'How awful!' She rose. 'I must go now. Goodbye and— I don't know how to thank you for the steak.'

'It was a pleasure. I'll walk with you to the end of the street. This neighbourhood isn't safe for a young woman alone.'

They went down the greasy stairs together, out into the cold windy night. The shadowy figure of the boy on guard had vanished from the doorway. In the moon's light the street seemed empty—as empty as a lunar landscape.

I hope he's not going to kiss me, thought Ella, just because he met me in a speakeasy.

She halted with a gasp. She was looking across the street to a car parked at the kerb, a black car with white letters on one side—the dread letters A.E.P.

'That car!' Ella's voice shook. 'You know what those letters mean?'

'Advertising Enforcement Police.' His voice had changed. It was no longer the lazy, confidence-inspiring drawl of a man weak enough to indulge himself in bootleg steak. It was now the stern voice of a dedicated moralist. Even his eyes had changed, and he made no effort to hide the deep contempt in them.

'I'm an inspector of the A.E.P.' In his hand she saw the identity card—signature, photograph, government seal. 'I've been following you for some time.'

'So that's why your face was so familiar!'

'Tonight I recorded your conversation with me in the speakeasy. My ring is a microphone.'

'But it has no wire connection!'

'You little fool! As long ago as 1963, they had microphones without wire connections. You're under arrest.'

'But . . . you led me on! You're a member of the secret police——'

'Of course. How else could we ever make an arrest?'

'And the charge?'

'Subversion of the whole economy by failure to perform your duty as a consumer of synthetics willingly, cheerfully, and patriotically. Conviction is certain. With Full Automation and computors on the Bench, a miscarriage of justice has become impossible.'

'And the penalty?'

'A deep-freeze cell for life. We can't have people like you around. This sort of thing might become contagious.'

'May I call my husband? Please!'

'No.'

Ella screamed as he shoved her into the car. She was still screaming as the A.E.P. car drove away in the moonlight.

INFRA DRACONIS

G. GUREVICH

It was a tragic disappointment for the space-travellers, who had spent 14 years on the quest, to be given only a hint of the wonders which the black sun of Infra Draconis might hold.

A black circle floats over the shining sea of stars—a matte saucer with rather misty edges. At one edge the stars are eclipsed, only to be born again at the other edge half an hour later. Familiar constellations, only here they are brighter and their pattern more complicated and delicate. Only one of them—the Flying Fish—has an extra star, the brightest in the sky, the most beautiful—our own sun.

But we are not looking at the sun, or enjoying the delicate pattern of stellar embroidery. Our eyes are fixed on the black circle, although no details are distinguishable in the dense obscurity, either with the naked eye or through the telescope. There are six of us—the entire crew of a spaceship: Charushin, the old man leading the expedition whom we call Grandpa, the Varentsovs—husband and wife, the Yuladshevs—also husband and wife, and myself, Rady Blokhin.

'Well, shall we go back?' asked Grandpa Charushin.

'There's nothing for it,' replied Tolya Varentsov, the chief engineer. 'The rocket is adapted for landing on dry land, and over there it's water, nothing but ocean. We have hand-lathes, home-made at that, and six people to work, all semi-skilled. We would be hanging about for a year contriving something and then we'd drown when making the landing on the water. We can't take the risk.'

'What's more, our fuel's running out,' added Rahim Yuldashev. 'We calculated it with you. A landing means a delay of seven years. We haven't enough air for an extra seven years. And we're not young.'

Ayesha tugged at his sleeve. Rahim had forgotten it was not polite to mention age in front of Grandpa. The old man was already over ninety.

'After all, we won't be going back empty-handed,' remarked Galya Varentsova.

Then Charushin put in a word.

'Then there's only one way out.'

We looked at our chief, puzzled. Ayesha was the first to catch on to his meaning.

'On no account!' she almost shrieked.

'Life is measured in deeds, not words.' I first heard Grandpa use the words seventeen years ago. I remember the first time I visited him. It was late autumn. There was a damp, penetrating wind. The pocket plane carried me over black fields of trampled grass, over bare trees, over the leaden waves of Kuibyshev Sea. Then I spied a bright blue fence on a clay escarpment, a little house of green, glassy brick, and an old man at the gate in a warm jacket of artificial ermine. His thick grey hair appeared to be whitish-grey as though it, too, was synthetic. I recognized him from a photograph. I switched off the pocket plane and landed awkwardly at his feet, straight into a ditch.

'Come and get changed, then you can introduce yourself,' he said, offering me a hand.

That was my introduction to Pavel Alexandrovich Charushin, the famous space captain, one of the crew of the first flight to Venus, commander of the first expedition on the Jupiter sputnik, first on Saturn, first on Neptune, and so on and so forth. Here on the shores of Kuibyshev Sea he was spending the last years of his glorious life.

I was myself connected with the stars, indirectly that is. By education I was a building engineer and worked on the construction of the Chief Inter-Planetary Station on Mount Kilimanjaro in East Africa. When a specialist finds himself in a strange sphere, he is tempted to alter things to suit himself. In addition I was young and self-confident. I was drawing up a plan for the reconstruction of the solar system. At that time, the beginning of the 21st century, it was already obvious that all the planets were unsuitable for habitation and almost all of them of no use to us. So I was suggesting that they should be shuffled around. Venus and Mars were to be driven into the Earth's orbit, Mars to be supplied with an artificial atmosphere and Venus's atmosphere to be purified of carbonic acid gas. I had further proposed that Saturn, Uranus and Neptune should be split up into parts to reduce the force of gravity there, and the various parts driven singly closer to the Sun, by means of atomic explosions. I proposed settling a colony of explorers on Triton and sending them out on an interstellar cruise. According to my calculations, Triton could circumnavigate all the neighbouring stellar systems in about a thousand years. In addition I intended educating children on Jupiter in conditions of heightened gravity, so that their young bones and muscles would grow strong, and then they would all be strong men on the Earth.

To my great surprise all these magnificent projects were invariably turned down. However, I did not give up but stubbornly traipsed from one institution to the next and called on prominent experts. It was natural that I should also turn to Charushin, and so I went to the trouble of flying out to the Kuibyshev Sea. Many people turned to him: young people who dreamed of working in outer space, authors of books, budding scientists, and the people of the local region whom he represented as a deputy. His name, too, constantly appeared in the newspapers. Charushin's signature was appended to the treaty on the Final Disarmament of Nations. At the world Peace Celebrations, Charushin travelled with Chinese, Americans and Germans on the first wagon-load of machine-guns and mortars en route to the open-hearth furnaces for smelting. Without doubt he was one of the most prominent people of his time.

Like many other people, the old man listened to what I had to say with a smile that was benevolently condescending.

'The trouble with you, Rady Grigoryevich,' he said, 'is that you're rushing too far ahead. There's no need for us to settle ourselves all over the solar system, there's enough room here on the Earth where it's comfortable. Your ideas will be needed in three hundred years' time. No doubt you say to yourself: see how perspicacious I am! And all to no purpose. No good comes of occupying yourself with problems not of our time. When it becomes necessary and possible, people will set about reconstructing the planets. And then they'll easily think of all the things you are so occupied with today.'

I did not agree with the old man, but I did not take offence. I felt it was praiseworthy to live in the future in one's own thoughts. So I continued to bore Pavel Alexandrovich with the details of my project. With a smile, Grandpa tore holes in my ideas, but he invariably invited me over on my next free day. He probably liked my youthful cocksureness. And he found the country cottage a solitary place enough. It was different in the summer months when his grandchildren and great-grandchildren took possession of it and the chatter of children's voices filled the garden. But in the winter months there were only letters and telephone calls.

So Pavel Alexandrovich used to listen to me and then I would listen to him dictating his famous memoirs to an electronic shorthand machine. They had just begun to be printed in the *Komsomolskaya Pravda.* You recall, of course, the beginning, the first few lines:

'Our expedition flew to the Moon to begin preparations for. . . .'

I remember saying to the old man at the time:

'You can't start off like that, Pavel Alexandrovich. People start their memoirs with childhood, the day of their birth, or even with a genealogical table. And here you are leaving out a quarter of your life and beginning: "Our expedition flew. . . ." '

It was then I first heard him say:

'Rady, we space experts have our own way of counting. We measure life not in years, but in discoveries, explorations. So I've begun my book with the story of the first occurrence.'

'But the reader is interested in knowing what sort of person you are, what your childhood was like and how you came to explore the planets.'

The old man would not agree.

'You're wrong, young man. People are not interested in me, but in what I do. Every epoch has its favourite profession. One honours sailors, another—writers, airmen, inventors. We space navigators are the favourites of the twenty-first century; we are always remembered, are the first to be sent invitations, are given seats in the front row.'

These words are to be found in the postscript to the first volume of the *Memoirs,* and also the following:

'I was lucky enough to be born at the dawn of the epoch of great discoveries in outer space. The years of my childhood coincided with the infancy of astronavigation. Before I reached manhood the Moon had been mastered by man. As a young man, I dreamed of meeting Venus; as a mature man of years—Jupiter; as an old man—Old Man Neptune. Technical progress made my dreams come true. In less than a century, during my lifetime, speed increased from 8 to 800 kilometres a second. Man's command of space became immeasurably wider. In the middle of the last century he had one planet—a sphere with a radius of 6,300 kilometres; today he has a sphere with a radius of 4,000 million kilometres. We have become stronger and wiser; we have enriched physics, astronomy, geology, biology, by comparing our world with others. Only one dream has not been fulfilled: we have not met other rational beings. We have not grown tired, but at present it is not possible to go farther. We have already reached the limit of the solar system, visited all the planets; ahead of us now is inter-stellar space. A distance of four light hours has been covered, but it is four light years to the nearest star. We have a speed of 800 kilometres a second, we need a hundred times more. Obviously we shall not soon move to other suns, some people say we never shall. The photon rocket and other still bolder projects are so far only projects. The era of discoveries in outer space will suffer an interruption of probably three or four centuries.'

People journeyed into outer space for various reasons. I for example, as an engineer was attracted by the idea of building on an unprecedented planetary scale. And Pavel Charushin had hoped to discover rational beings. Hoping to meet them, he had flown off to discover new worlds. Now we had come to a dead end. There was nothing more to discover, and he did not want to become merely a cosmic pilot. Peace, honour, grandchildren, memoirs, the country home. . . . And he would have ended his life there in a backwater, but for the sudden idea of the possibility of infra-suns that came into my head.

Actually it was he who in some measure suggested the idea to me; he could not reconcile himself to the idea that there was nowhere else to fly to.

How did I reason it out?

To the limits of the solar system it is four light hours, to the nearest star—four light years. A vast ocean of void. But is it certain that it is all void? We only know that there are no bright stars there, otherwise they would be visible. But perhaps there are dark, not bright, bodies there. Perhaps our celestial maps, like most of our terrestrial maps, indicate only the star capitals, and leave out the star-villages.

Take, for example, a sphere with a diameter of 15 light years. There will be four suns in it—our Sun, Alpha-Centaurus, Sirius and Procyon. We can reckon that there are seven suns, because apart from our own, all the others are double stars.

But in the same area of space there are some scores of feeble, dim stars—red-dwarfs, sub-dwarfs, white-dwarfs. These are the stars next to us, but almost all of them are invisible to the naked eye and it was only in the twentieth century that we learned that they are so near.

Thus, there are isolated stars visible to the naked eye, and dozens more visible through the telescope. Could there not be in the same space hundreds of heavenly bodies which the telescope has not noticed? It is, of course, terribly difficult, among the thousand million feeble stars known to us, to pick out a hundred small ones that are near us!

And the temperatures suggest the same conclusion.

In the world of stars the rule is: the larger the star, the hotter it is; the smaller—the cooler. The red-dwarfs are ten times smaller than the Sun, their temperature is 2000°–3000°C. Let us suppose that there exist some bodies ten times smaller than the red-dwarfs. What would their temperature be? Probably 1000°, 600°, 300° or 100°C. The luminosity of the largest would be insignificant, that of the others—nil. With a temperature of less than 600°, bodies send out only invisible infra-red rays. Invisible, dark, black suns! And among them of special interest to us dark, warm planets heated from within, with a surface temperature of 30°C above zero.

Why have they not been found before? Partly because no one looked for them, partly because it was difficult to find them. In general, from the Earth it is impossible to see dark planets. For our earth radiates infra-red light, we live in a sea of infra-red flame. It is hardly possible to live in a flame and yet notice the light of a distant small star!

Timidly, I outlined all this to Pavel Alexandrovich. Out of the corner of my eye I watched the condescending smile fade from the old man's face, the shaggy eyebrows form into a frown. I thought I was reasoning so logically. Could there be some unforeseen objection? I somehow floundered on to the end; then I waited to be routed.

'Now that is interesting, Rady,' he began. 'A planet heated internally, a world inside out. And everything different from what it is on Earth. There will be life there, don't you think? Of course, if there is no light, there cannot be vegetation. But animal life? On the Earth there are animals that live in the darkness, in caves and in the ocean depths. But photo-synthesis, what about that? Can higher forms arise in eternal darkness?'

Then he burst out laughing and clapped me on the shoulder.

'Perhaps you and I will be off into outer space again,

Rady! Are you ready to fly off in search of your infras?'

'What about you, Pavel Alexandrovich?'

He chose to interpret the question in his own way and was offended.

'Why not? I'm not old yet. I'm still not eighty. And our statistics put middle age at ninety-two and a half years.'

Even I was astonished when, six months later, the Central Lunar Observatory announced the discovery of the first infra.

Without Pavel Alexandrovich, all this would have happened much later. But he abandoned all his affairs and diversions. He stripped the greenhouse of its luxuriant flowers and turned it into a workshop. He dropped the memoirs in the middle of a sentence. The electronic shorthand machine did nothing but write letters to scientific and public bodies, to old friends interested in outer space, to comrades, pupils, to the Moon, Mars, Yunon and Io, to long-distance space-ships, all with the convincing, insistent, enthusiastic request to organize a search for black suns.

I had to admire the old man's energy. It was as though he had only been waiting for the signal while sitting at home in his country cottage. Perhaps he was really waiting. And then the great aim arrived—undiscovered worlds: he could fly off into outer space, he could search and make discoveries.

Infras were found in the constellations of Lyra, Sagittarius, the Little Bear, Tucana, Telescopium. . . . And the nearest and most interesting for us was in the constellation of Draco, the Dragon. Its surface temperature was 10°C above zero, the distance to it was 'only' seven light days. 'Only' forty times as far as to Neptune. A space-rocket could cover the distance in fourteen years.

A year later the rocket took off. In it were the Varentsovs, the Yuldashevs, Pavel Alexandrovich and myself. Only I know what it cost the old man to persuade the authorities to include himself and me in the crew. In his case, age was against him, in mine—my youth and inexperience.

The first days of the flight were just like my first excursion to Moscow: enthrallingly interesting, everything perfectly familiar. I had read about it all a hundred times and seen it all a hundred times at the cinema. From a height, the Earth appears as a gigantic globe casting a shadow across the sky. Fourfold gravity, then the miracle of weightlessness. The Moon was a strange, black-and-white world, its face pockmarked. Smooth lunar slopes, deep black shadows, abysses, age-old dust. I had read about it, imagined it; now I saw it and was astounded. Then came the monotonous days of our everyday life, which the writers omit from their descriptions. A tiny sleeping-cabin, three metres by three, hammocks, a table, a cupboard. Beyond its wall, a work-room just a trifle larger containing a telescope, the control panel, instruments, computers. Farther on—the stores, the engine-room and half a kilometre of cans with fuel. If you like, you can take a walk alongside the cans; if you like, you can get into a flying-suit and tumble about in space. Then once more the hammock, the table and cupboard. In fact—a prison cell. Thirty years in close confinement.

Darkness and the stars, the stars and darkness. There are 24 divisions on our watches, otherwise we could get confused. Day or night, there is no difference. Electricity by day in the cabin, at night—more electricity. Stars through the windows by day, stars by night. Silence. Peace. Yet actually we are flying—a state of steady movement in a straight line, almost one and a half million kilometres an hour, 35 million each day. We write up the log: 'May 23, we have traversed a thousand million kilometres. June 1, we have crossed Saturn's orbit.' When that happened we had a ceremonial dinner, sang songs and celebrated. But actually it was a purely conventional milestone because there was nothing but void before reaching the orbit and nothing but void after it. In point of fact the orbit itself was far away on one side of us. And Saturn was no more clearly seen than from the Earth, looking like an ordinary little star.

It was Pavel Alexandrovich who devised all kinds of ceremonies. He was a past master at filling up the hours. Even in the space-rocket there was never enough time for him. After sleeping—space drill for at least an hour. Without this the muscles would become atrophied from the perpetual weightlessness. Then a compulsory airing in space, an examination of the rocket, first externally, then internally. Work at the telescope. Dinner. Then two hours during which he dictated his reminiscences. He dictated to me. We had been unable to take the electronic shorthand machine with us on account of the extra weight. Then reading from microbooks. Grandpa read for one hour exactly and always laid the book aside at the end of it. It was partly recreation, and at the same time a struggle to keep our spirits up. 'We must patiently wait for the morrow,' he said frequently. As for me, I did my best to follow his example. I realized it could not be otherwise. If one indulged in bad temper, then one let oneself go. First it would be spleen, then laziness, then illness. Then one would give up working and forget one's duties. There had been tragedies in outer space: people had allowed themselves to become demoralized and had even been known to turn back before reaching the goal.

Work was the only cure for spleen. But there was not much work to do. Inspection and running repairs do not take up much time. I used to work on my plan for reconstructing the planets, but more for my own satisfaction than anything else. One cannot, in isolation, outdo such a mighty collective as mankind. And with each year of our flight my knowledge became more and more out of date by the standards on Earth. There they were forging ahead but I knew nothing of it.

The only rational occupation was astronomical observations. We compiled a catalogue, measured the distance to the stars. Usually they are measured by a triangle. The base of the triangle is the diameter of the Earth's orbit, the two angles—the direction to the star. The height—the distance to the star—is determined by the side and the two angles. But the narrower and longer the triangle, the greater the possible error, hence this method is only suitable for the nearest stars. It was easier for us—we were now a thousand times farther from the Sun, the base of our triangle was a thousand times larger, the distances could be measured a thousand times more accurately. That applies, roughly speaking, to all the stars that are visible in the telescope. Here then was an occupation to last us for the whole journey: measuring and calculating, measuring and calculating. Then the entries in the log-book: Catalogue No. so and so, spectral class AO, distance—7118 light years. Sometimes as we wrote we would get infuriated. We were spending a whole lifetime on seven light days, and here we were dealing with seven thousand light years. No one would ever fly such a distance, to this sun of class AO.

Boredom, tedious monotony, and yet—continual vigilance. Nothing happens for whole years, yet every second might bring a catastrophe. For space is not entirely empty, there were meteorites and meteorite dust flying about. At the speed at which we were travelling even gas clouds would be dangerous; it could be like plunging into water. We did encounter in outer space some dense zones unknown to science. When we entered them, everything started shifting and one's chest felt constricted. It is not clear why. Meteorite dust corrodes the sheathing, metal gets fatigued, and stray currents appear. So gradually everything wears out. Then we find an air leak, or the steering goes out of order, or the instruments let us down. For years nothing happens, then suddenly. . . . Consequently, someone has to be on duty all the time.

The hours of solitary duty are worst of all. You think of the Earth. You want to walk in the fields and woods. You want to see moondaisies in bloom and larks singing in the blue sky. You long for crowds, the Metro, the sports stadium, meetings. You want to hear loud shouting, not silence, to have your elbows jostled by the crowds round you, lots and lots of people, all strangers to you, and women and girls. You close your eyes—the Red Square, the Kremlin, demonstrations, bright banners . . . you open your eyes—the hammock, the table, the cupboard and through the window the stars and darkness.

And so day after day, month after month. There were six of us in the space rocket. We worked in shifts, keeping watch for two hours, sleeping for four. Artificial sleep, of course, with cooling.

I could stand being wakened all right, but Grandpa not so well. After all, he was an old man, his heart was wearing out. The first time it passed off all right, but after the second, he had fainting fits, pains round the heart, pain in the left shoulder. For four hours our doctor, Ayesha, nursed him. Then she announced that if he undertook a third shift, she would not answer for the consequences.

For fourteen years we had been hurtling towards an invisible point and at last the moment came when we could distinguish the goal—a small dark circle that eclipsed the stars. We had arrived accurately at our goal. The observations of the astronomers on the Earth had been correct. But one thing they had not foreseen: it turned out that Infra Draconis was not a single, but a twin body. There were two black suns there—A and B. A was smaller, B slightly larger. A was nearer to us, B a little farther away. 'A little' in cosmic terms, of course. Actually the distance between them was greater than the distance from the Earth to Saturn.

We were all bursting with impatience and especially Pavel Alexandrovich, although he showed no sign of it. He had already prepared a whole arsenal for interplanetary conversations: light signals, infra-red searchlights. There was also an alphabet with pictures in relief, a collection of geometrical figures.

The great day of our encounter arrived.

In the morning we began to put on the brake. Top and bottom appeared, things forgotten in the air fell on the floor. By midday the dark Infra spot began to grow perceptibly, the stars were extinguished one after the other. Finally, the black saucer hung before us. We came to a halt. We had become Infra's temporary satellite.

Then, imagine our disappointment: our astronomers had made a slight error. They had determined the surface temperature as 10°C above zero, but it turned out to be 6°C below. There were gases in the atmosphere: methane and ammonia as on Jupiter, carbon dioxide as on Venus, a great deal of hydrogen and water vapour—dense clouds. Beneath them was a frozen ocean—ice, snow-fields, ice-hummocks. The ice was tens and hundreds of kilometres thick. We used explosives to measure it.

Was it worth while flying for fourteen years to see an ordinary arctic night!

Grandpa was thoroughly despondent. The last attempt had failed! The dream of his life had not come true.

It was then we came to the decision to visit Infra B as well.

At first glance this seemed natural enough. We were near it, so why not go there. But outer space has its own basis of calculation. There everything depends on fuel. On the Earth, fuel determines the distance traversed, the kilometres, but in outer space it determines only the speed. Fuel is not spent all the time, only when taking off and slowing down. Most frequently enough is taken for two take-offs and for slowing down twice. To visit the second Infra meant delaying our return for three or four years. We did not want to add extra years to the journey, but where thirty years have already been spent, three years do not count much. None of us wished to turn his back on the unexplored world.

For a whole year we slowly crept from one Infra to the other, and now the black spot had enlarged and become a coal-black disc. We slowed down again, became a temporary satellite, and sent the automatic scout into the darkness. We saw for ourselves, for this time the darkness was not complete. There was summer lightning and at times storms in the atmosphere. Cloud contours were visible on the screen. A radio report came from the automatic scout —the air temperature was 24°C above zero. Perhaps astronomers on the Earth had made their mistake because they had combined the rays from the ice-bound Infra with this stormy Infra. It turned out that an average of 10°C above zero was not so far off the truth.

But we must have omitted something in our calculations, for we lost our scout rocket; apparently it sank. At the last moment we saw an expanse of water and high, slanting waves on the television screen. We sent out a second rocket which flew several times round Infra. We saw clouds and rain—falling straight, not slanting as it usually does on the Earth. Even the drops on Infra were heavier. Again we saw waves. It was only sea, sea everywhere, not a single islet. An ocean at the equator and an ocean at the poles. No ice at all. That was understandable. Warmth comes from the interior on Infra, and the climate there is the same everywhere, not colder at the poles.

There were no continents, no islands, not even the summit of a volcano. Ocean, ocean everywhere.

What a vast number of surprises there are in this outer space; it is incorrect to speak of monotonous uniformity and boredom. What was it we had counted on? That there would be dry land and oceans on the Infras, just as there are on the Earth. Rational beings (and in our hearts we had all hoped to meet them) have only developed on dry land, naturally. We intended making a study of the ocean, but only from the coast; to swim out and let down a small bathysphere. And our star-plane could only land on terra firma.

And so now a black circle floats over the shining sea of stars—a matte saucer with rather misty edges. At one edge the stars are eclipsed, only to be born again at the other edge half an hour later. Familiar constellations, only they are brighter and their pattern more complicated. Only one of them has an extra star—our own Sun.

But we are not looking at the Sun, or enjoying the delicate pattern of stellar embroidery. Our eyes were fixed on the black circle, although no details are distinguishable in the dense obscurity, either with the naked eye or with a telescope.

'Well, shall we go back?' asked Grandpa Charushin

For the hundredth and thousandth time the same question is asked. Yes, we shall have to go back, we cannot contrive anything to meet the situation.

'Then there's only one way out,' Grandpa announced.

We looked at our chief, puzzled. Ayesha was the first to catch on to his meaning.

'On no account,' she almost shrieked. 'I know, you want to go down in the bathysphere.'

We were all filled with consternation. It was quite possible to make the descent in the bathysphere, but the question was how to return. The automatic scout cannot fly. The bathysphere would remain there for ever . . . and with a man inside it.

'We simply won't let you!' insisted Ayesha.

But Grandpa merely shrugged his shoulders.

'You know, Ayesha,' he said, 'you're stuffed with medical prejudice. You imagine a man only has the right to die of some serious illness. We space experts have our own calculation of life. We measure it in deeds, not years.'

'It's an unnecessary sacrifice!' declared Rahim. 'We must work consistently, return to the Earth and report. The next expedition will be specially prepared and will make a study of the bed of the ocean.'

The next! But when? In thirty years' time?

Tolya Varentsov was about to intervene and volunteer to go himself. Galya seized him by the sleeve. Then I insisted that I should be the candidate.

'The decision has been made,' announced Grandpa. 'So don't waste time arguing about nothing. I command you to start preparations for the descent.'

The last preparations were in progress, yet we still could hardly take it all in. The eve of the take-off arrived.

The old captain gave orders for a farewell supper; he drew up the menu himself. We played our favourite record—from the newsfilm *On the Streets of Moscow*. Then we listened to Beethoven's Ninth Symphony. The old man was fond of it because it was a rousing symphony, a call to struggle. We drank champagne. It's quite a problem drinking champagne in a weightless rocket; it has a habit of floating away into the air. Then we sang songs. Our outer space hymn, no one knows who composed it:

Perhaps we need eternity
To discover the whole of infinity
But before the goal is reached
The captain departs from us,
But others will be found, if need be. . . .

Ayesha and Galya wept. I got a bit tipsy and asked: 'But aren't you scared, Pavel Alexandrovich?' And he replied: 'Rady, young man, I'm terrified, but most of all I'm afraid I'm doing this in vain, and I'll see nothing but black water. . . .' I gripped his hand and said: 'Pavel Alexandrovich, it's true there may be nothing at all. Take back your orders, please!'

And now there were only five of us, standing with lips compressed in front of the loudspeaker, which was emitting a sound of rolling thunder, whistling, hooting, howling. The atmosphere of Infra is saturated with electricity, that's the obstacle.

At last Charushin's voice broke through the din of atmospherics. Our Grandpa was with us! The familiar husky bass filled the cabin.

'I've switched off the searchlight,' he was saying. 'It's not absolutely dark. There is sheet and forked lightning all the time. By the light of the flashes, flat clouds like a blanket can be seen. They are like those on Jupiter. Cumulus clouds at the edges. The air is dense and there are whirlwinds at the edges of the air streams.'

There were more atmospherics; isolated words and whole phrases were inaudible. Then audibility improved.

'The air is becoming clearer,' said Grandpa. 'I see the sea. An enamel-black surface. Small waves like ripples. I'm falling slowly, the air is very dense. The gravity is incredible, it's difficult to move. It's the same as on the Infra glaciers. It's even difficult to move my tongue.'

Suddenly there was a joyful exclamation:

'Birds! Luminescent birds! Another, and another. Three at once. They flashed by and were gone. Does the television screen show it? I managed to see a round head, thick body and small, fluttering wings. They look rather like our flying fish. Perhaps they are fish, and not birds. But they were flying high.'

A heavy splash, then a pause.

'Did you hear that noise? It was me, falling into the water. I struck it hard. Still, it doesn't matter. I've switched off the light. I'm getting accustomed to the darkness.'

And then a little later:

'I'm going down slowly, at the rate of two metres a second. I've switched on the searchlight again. Through the window there's fiery blizzard—shining whirlwinds, waves, clouds. What a lot of small creatures there are here! Probably similar to our shrimps. The deeper I go, the thicker they are. It's just the opposite on the Earth, where life is scarcer deep down. But there, the warmth comes from the top, here it's from below.

'And what's this? Long and dark, no head, no tail. A whale, a sperm-whale? It moves quickly, a shining stream in its wake. A row of lights along the sides, portholes as it were. Could it be a submarine? Or something else, not comparable to anything. I'll give it a signal from the searchlight in any case: two-two-four, two-three-six, two-two-four.

'It paid no attention. It has gone off to the right. It's out of sight.

'Here are some more monsters—something between a turtle and an octopus. I'm calling them octopuses by way of comparison, actually they have five legs. Five tentacles, one at the back like a rudder, four at the sides. The ends are thickened, with suckers. One of the front tentacles has a strong luminous organ. Like a headlight. Its straight beam is shining on seaweeds. It has a carapace on its back. It has crab-like eyes on movable stalks. The mouth is trumpet-shaped. I'm describing it in such detail because these creatures are swimming towards me. Now they are looking straight into my headlight. It's an eerie feeling—the look in their eyes is perfectly intelligent, the pupil has a crystalline lens, and the iris gives a phosphorescent, dead-green light, like that of a cat. I once read that the terrestrial octopus has a human look in its eyes, but I've never seen one, so can make no comparison.

'The searchlight is sweeping the ocean bed. There are some knotted roots on it, like corals or sea lilies. I can see thick stems, little cups hang downwards from their branches, some resting on the bottom. Our sea lilies hold their cups upwards, they catch descending food. What are these looking for in the silt? Decaying remains? But they don't all reach to the bottom. Could they be absorbing warmth? But then they are plants. Plants without light? It's impossible. Incidentally, there is infra-red light coming from the ocean bed. Is it possible to use the energy of infra-red rays to construct albumen, decompose carbon dioxide? There's not much energy, it needs to be accumulated. But green leaves on the Earth also accumulate energy. Actually, visible rays do not of themselves decompose carbon dioxide.

'I've had a delay,' continued the old man. 'I'm caught in the weeds on the bottom. I can look around at my leisure. I'm more and more convinced that there are plants below me. Here's a fat, headless fish chewing at the shoots. Another—toothy and long—has seized the fat one and has swum upwards. The flow of food here goes from the bottom to the surface. The luminescent birds in the last instance.'

There was a sound of scraping and dull thuds on metal. What did it signify?

'The bathysphere has shifted,' announced Grandpa. 'Something has seized it and is dragging at it. I can't see what. There's nothing in front of the headlight.

'The sea bed slopes. There's no end to the weeds. But the strange thing is that the plants are in straight rows as in an orchard. Something enormous is slowly moving, cutting down whole bushes at the roots. The voracious monster is swallowing the bushes. I can't see very well, somewhere to the side this living combine is creeping along. There's a heap of rock ahead. We've sailed through it. A black chasm. The bathysphere is going down. The pressure is increasing. Goodbye! Greetings to Moscow!'

A second's pause. Then suddenly a shout, almost a yell.

'A crack!!!'

There was a sound of ever more frequent ringing blows. Evidently water had burst into the chamber.

The old man gulped. Probably he had swallowed some water, too. Then a stream of words came tumbling out in swift succession.

'There are buildings at the bottom of the chasm. A town. Street-lights. A dome, spheres. Swimming turrets.

Strange creatures . . . they're everywhere. . . . Can they possibly be. . . .'

A loud crash. A cry of pain. A gurgling sound.

Then the triumphant, prolonged howling and loud whispering of atmospheric interference.

In profound silence five people watched the black circle though there was nothing to be distinguished with the naked eye or through the telescope.

'We'll come back here in thirty years' time,' said Tolya Varentsov, now chief of the expedition. And Galya softly sang:

Perhaps we need eternity
To discover the whole of infinity
But before the goal is reached
The captain departs from us,
But others will be found, if need be. . . .

Will they be found?

THE ENORMOUS ROOM

H. L. GOLD & ROBERT KREPPS

Only just in time the ill-assorted company, kidnapped from Earth, learned why they were in the Enormous Room, and found the true explanation of the extraordinary behaviour of its huge and alarming occupants.

I

The roller coaster's string of cars, looking shopworn in their flaky blue and orange paint, crept towards the top of the incline, the ratcheted lift chain clanking with weary patience.

In the front seat a young couple held hands and prepared to scream. Two cars back, a heavy, round-shouldered, black-moustached man with a swarthy skin clenched his hands on the rail before him. A thin blond fellow with a briefcase on his lap glanced back and down at the receding platform. Behind him was a Negro youth, sitting relaxed with one lean foot on the seat; he looked as bored as someone who'd taken a thousand coaster rides in a summer and expected to take ten thousand more. In the last car, a tall broad man stared at the sky without any particular expression on his lined face.

The chain carried its load to the peak and relinquished it to the force of gravity. The riders had a glimpse of the sprawling amusement park spread out below them like a collection of gaudy toys on the floor of a playroom; then the coaster was roaring and thundering down into the hollow of the first big dip.

Everyone but the Negro boy and the tall man yelled.

These two looked detached—as though they wouldn't have cared if the train of cars went off the tracks.

The cars didn't go off the tracks. The people did.

The orange-blue cars hit the bottom, slammed round a bend and shot upward again, the wind of their passage whistling boisterously. But by then there was none to hear the wind, to feel the gust of it with watered eyes or open shouting mouths. The cars were empty.

'Is this what happens to *everybody* who takes a ride on the coaster?' asked a bewildered voice with a slight Mexican accent. '*Santos*,' it continued, 'to think I have wait so many years for this!'

'What is it?' said the young woman. Was there an accident? Where are we?'

'I don't know, dear. Maybe we jumped the tracks. But it certainly doesn't look like a hospital.'

John Summersby, the big man who had been in the last car, opened his eyes. The room didn't look like a hospital. It didn't look like anything that he could think of offhand.

It was about living-room size, with flat yellow walls and a grey ceiling. There was a quantity of musty-smelling straw on the floor. Four tree-trunks from which the branches had been lopped were planted solidly in that floor. Near the roof was a round silver rod, running from wall to wall; over in a corner was a large shallow box filled with something that might have been sand. An old car tyre lay in the straw near by, and a green bird-bath sort of thing held water that splashed from a tiny fountain in its centre. Five other people, four men and a woman, were standing or sitting on the floor.

'If it was a hospital, we'd be hurt,' said the thin yellow-haired man with a briefcase under one arm. 'I'm all right. Feel as good as I ever did.'

Several men prodded themselves experimentally, and

one began to take his own pulse. Summersby stretched and blinked his eyes; they felt gummy, as though he'd been asleep a long time, but his mouth wasn't cottony, so he guessed that the blacked-out interval must have been fairly short.

'Where's the door?' asked the woman.

'There isn't any door,' said a Negro boy. 'Hey, there isn't a door at all!'

'There must be a door,' said the heavy man with the Mexican accent.

Several of them ran to the walls. 'Here's something,' said the blond man, pushing with his fingertips. 'Looks like a sliding panel, but it won't budge. We never came in through anything *that* small, anyway.' He looked over at Summersby. 'You didn't, at least. I guess they could have slid me through it.'

'They?' said the woman. 'Who are they?'

'Yes,' said the heavy man, looking at the blond man accusingly, 'who put us here?'

'Don't ask me,' said the blond man. He looked at his watch, held it to his ear, and Summersby saw him actually go pale, as at a terrible shock. 'My God,' he gasped, 'what day is this?'

'Tuesday,' said the Negro.

'That's right. We got on the coaster about eleven Tuesday morning. It's three o'clock Thursday!' His voice was flat and astonished as he held up the watch. 'Two days,' he said, winding it. 'This thing's almost run down.'

'How do you know it's Thursday?' asked Summersby.

'This is a chronograph,' said the blond man.

'Calvin, we've been kidnapped!' the woman said shrilly, clutching at a man—her husband or boy friend.

'No, no, dear. How could they do it on a roller coaster?'

'*Maria y José!*' said the Mexican. 'Then for two days

that idiot relief man has had charge of my chili stand! It'll go to hell!'

'Our things at the hotel,' the woman said, 'all my new clothes and the marriage licence.'

'They'll be all right, dear.'

'And where's my bag?'

The blond man stooped and picked up a leather handbag from the straw. 'This it?'

She took it and rummaged inside before she said: 'Thank you.'

'I don't like all this,' said the Negro boy. 'Where are we? I got to get back to my job. Where's the door?'

'Come on,' said the man with the briefcase shortly; 'let's get out of here and find out what's what.' He was going along the wall, pushing and rapping it. 'How did they cop us, that's what I'd like to know. All I remember is hitting the bottom of that big dip, and then waking up in here.' He stopped, then said sharply, 'I hear something moving. It sounds as big as an elephant.'

Then the wall began to glide noiselessly and smoothly to the left, and he scuttled back, looking over his shoulder.

The entire wall slid sideways and vanished, leaving an open end to the room through which Summersby could see a number of large structures that seemed to be machines, painted various colours. There was no sign of movement. He wondered, in a quiet, detached way, what sort of people might be out there.

'It sounded big,' said the blond man again, and looked up at Summersby.

An unknown thing moved beyond the room with a shuffling sound and then a hand came in through the open end. It was on an arm with a wrist the thickness of Summersby's biceps, an arm two yards long with no indication that it might not be even longer. The hand itself was a foot and a half broad, with a prehensile thumb at either side. Summersby did not notice how many fingers it had. The backs of the fingers and the whole great arm were covered with a thick grey-black thatch of coarse hair, and the naked palm was gunmetal grey. Between one thumb and finger it held a long green rod that was tipped by an ivory-coloured ball.

There was no sign of anyone looking in, only the incredible arm and hand.

The others cried out and drew together. Summersby stood still, watching the hand. It poked the stick forward in short jabs, once just missing his head. Then it made a wide sweep and the stick collided with the fat Mexican. He squealed, and at once the hand shot forward, exposing still more of the thick arm, and prodded him away from the group. He skipped towards a far corner, but the stick had him now and was tapping him relentlessly towards the open end.

'*Amigos!*' he yelled, his voice full of anguish. '*Por favor*, save me!'

'Go along with it peaceably,' advised the Negro youth. 'Don't get it annoyed.' He was shaking and his glasses kept sliding down his sweaty nose so that he had to push them up continually.

'What is it?' the woman was asking, over and over.

The Mexican was driven to the edge of the room. The place beyond seemed to be much larger than their prison. He waved his hands despairingly.

'Now, quick, you have only a *momentito* to save me! Don't *stand* there!'

The stick touched him and he jumped. The wall began to slide into place again.

'Let's rush it,' said the man with the briefcase suddenly.

'Why?' asked Summersby. The wall closed and they were alone, staring at one another.

'There wasn't anything we could do,' the Negro boy said. 'It happened too quick. But if it comes in again we better fight it.' He looked around, plainly expecting to be contradicted. 'We can't get split up like this.'

'Possibly one of us can suggest something,' said the husband. He was a sober-looking man of about twenty-eight or thirty. 'We should make a real attempt at escape.'

'We know where the door is, at least,' said the blond man. He went to the sliding wall and threw his weight obliquely against it. 'Give me a hand here, will you, big fellow?'

'You won't move it that way,' said Summersby. He sat down on the car tyre, which seemed to have been chewed by some large animal. 'It's probably electrically operated.'

'We can try, can't we?'

Summersby did not answer. In one corner, six feet off the floor, was a thing he had not noticed before, a network of silver strands like an enormous spider's web, or a cat's cradle. He stared at it, but after the first moment he did not actually see it. He was thinking of the forest, and wishing dully that he might have died there.

The woman spoke sharply, intruding on his detachment; he hoped someone would sit on her. 'Will you please *do* something, Calvin! We must get out of this place.'

'Where are we, anyway?' asked the Negro boy, who looked about nineteen, a tall, well-built youth with beautiful hands. 'How'd they get us here? And what was that thing that took the Mex?'

'It doesn't matter where we are,' snapped the woman.

'Yes, it does, ma'am,' said the youth. 'We got to know how they brought us here before we can escape.'

'The hell we do,' said the blond man. 'We can't guess our location until we get out. I think you're right about the door,' he told Summersby. 'There isn't any lock to it you could reach from inside. The mechanism for sliding and locking must be in the wall itself. Nothing short of a blow-lamp will get through to it.' He came over to Summersby. 'We'll have to jam it next time it opens.'

'With what?' asked the woman's husband.

'Something small, so it won't be noticed.'

'Your briefcase?' suggested the husband, who had a hard New England twang.

'No, chum,' said the blond man, 'not my briefcase.'

'What happened, anyway?' asked the Negro. 'I remember the coaster hitting the dip and then nothing, no wind or motion, until I woke up here. And it's two days later.'

'Something was done to knock us out,' said the blond man. 'Then we must have been taken off the cars at the end of the ride, and brought here.' He rubbed his chin, which was now covered with stubble. 'That's impossible, on the face of it,' he went on, 'but it must be the truth.' He grinned; it was the first time Summersby had seen any of them smile.

'Are we in South America? Or Africa?' asked the Negro.

'Why?'

'That hand!'

'Yeah,' said the blond man, 'that never grew on anything American. Could it be a freak gorilla?'

'That size and with two thumbs?' asked the Negro boy. 'And what would it be doing roaming around loose?'

'Could it be a robot?' asked the husband. His wife screamed, and Summersby got up and went over to the door, getting as far as possible from them. He wished he were a thousand miles away. Anywhere.

'That hand was alive,' said the Negro. 'I never saw

anything like it in biology. Did you see those two thumbs? I don't know any animal that has two thumbs.'

'Would you come over here, sir?' called the New Englander. Summersby realized he was talking to him. 'We must plan a course of action.' Reluctantly Summersby joined them. 'My name is Calvin Full, sir, and this is Mrs. Full.'

Summersby took his hand; it was dry and had a preciseness about its grip that irritated him. 'John Summersby.'

'I'm a milk inspector. My wife and I were on our honeymoon,' said Full.

'I'm a forest ranger,' said Summersby. Retired, he thought bitterly, pensioned off to die with a rotten heart. They couldn't even let a man die on the job, in the woods.

'My work,' said Calvin Full, 'consists of watching for unsanitary and unsterile practices, making tuberculin tests, and so forth. I'm afraid I'm not much good at this sort of emergency.'

His wife's almost-pretty face, cleared of fright, was swept by pride. 'You're as brave as the next man, Calvin, and as clever. You'll get us home.'

'I hope so, dear. But Mr. Summersby must be a great deal more used to problems of this sort.'

They all gaped at him expectantly. Because of his size, of course; he was the big born leader! The hell with them! He kept his mouth shut.

The blond man with the briefcase said, 'I'm Tom Watkins.'

'Adam Pierce,' said the Negro.

'What do you do, Adam?'

The boy pushed his glasses up on his nose again, frowning. 'University, but summers, I'm the Wild Man from Zululand in the sideshow, and on the coaster when I'm not on duty. It helps out my family some, for me to be making money in the vacation.'

'Are you taking subjects that might help us?' asked Full.

'I major in English. I'm going to teach it when I graduate. Then I take psychology and biology, the usual courses.'

'Hmm,' said Tom Watkins, looking at the end of the room through which the Mexican had been taken. 'Psychology and biology. Could be some use here.'

'What we need is a locksmith,' said Summersby. He felt himself unwillingly drawn into the group, sharing their problems that were not his, and it angered him. He fished out a bent packet of cigarettes, lit one and was about to put the rest away.

'Nothing but a blow-lamp would help. I know a little about locks myself.' Tom Watkins grinned genially. 'I'm out of smokes,' he said, and Summersby gave him the pack. He took one and passed it to Full, who declined. Adam took one.

The coloured boy reached up and pushed at his glasses again. 'Say,' he muttered, 'is this room a little wobbly, or is it my eyes?'

'Wobbly?'

'Wavy. See how those tree trunks are blurred?'

'You need your glasses changed, Adam,' said Watkins.

'No, sir.' Adam took them off and started to polish them on a handkerchief; then his brown eyes opened wide. 'I can see!' he said. The others stared at him. 'My astigmatism's gone! I can see plain as noon without 'em. I've had astigmatism since I was a kid!'

'What happened?' asked the woman, addressing her husband. 'How could that be, Calvin?'

'Don't know, dear.'

'My headache is gone,' she said. 'I never realized it till this boy mentioned his eyes.'

'Mrs. Full has suffered from an almost constant headache for years,' said Calvin, and sniffed twice. 'My post-nasal drip is missing, too. Do you suppose my sinus trouble is cleared up?'

'That's what must have been happening those two days we were out,' said Watkins, knocking ash from his cigarette. 'We were put through a hospital or something. I feel good, even if I'm damned hungry.'

Summersby looked from one to another, detesting them against his will. He had a heart for which there was no help, a heart no two-day period of miraculous cures could touch. Their puny ailments had been relieved, but he was still at the slow, listless task of dying.

'Listen,' said Watkins jubilantly, 'whoever or whatever brought us here, it's a cinch they don't mean to harm us. They wouldn't mend us if they were going to hurt us, would they?'

'In two days,' said Adam, nodding hard. 'Two days!'

There was an air of near-gaiety about them that repelled Summersby. 'What do you do to a duck before you cook it?' he asked. 'Clean it. Think that over.'

Adam Pierce looked at him levelly. 'No, sir. If that duck has sinus trouble or bad eyes, you don't have to fix that up.'

'What about the Mexican?' Summersby asked.

At that very moment the wall slid open again and they all started forward; Summersby looked after them bitterly, feeling the resentment drain out and leave only the old hopelessness, the apathetic disregard of everything but death.

II

Porfirio Villa's wife had told him to stay off the roller coaster, but he had sneered. What could happen? The people always got off again, laughing and wiping their brows. He had the bad burn on his left hand, caused by an accidental smacking of the steam table in a rage at his fool of a helper—that idiot who now had had charge of the stand for two days, *lodo feo!* So, forced to take a holiday, he had gone crawling up that terrible incline, giggling nervously, and then rushing madly down the other side. He should have stayed in his chili stand and dreamed of the ride.

Por Dios! What a terror the rising, what a discomfort the drop, what a fearful thing the awakening in this place . . . this place a man could not believe in, though he stood upon its floor and gazed upon its size, its devices for unknown purposes, its impossible inhabitant!

The thing was twelve feet tall. Was it a machine? He had seen machines in the *revistas* and the cinema, looking much like this one, a clumsy copy of a man moving, speaking, tearing people to pieces. There was also King Kong, who resembled this thing.

If it was not alive, it moved very creditably. The grey-furred legs were long and thin, placed on the sides of the body at the waist; the arms, much thicker than the legs, swung very low, and must be fully eight feet long. It was backing from him slowly, holding out one hand—six fingers and two thumbs, *demonio!*—with the green stick. That stick stung like a bee when it touched you.

The monster was already a good distance away. Porfirio cast his eyes slowly to one side and the other. There was a complication of machinery so great that even a teacher of mechanics would be dismayed.

There! A hole between two pink walls. He glanced once at the thing, standing now with its impossible face turned down to him, and then he ran for the hole.

It was after him with a short cry, but he reached the hole and scuttled through. Four paths faced him. What a time for decisions! He took the left-hand path, went round several turns, came to two more openings. The pink walls were smooth and featureless, well over his head so that he could not tell where he was. He ran like the mouse in the game next to his chili stand, the game in which suckers bet on which escape—the red, green, blue or white—the mouse would choose. Paths opened and Porfirio plunged on, losing his sense of direction, becoming more terrified as he went.

He panted past two doorways and abruptly the green stick shot down before him, held in that monstrous grey hand!

The stick appeared and disappeared, herding him, chivvying him from place to place, all places looking alike, till finally the great room lay again before his eyes. Whimpering, he stepped out of the pink maze and leaned against the wall. He was done. Let it murder him. A man could not run forever.

The brute stood over him. Cautiously it brought its face down to peer. Its eyes were set in deep pits, there was a hole between them, and far below in the watermelon-shaped head, a mouth like a man's with lips the colour of rust on iron.

Panting, he gazed at it, then flung out one arm in a futile blow that fell short by two feet. The thing was angering him. Let it watch out for itself!

A hand, unnoticed, had crept round behind him and now took him by the back of the shirt, belt, and trousers, and lifted him off the floor. He regretted the useless punch. Now he would be dead.

The monster inspected him, prodding aside his bedraggled collar points and digging gently at his belly with the rod, which did not sting him this time. It made a sound from its mouth like the last weak bellow of a dying *toro*—'Mmwaa gnaa!'—then set him down once more with a thump that jolted his teeth, nearly fractured his ankles.

Maria y José, but it moved as fast as a lizard's tongue! Escape was beyond hope.

It backed away from him, stood by a huge box and gestured him with the green stick. It wanted him to come. He walked towards it. The box was enormous, oblong, like a huge shoe-box. Only when he had come to it did he realize it was the room in which he had awakened earlier.

In this hall it was lost. Untouched by the monster, he looked at the hall with seeing eyes for the first time. It had yellow walls and a grey roof, like the box. He clapped a hand to his head. Like a theatre without seats, thirty feet by seventy-five by a hundred! Scattered here and there in staggering confusion were the machines, the gadgets, the unknown things. All the colours he had ever seen were there. It was gaudy as the amusement park, but fresher-looking.

The creature laid a hand on the box, and the wall began to slide open. Porfirio looked up, and it gestured, telling him as plainly as words to go in. He was to enter again.

He braced himself. *He* had emerged, while *they* had cowered behind. Worms that they were, he would show them the bearing of a hero, one who had braved mysterious dangers. He sucked in his belly, threw forward his chest, placed his fists carefully on his hips and strutted into the strawed room, turning his head proudly from side to side. He heard the wall close behind him.

The worms came crowding to him.

'What is it? What happened?'

Porfirio Villa, adventurer, laughed. The relief that washed through him was making him shake, his empty stomach still heaved after the panic, but from somewhere he dredged up a casual laugh. 'Very little happened,' he said. 'Truly very little of interest.'

III

Mrs. Full sat on the straw. She pulled her skirt lower over her folded legs, and then she deliberately put one hand flat on the floor so that she would not appear to be nervous. She wanted Calvin to be as proud of her in this terrible crisis as she was of him. Calvin was calm, at any rate.

'We've got to slam something into that opening next time the wall slides back,' said Watkins. She nodded at him approvingly. There was a man who might be of some help.

'What do you think these creatures are, Mr. Watkins?' she asked quietly, though she felt like screeching the question.

'I haven't the least idea, ma'am.'

'Freak gorillas,' said Calvin.

'No, sir,' said Adam. 'I've been thinking. Wasn't the Java Ape Man about nine feet tall?'

'Five and a half's more like it,' said Watkins. 'At least that's how I remember it.'

'Well, *some* fossil man was nine feet tall,' said Adam dogmatically. 'There's plenty of places in the world where a race of people or animals could have developed without Homo sapiens being any the wiser. Now suppose they got hold of us?'

'How?' asked Calvin.

'Through people working for 'em. We might all have been doped and put on a plane and we might be on an island somewhere now, or in the middle of a jungle, with these whatcha-may-call-'ems.'

'How were we doped?' persisted Calvin.

'Gosh, I don't know that!'

'And what the devil do they want with us?' asked Watkins.

Mrs. Full did not hear what Adam said. She was wondering, with a cold horror, if the creatures were near enough human to desire white girls—as mates! 'Calvin, we've got to get home!' she cried.

'We will, dear.' He patted her shoulder. 'Don't you worry.'

'Someone has to worry.'

'We all are, ma'am,' said the pleasant Watkins. 'Except you, I guess, Summersby,' he added accusingly.

Summersby stared at him, seemed about to speak, then looked away. Mrs. Full was afraid of this great man. He might be a lunatic, with that lined, tormented face.

'We might be in the East Indies somewhere, some place near Siam,' said Adam vaguely. 'Question is, if we're there, or any place else for that matter, *why* are we?'

A number of reasons shot through Mrs. Full's mind. They might be potential mates for these incredible animals, or slaves, or food, or. . . . She was surprised at herself for thinking of such things.

She rose and walked aside, ostensibly studying the green fountain. 'Oh, Calvin,' she said.

He came over to her. 'Yes, dear?'

'Calvin, I——' she halted, unable to phrase her question. But he did it for her.

'I've been thinking: if there are—certain basic needs—I mean, if you find it necessary to——'

'I do, Calvin,' she said gratefully.

'Well, there is the, hmm, sand box. I believe it's meant for such, ah, purposes.'

'Calvin! In front of you, in front of these strangers?' She was shocked.

'We'll ask them to turn their backs. After all, such things must be attended to.'

'I'd rather die,' she said, but not at all certainly.

'There are sacrifices to be made in this predicament, and modesty is one,' he clipped out. 'Er, gentlemen.'

Watkins said: 'I know, it just hit me too.'

'What?'

'I've got to go to the john.'

'Yes,' said Calvin stiffly. 'I suggest we retire to the farther end from the sand box, while one by one——'

'We could rig up a screen or something, but there isn't anything to do it with,' said Watkins. He walked away; despite his outspoken manner, he seemed to have the proper instincts.

Adam followed him. Summersby turned his back, Calvin looked at the Mexican. 'Come along.'

'Why?' asked Villa, raising his black brows. 'What is there in a simple relieving of——'

Calvin strode to him, catching him by the nape, lifted him bodily from the floor, and sent him reeling after the others. He half turned, then walked on, muttering, 'Crazy *gringos!*' Calvin went and stood a little behind the others, his back to her.

The minutes following were interminable, horrible, embarrassing. At last she touched his shoulder. 'All right, Calvin,' she whispered.

One by one the others used the sand box. By the time they were through with the unspeakably primitive ritual, she had become admirably calm. There were unsuspected resources in her nature, she thought.

'When do you suppose they feed us?' asked Watkins. He was still holding his tan briefcase under his left arm; he hadn't once laid it down. 'I'm so empty I rattle.'

'Soon,' said Calvin firmly, and his wife felt reassured.

Summersby was standing by the door-wall, his great hands working along the seams of his trouser legs. A violent temper, held in check, thought Mrs. Full. He was the worst of the problems facing them, except for the unknown animals.

Even as she looked at him, the wall opened again. This time no one jumped or shrieked, though she felt her breath hiss back over her tongue. Watkins said: 'Well, Viva, here's your pal again.'

The Mexican glared. Evidently the joke was a stale one to him. 'My name is Villa, not Viva. I hope you get a good taste of that green stick, you little man!'

'Viva Villa,' said Watkins. 'Lead on. You know the way.'

The awful arm came in like a hairy python, groping blindly with the rod.

Summersby, standing near the opening, was the first to be touched. It tapped him lightly, and he walked out of the room, really very bravely, thought Mrs. Full. The rod discovered Adam. The boy backed up, too frightened to put on a show of boldness. The rod slapped him impatiently, and he yelled and darted forward into the huge room. He and Summersby stood together, staring up at something that could not be seen from inside the prison box.

'It's electrical,' said Calvin.

'Yes, dear,' his wife said automatically.

'We may as well go out. I don't want you shocked.'

'All right, Calvin.' She took his arm. Watkins had been caught and herded out. As they stepped forward after him, she glanced sideways at her husband. She would have liked to tell him she loved him, but it would have been too melodramatic. She pressed his arm tightly, affectionately. They walked out into the great hall.

Villa's cursory description had not prepared Calvin Full for the reality of the huge beings.

There were three of them. They stood absolutely motionless, grotesquely humanoid figures with smallish, sunken eyes fixed rigidly on the people some yards away. Then, as Calvin watched, two of them thrust out their hands holding the ball-tipped rods. The gestures were almost too swift to follow.

He stared at the central figure, and it gazed back with its withdrawn, pupil-less, rust-red eyes. Its head was, as Villa had told them, the shape of a watermelon, with the eyes wide-set on either side of a gently agitating orifice that was probably a nostril. The mouth, very human in shape, with full lips the colour of the eyeballs, was quite low in the face. There was a rough growth of grey-black hair on the crown of the big head, and a fuzz of it, less dark, on the face itself. There seemed to be no ears.

Its body, long and thick, was dwarfed by the tremendous arms. Its feet were large, toeless, and flat; its legs joined smoothly to the trunk about halfway up. It wore a clothing of a sort, which surprised Calvin Full, perhaps more than anything else about the being. There was a kind of short sleeveless jacket of amber colour caught at the front by a long silver bar, and a white skirt worn under the legs, reaching from just below the hip joints to the bottom of the torso.

Its companions were almost identical with it, except for clothing of different hues and varying cut.

The thing in the middle now opened its mouth and made a noise that reminded Full of an off-key clarinet.

'Gpwk?' it said, with a rising inflection. 'Hummr gpwk?'

Abruptly it came forward, its long legs carrying it rhythmically, but with a hint of gawkiness; Calvin thought of a galloping giraffe he and his wife had seen in a travelogue. It towered over them, bending at the hip joints.

'Steady, dear,' he said.

'I'm all right,' his wife said shakily.

'Wish I could say the same,' said Adam, the Negro boy. 'What a specimen!'

'Look like anything to you?' asked Watkins.

'Hell, no. Unless it's something from Mars.'

'Maybe we're on Mars,' said Watkins conversationally, but no one responded.

The East Indian suggestion is as sensible as any, thought Calvin. He had not the slightest idea where they were, and he saw no sense in worrying over it until they had more information.

The beast making no further move, his wife at last leaned towards him and said in his ear, 'Calvin, can you tell what—I mean whether it's male or female?'

He studied it carefully. He couldn't even make a guess. He shook his head.

Then it reached forward its stick and thrust it directly at Calvin's face. He backed off, startled and somewhat frightened. At once the rod touched Mrs. Full, as if to separate her from the knot of men.

She cried out in pain, and Calvin leaped forward; he

had a vision of the great paw coming at him with the prod aimed for his face again. It touched his forehead, he felt an intense shock, and then he was powerless to move.

His mind screamed, but he was paralysed in an attitude of charging; he knew his face must be twisted in horror and rage, but he could feel nothing. Only his mind and eyesight seemed wholly clear.

He saw his wife taken off, stumbling unwillingly and looking back at him over her shoulder. Watkins said (Calvin could hear plainly, he found), 'Watch it, he's falling!' Then the paralysis left him and he slumped as though all his bones had been extracted. Someone caught him under the arms, holding him up. He tried to move, but apart from rolling his eyes and lolling his tongue out, he was helpless.

Summersby, behind him, said, 'Are his eyes open?'

'Yeah.' Watkin's face appeared before him. 'Poor guy looks half dead.'

Calvin blinked and made a try at speech, but nothing came out but a flop-tongued drooling sound.

The two creatures remaining near them squatted down and observed them, making fragmentary noises to each other. Watkins started to walk after the third, which had escorted Mrs. Full across the wide room and was on the point of making her get on to a low platform on which there were a number of structures of purple tubing and crimson boxes and small varicoloured contrivances. One of the pair flicked its goad across Watkins' path.

Villa said, 'Come back, you fool, do you think you can take that stick?' He sounded furious, probably because he was afraid of the beasts becoming enraged.

Watkins said, 'Blast it, Viva, we don't know what the thing might do to her.'

'Come on back,' said Summersby. 'Do you want to get this?' He hefted the limp Full.

Calvin writhed and managed to move his hands up and down.

'He's regaining consciousness,' said Watkins, coming back.

'Those rods pack a wallop,' said Adam. 'What sort of power can they have in 'em? Seems to me they're away beyond our science.'

'They're not hitched to batteries,' said Watkins. 'Say, look at all this machinery. If these animals built it, they're a pretty advanced race.'

Mrs. Full was seated now on a large thing like a chrome-and-rubber chair, one of those modern abominations which she and Calvin so cordially detested. The twelve-foot brute was moving its fingers before her, evidently telling her to do something. Calvin could not see her face, but heard her say plaintively, 'But what *is* it?'

Summersby hoisted him up and feeling began to come back to his limbs with a sharp, unpleasant tingling. He said, 'Help her!' quite distinctly.

'Nothing's happening to her,' said Watkins. 'Take it easy.'

Mrs. Full was apparently pulling levers and moving blocks of vividly coloured material back and forth on rods like an abacus, thought her husband.

Suddenly one of the other pair of creatures gave a cry, 'Brrm hmmr!' and pointed to the left. From a muddle of gear rose a small airship, orange, with a nose like a space-ship and streamlined fins, and a square box on its tail. It made no noise, but rose straight towards the ceiling, moving slowly, jerkily.

Calvin's wife had her back to it. He heard her give an exasperated, bewildered cry. 'What on earth . . . what are you *doing*?' She spoke to the creature as if it understood. 'I don't see why you——'

Calvin pushed free of Summersby. He could stand now, shakily. The beast indicated a blue block on a vertical bar. Mrs. Full moved it down, the airship halted and began to sail towards them. 'Do you see the toy ship?' called Calvin. 'You're flying the ship!'

'Oh, my!' she said helplessly. 'What shall I do now?'

'This is crazy,' said Watkins.

'Go on moving things,' Calvin called to his wife. 'Experiment. It wants you to fly it.' He rubbed his tingling arms and hands, hoping she wouldn't crash the ship. Villa and Adam Pierce were calling encouragement to her as the orange thing drifted up and down.

Now the twelve-foot being gestured briefly at a portion of the apparatus. Mrs. Full caught his meaning and moved something, and the ship tilted and flew along the wall without touching it. The three creatures uttered sounds that might be taken for words of pleasure.

'Good girl!' yelled Watkins. 'Keep it up!'

She turned to them and Calvin saw she was smiling. 'There's really nothing to it,' she said. The airship bumped into the wall and fell. The animal above her squawked and pressed down a lever, which evidently sent out a beam or impulse that caught the ship in mid-air and held it suspended. Then it grasped Mrs. Full and carried her, flailing her limbs, over to the corner.

Calvin started forward, apprehensively.

'Hold it, Cal, you don't want another shock.' Watkins took his arm.

The creature kicked aside a mound of small gadgets, sending them helter-skelter, picked up what looked like a big five-legged stool and set it on its feet. It was perhaps ten feet high. Then he deposited Mrs. Full on its smooth round top and turned her bodily so that she faced the wall.

'Help her!' snapped Calvin.

'Just wait a minute, sir,' said Adam. 'He's leaving her alone. I don't think he'll hurt her.'

She twisted her head around, looking frightened. Her legs hung over the edge. The being strode back with its curious gawky-graceful walk, and firmly turned her face to the wall again, using one big rubbery finger. 'Oh!' she said, in a small voice, and remained staring at the wall, like a naughty child on a dunce's stool. The beast came over to the group.

The three creatures talked among themselves, glancing at the men. The airship hung on its invisible beam of energy, ignored. Mrs. Full patted up her hair. She must be terrified, thought Calvin.

The three came to them, their skirts swishing like taffeta. They knelt—it was an odd movement, their high-hipped legs angling to their sides, their bodies slanting forward as their heads dropped towards the humans—and stared at one and then another. The one who was evidently the leader put out his green goad, but slowly, as if showing no harm was intended, and pushed at Calvin's jacket. The ivory ball touched his chest but no shock followed. The creature made noises, perhaps comparing Calvin's clothing with its own.

'Take it off, Cal,' said Watkins.

'Why?'

'He'd like to see it. Be friendly.'

'That's it,' agreed Adam, 'be friendly.'

Calvin removed his jacket and handed it to the brute, who received it dubiously, fingered it, exhibited it to the other two, and dropped it. Calvin bent to pick it up; the goad barred his way. Two large fingers plucked at his trousers. He felt himself flush with outrage.

'No!'

Watkins chuckled. 'I'll bet you will.'

'Don't make it mad,' said Adam.

'I won't take my trousers off.'

Next moment the creature had lifted him high in the air, and was peering closely at the trousers and tugging at them. 'Ouch!' said Calvin. The beast would tear them off; the humiliation of that would be worse than removing them himself. It might rip them to shreds. He loosened his belt and unbuttoned and unzipped just in time; they came off over his shoes and were held up in front of the sunken red eyes. Calvin was set down, carefully enough, and the garment was handed to the other monstrosities. Calvin cast a look at the stool. He was glad his wife was not witnessing his shame.

'Nice shorts,' said Villa.

Full whirled on him, angry enough to bark out an insult, even an oath, but the man was evidently sincere in his praise. 'Thank you,' he said stiffly.

His trousers were thrown to him and he shoved his feet into them and secured them once more. He put on his jacket.

One of the beasts which had not taken an active part in the business now walked to Mrs. Full and picked her up by the back of the waist, as though she had been a cat, and brought her over. For one ghastly moment Calvin thought it was going to divest her of her skirt, but after scrutinizing her a while, it set her down among them.

He took her hand. 'Are you all right, dear?'

She was amazingly calm. 'I am, Calvin, I am. I don't believe they mean us any harm, after all.'

The first great animal pointed at the box, waving his prod.

'We're supposed to go in again, I guess,' said Watkins.

'Let's go, then,' said Adam. 'No sense in getting shocked.'

They trooped in, and the wall closed behind them.

IV

Adam Pierce had an idea. It had begun to grow in his mind while the woman was running the miniature spaceship, but he had thought it over until he was certain it wasn't so silly as to make the others laugh at him. Now he felt sure he'd hit on the truth.

'I have an idea,' he said.

'To get out?' asked the woman.

'No, ma'am. I think I know where we are.'

'Where?' asked everyone, except the big man, Summersby, who was sitting on the tyre, looking away from them.

'In a lab! This is a laboratory, and those big things are some kind of scientists!'

'You could be right,' said Watkins reluctantly. 'My God, what a spot, if you're right!'

'Sure. That's why we were snatched off the coaster, however it happened. They wanted to experiment on us, and study us. They got this lab some place where it's secret, and they make tests——'

'There was a contrivance like a milking machine,' said Full.

'You don't know *what* it's used for,' said Adam darkly. He imagined it might be an especially nasty way of picking over a man's brains or body. 'Look, it all fits. That stool, that's a funny way to punish a person, but all their stuff is a little cock-eyed.'

'By our standards,' added Watkins.

'That's what I meant. Look, you punish a guinea pig when it does something wrong, if you're trying to teach it some trick or other; I mean, suppose you want to determine its intelligence, you give it a problem, and if it does the thing wrong it gets a shock, maybe, or a bat on the nose. That stool was punishment. If you hadn't crashed the rocket,' he said to Mrs. Full, 'it might have given you a reward.'

'Maybe some food,' said Villa.

'Here's another angle,' said Watkins, who obviously knew something about lab work. 'They may be trying to give us neurosis. Scientists induce neurosis in all kinds of critters, by punishment and complex problems and——'

'You mean they might be trying to drive us mad?' said the woman in a scared voice.

'I doubt it,' said Calvin Full.

'They might be,' said Watkins.

'Anyway,' Adam went on, 'that could explain why we were fixed up before they woke us—like—quarantine. They wouldn't want sick animals.'

'Who was fixed up how?' asked the Mexican suspiciously.

'My astigmatism,' said Adam, 'and this gentleman's sinus trouble, and his wife's headache.'

Villa peeled away the bandage on his hand. Now he gave a glad shout. '*Madre de Dios!* Look, the burn has gone!' He showed them his hand. 'Tuesday, a terrible scorched place; today, behold, it is well!'

The woman said, 'You know, this *might* be a laboratory. When I taught kindergarten we had our simple tests for the children that were somewhat like that remote control apparatus.'

Watkins pushed the big man, Summersby, on the shoulder. 'I wish you'd get into this,' he said irritably. 'We need all the brains we have to get out.'

Summersby looked at him. 'You think we'll get out?' he asked.

'Why not?'

'Why?' Summersby sounded tired, and as if his mind was a long way off. 'If these are scientists, they'll keep a fairly close watch on their lab animals.'

'You're a forest ranger, man. Don't you have to meet emergencies all the time?' Watkins was exasperated. Adam thought, I wouldn't talk to the big fellow that way; he looks as wild as a panther.

'I'm sorry,' said Summersby, turning away again. 'I don't think we can escape, or plan to, until we have more information.'

'You needn't inflict your morbidity on us,' said Full. 'Because you're a defeatist is no reason for us to be.'

Summersby stood up. He looked to Adam as tall as one of the monsters. 'If we're guinea pigs, we'll end up as guinea pigs,' he said. 'And what do experimenters do with guinea pigs, finally? They infect or dissect them. Now leave me alone!' He walked to the farthest corner and sat down.

'That's a thought,' said the coloured boy. 'We'd better bust out as quick as we can.'

'Adam, you're nearer to college courses than I am,' said Watkins. 'How many places in the world are there, big enough and unexplored enough to hide a race of giants like these?'

'I guess parts of Africa and South America, maybe the Arctic, some islands. I don't really know.'

'Perhaps we aren't on the earth at all,' said Mrs. Full. 'I read a book once in which a party of people discovered a land beneath the earth's surface,' she went on, blushing a little. 'It was a trashy sort of book—but I thought possibly there might be something in the idea.'

'There might,' said her husband.

'Wherever we are, we've got to get out of this box before we do anything else,' said Adam. The realization had sunk into him of what they might be in for, in this alien lab, under the care of scientists that looked more like apes than anything.

'Look!' shouted Villa. Adam whirled and saw the small panel, that Watkins had discovered earlier, just sliding open. A large platter came through, heaped with what looked like a collection of junk. The huge hand which had pushed it in withdrew, the panel slipping shut after it. Villa was the first to reach the platter. '*Santos*,' he muttered. '*Santos y santas!*'

The platter was two feet square, of sky-blue plastic, and on it lay seven pies, several dozen cupcakes, a double handful of macaroon biscuits, and a quantity of broken glass. Some of the pies were upside down.

'What on earth. . . .' said Mrs. Full.

'Looks like the contents of a bakery window,' said Watkins, leaning over with his briefcase clamped to his thin chest. 'Window and all.'

Villa picked up a custard pie. It had been smeared up by rough handling but it looked good to Adam. He chose one for himself, and Watkins handed Mrs. Full an apple pie. She thanked him. They all took tentative bites.

'What do you make of this?' Watkins asked Summersby, still trying to drag him into their group.

The big man shrugged.

'The glass,' went on the blond fellow, 'that doesn't make sense. Do they think we eat glass?'

'Possibly,' said Calvin Full.

Among the six of them, they consumed all the eatable contents of the tray. Almost immediately Adam felt his eyelids drooping. 'I'm sleepy,' he said, yawning.

'So am I,' said Villa. He lay prone and closed his eyes at once.

Adam sat down, more heavily than he had meant to. He was vaguely disturbed by the sudden tiredness.

'Someone ought to stand guard,' said Mrs. Full.

'I will,' said Summersby unexpectedly.

'I'll do it,' said Watkins. He started to pace up and down. 'I'm a little groggy myself, but I'll take first trick.'

V

When they were let out of their prison box next morning—nine o'clock Friday, by the watch, and they had slept another fifteen hours—there were five of the gigantic beast-creatures waiting for them. Any hopes that Tom Watkins had had of looking round the big hall for a way of escape died. There must be well over a ton of enemies there, with their caverned red eyes peering down at the humans.

The boss of the alien scientists—Watkins recognized it, or him (or was it her?), by the clothing and by certain differences in facial structure—came and bent over them. Watkins was smoking a cigarette he had cadged from Villa, Summersby's having given out the day before. He took a hearty drag and blew out the smoke, which unfortunately lifted right into the creature's eyes. It shook its head, made a squawking sound, and flipped its green prodder into Watkins's belly. He abruptly sat down, with the sensation of having stuck his finger into a lamp socket. Calvin helped him up.

Summersby walked off toward a twenty-foot-high door. None of the beings tried to stop him. The boss motioned Watkins to come, so he shakily followed it across the room.

Before him was a gadget that resembled a five-manual organ console. The banks of keys were broad and there was a kind of chair, or stool, fixed on a horizontal bar in front of them. The giant indicated that he was to get on to it.

'Now what?' he said, when he had been stopped directly in front of the apparatus. 'Expect me to play this? Look, Buster, I'm tone deaf, and I'd just as soon dance a polka as play you a tune.'

The creature pressed down two of the keys—they were of an amethyst colour, longer and more tapered than those of an organ—and looked at Watkins.

'Drop dead,' he said to it.

It hit him on the head with a couple of its big rubbery fingers. He felt as if a cop had sloshed him with a blackjack, and all the hostility went out of him. He leaned forward and pushed down half a dozen keys at random.

There was no sound, at least none that he could hear, though he remembered the whistle he had at home to call his dog, and wondered if the notes of this organ were sub- or supersonic. Certainly there was no reason to suppose this race of creatures was limited to the same range of hearing that humans were.

The creature went down the hall some yards and folded itself into a sitting position before a large white space on the wall. When Watkins did nothing, it gestured angrily with its goad. When he pressed more keys, it jerked its head around and stared at the white space.

Accidentally he discovered that by pressing with his calves on certain pedals below the stool he could manœuvre the seat to either side. The gadget began to intrigue him.

He had never played any musical instrument, but had always had a quiet desire to produce music. He couldn't hear this organ's sounds, but he could go through the motions enthusiastically. He did.

The boss scientist gazed raptly at the wall screen; was it concentrating on what he played? Did his random selection of keys indicate something to it, something about his mental powers or emotions or—what?

Or was it possible that the playing produced images or colours on the blank space? Watkins craned his neck, but could distinguish nothing. Pounding on, he called over his shoulder, 'Come here, somebody!'

No one answered. Pushing keys at random he turned to look for the others. Each of them was doing something under the supervision of a twelve-foot beast, except for Summersby, who was still examining the door. 'Hey!' he yelled. 'Summersby! Come here!'

'What is it?' said Summersby in a moment, standing below his seat.

'Take a squint at that screen the old boy's gaping at. I want to know what the devil I'm doing.'

Summersby walked over and stood beside the scientist.

'What's happening?'

'Nothing.'

'Nothing at all?'

'Well, the screen's mottled grey and white, and the pattern's swirling slowly; but that's all.'

'Is it particularly beautiful?' asked Watkins.

'No. It's hardly distinguishable.'

Sliding right and left on the bar, striking first one and then another of the manuals, Watkins said to Summersby, 'What do you figure these scientists are, anyway?'

'Mammals,' said the big man. 'They have navels. They weren't hatched.'

'Oh.' Watkins hadn't noticed that. 'Where are we, then?'

'I don't know.'

Another scientist wandered over and sat down beside the first. Shortly they seemed to get in each other's way, and there was a lot of shoving and squawking. At last one of them hit the other on the face with an open hand. Then they were rolling on the floor, snatching at one another's hair and pummelling the big bodies and heads with those gargantuan fists. It sounded like a brawl between elephants. Watkins swivelled round to watch. Mrs. Full said to someone—Watkins heard her distinctly in a lull in the rumpus—'If these are scientists, what are the common people like?' He grinned and stopped playing the organ. The other scientists had gathered around the fight and were uttering strange cries.

Adam came over. 'Mr. Watkins,' he said, 'could we have been wrong? Do you think a scientist would act like that?'

'They sure seem to be a quarrelsome race, Adam,' he said. 'Anyway they're not noticing what we do. Suppose you go look for a way out.'

The boy ran down the hall.

The giants arose and straightened their clothing. They had patched up their argument in the midst of fighting over it. The leader walked toward a tall device of pipes and boards and steps, motioning Mrs. Full to follow.

Apparently Watkins had been forgotten. He took his briefcase off his lap, where he had held it all the time he played, and, slipping down from his stool, went to investigate the room.

Before he had done more than glimpse the enormous door, he was picked up kitten-fashion by a scientist, who carried him off, dangling and swearing, to another machine.

For a couple of hours they were put through paces,

all of them; sometimes one man would be working a gadget while all the scientists and humans watched him; at other periods they would each be hard at work doing something different.

The purpose of several of the machines could be guessed at. The sleek modernistic machinery which directed the airship was plain enough. There were certain designs and arrangements that made it fly up and down the room. They were hard to memorize but Mrs. Full and Summersby became adept at them. There was a remote control device that played 'music'—weird haunting all-but-harmonies that sounded worst when the creatures appeared most pleased, and earned the punishment stool or a brutal cuffing for the operator when he did manage to produce something resembling a tune. What the human ear relished, the giant ear flinched from.

There was a sort of vertical maze that verged on the four-dimensional, for when they thought they were finding a way out of the top they would come abruptly to the side, or even the bottom, and have to begin anew. It must be one of the ways in which the scientists induced neurosis in their experimental subjects, thought Watkins. He had a quick mind for puzzles and intricacies of any kind, but this one stumped him.

'You think it's calculated to drive you crazy?' he asked Calvin.

Calvin pondered. At last he said, 'Not if we don't let it.'

'I could develop a first class neurosis,' said Watkins to Mrs. Full, 'if I let myself really go.'

'We must all keep our heads, Mr. Watkins,' she told him. 'Those of us who have not given up'—she glanced at Summersby with a frown—'must keep a tight rein on ourselves.'

'That's right, ma'am,' he said. They all called her 'ma'am'

or 'Mrs. Full.' Nobody knew her first name. He wondered if she'd be insulted if he asked her, and decided that she would.

Capriciously, after a series of punishments, the head scientist went out of the room and came back with food for them. It flung the food—three chickens—on the floor. Villa snatched one of them up with a happy shout, but at once his dark face soured. 'Raw? How can we cook them?' His hand with the fowl dropped limply to his side.

'We can make a fire,' said Calvin.

'A fire of what?' asked Villa, managing to look starved, helpless, and wistful, all at once.

Summersby said, 'There are plates of plastic over there, and plenty of short rods. I don't know what these beasts use them for, but if they're fireproof, we can construct a grill with them.' He went without further talk to a stack of the multicoloured slabs and dowels, which lay beside a neat array of what looked like conduit pipes, electro-magnets, and coiled cable. He picked up an armful. One of the giants put a hand down before him. He pushed it aside and strode back to the group.

'I'll cut some kindling from the trees in our room,' said Calvin. 'Who has a knife?'

Summersby handed him a large pocket knife, and set about making a grill over two of the plastic slabs. It was a workmanlike job when he had finished. He held his lighter under one of the rods, which was apparently impervious to fire. He nodded to himself. Looks more human, thought Watkins, than he has yet.

Villa was plucking one of the chickens, humming to himself. Mrs. Full was working on another, Adam on the third. Watkins sat down, running his fingers along the smooth side of his briefcase.

Calvin set a heap of chips and pieces of wood and bark

under the grill. Summersby lit it. The giants, who were grouped around them at a few yards' distance, mumbled among themselves as the shavings took flame. The plucked and drawn fowls were laid on the grill. Watkins' mouth began to water.

'Now if we only had some coffee,' he said to Adam. 'One lousy pot of greasy-spoon coffee!'

VI

'I have seen you,' said Villa to Adam, who was gnawing on a drumstick. 'You wear the wig and a bone in the nose, and a tigerskin around you.'

'Sure,' said Adam. 'I'm the Wild Man from Zululand. It's one job where my colour's an advantage.'

'A fine job!' said Villa. 'You should have come down to my stand. The best chili in New York.'

'I had a bowl there last week. Without my make-up, I mean.'

'I will give you a bowl free when we go home. With tacos,' added Villa generously.

'It's good stuff,' said the boy.

Calvin Full wiped his fingers and his lips on a handkerchief. He looked about at the hall, through which the giants had now scattered; some of them were tinkering with the machines, others were simply loitering as if bored by scientific research. They had lost their early wariness of the humans, and did not carry the green goads, but kept them tucked into holsters at the back of their swishing skirts.

At one point, one of them removed Watkins and set him to doing something with a pipe-and-block apparatus. The processes they went through with their strange mechanical and electrical gadgets and the end results they achieved, were a mystery to Calvin. And as the afternoon wore on, their conduct as a whole became even more mysterious. It was, by human standards, totally irrational. One would begin a test, analysis, or whatever it might be; he would follow it through its devious windings to its ambiguous result, or to no result, and suddenly leave it to begin something else, or come to watch the humans perform.

The longer Calvin observed their conduct, the more worried he became. Finally, after a good bit of hiding and spying, he found out something; then it seemed time for him to talk to someone.

Watkins had been peering into his briefcase. He zipped it shut quickly as Calvin approached, with a kind of guilty movement. What does he have in there, Calvin wondered.

'Mr. Watkins,' he said 'did you ever see a scientist, or laboratory assistant, skip from one thing to another as these creatures do?'

'I never did.'

'Nor did I. They don't take care of their equipment, either.'

'It might be junked machinery,' suggested Watkins.

'I doubt it.'

At that moment one of the giants made a raucous noise—*Brangg!*

'And how irritable they are, in addition to their capriciousness and sloppiness! I can't imagine a race of emotional misfits producing equipment of such complexity. Their science is beyond ours in many ways, yet look at this place.' He made a broad gesture. 'When we were let out this morning, it was clean and well ordered. I've inspected dairies that were far dirtier. Now it's a hotch-potch of scattered materials, upset stacks of gear, tipped-over instruments. What sort of mind can bear such confusion?'

Watkins smiled. 'The minds that conceived—that vertical maze, for instance—must be orderly after a fashion, even though it isn't the human fashion.'

'This is far from what I wanted to say, though. Have you been noticing the door?'

'There isn't much to notice. It's a sliding panel like our wall.'

'When one of the creatures leaves, he passes his right hand across what is evidently an electric eye beam, as nearly as I can place it about ten or eleven feet off the floor. That opens the door.'

'Good going, Calvin!' said Watkins. 'I hadn't seen 'em do it.'

'Our try for escape should be made as soon as possible,' went on Calvin in a low voice. 'The object of these tests and experiments may be to produce neurosis. There's also Summersby's suggestion about the fate of guinea pigs, so I think we'd better try to get out right away.'

'With five of them here?'

'If we have any luck, we may find an opportunity. Occasionally they get absorbed in something, and that door makes no noise.'

Watkins looked at his briefcase uncertainly. 'Okay,' he said, 'though God knows where we are when we do get out of the lab.'

Calvin congratulated himself on his choice of an ally.

In the next hour they managed to build a crude platform beside the door, of various boxlike things, nondescript plastic blocks and impedimenta. The giants didn't even look at them. They were, indeed, a strange race.

Now the platform was high enough for Calvin to feel he could reach the opening ray.

Summersby wandered over. 'What are you doing?' he asked, seeming to ask the question from politeness, not curiosity.

'We're going to make a break,' said Watkins. 'Want to help?'

'They won't let you,' said the big man.

'We can try, can't we?' asked Watkins hotly. 'You may be the size of a water buffalo, but if Calvin and Adam and I piled on you, you'd go down all right. Why don't you co-operate?'

Summersby stared at him a moment and Calvin thought he was going to say something, something that would be important; but he shrugged and went across the hall and into the prison box.

'What's eating him anyway?' said Watkins.

Calvin believed he knew, but it was not his secret; it was Summersby's. He said nothing.

'Watch it,' said Watkins. 'They're coming.' The two men scurried behind their rampart. The five giants marched, flat-footed, down the hall, their arms swinging. The door opened and all of them went out. It closed behind them.

'How about that!' said Watkins exultantly, a grin on his face.

'I'll get Mrs. Full and the others,' said Calvin. He felt a tingle of rising excitement. 'Get up there and be ready to open it. We'll give them five minutes and then make our break.'

'Right.' Watkins was already clambering up the boxes and blocks.

Calvin almost ran to his wife. She was standing in front of the colour organ. 'Dear,' he said, and halted.

'Yes, what is it, Calvin?'

'I don't know. I was going to say——'

A sluggishness was pervading his body, a terrible lassitude crept through his brain. What was it? What was happening?

'I was going to——'

He caught her as she slumped, but could not hold up her weight, and sank to the floor beside her. His eyes blinked a couple of times. Then knowledge and sensation vanished together.

VII

Tom Watkins awoke slowly. He had a cramp in one arm from sleeping on it, but otherwise he was conscious of a comfortable, healthy feeling, which told him he'd slept well and long. He stretched and brushed a few pieces of straw from his face.

Straw?

He suddenly remembered sitting down on their platform, very sleepy and worried because of the abruptness of it.

He sat up. Summersby had just stood, yawning. 'Did you carry me in here?' he asked the big man.

'I was going to ask that.'

'What happened?' He was wholly awake now. 'Did you drop off out in the lab?'

'Yeah.'

'So did I,' said Adam. He was sitting next to the Mexican whom he pushed gently. 'You okay, Porfirio?'

Villa grunted. The Fulls were looking at each other owlishly.

And then it hit him. Watkins twisted, looked at the floor, and saw nothing but straw and fountain and tree trunks.

His briefcase was gone!

He stared about wildly. Then he took four fast steps and grabbed Summersby by the coat. It was queer, but he didn't even think of anyone else having taken it. Summersby towered over him, but he could be brought down.

'Where'd you put it?' demanded Watkins.

'Put what?'

'My case! Where is it?'

'I never touched your damned case.'

Watkins could smell honesty, and here it was. That startled amazement was genuine. He glared at Adam, Villa, the Fulls. Not that last pair, surely! As rock-ribbed and honest as their New England coasts, and about as imaginative. Not the coloured boy, either, a good kid; and he didn't think it was Villa.

'We must have been carried in here by the scientists,' said Adam rationally. 'Maybe they left it outside.'

That was logical. But he'd had a death-grip on the handle when he fell asleep, just as he always did. He looked at them all again. He went from wall to wall, kicking the straw. Then he scowled at the sand box, the only place a thing that size could be stashed away. He was suddenly on his knees, tossing sand left and right.

Avoiding certain places, he checked the pile. Nothing! Not a scrap of leather nor a piece of green paper!

'If you are through,' said Villa heavily, 'I wish to use the box.'

'Go ahead, Viva.' Watkins walked across the room, groping for a cigarette, then remembering he had none left. 'Were we doped? Something in the chickens?'

'We were awake for a long time after we ate,' said Adam. 'Not even these people could drug six of us in the same minute, after that long; too many differences in metabolism. If that's the word I want.'

'They weren't even in the room when we dropped off,' said Mrs. Full.

That was a tip-off. Watkins momentarily forgot his loss. 'They left, and in a minute, we were asleep. They must have pumped some sort of gas into the lab. Sleep gas.'

'Is there such a thing?' asked Calvin. 'An anaesthetic vapour that would permeate such a large place so quickly?'

'Is there such a thing as a four-dimensional maze?' asked Adam shortly.

Watkins grinned. He wasn't the only one who needed his morning coffee.

Then he thought of his briefcase again. He tried to push the moving wall to one side; no go. He got mad again. 'It's no good to them,' he said. 'What do they want with it?'

'It couldn't have been so important that——' began Full.

'Important?' Watkins was yelling now, and although he disliked raising his voice and making scenes, he did it now, with furious pleasure. 'Calvin, you never saw anything more important in your life than that case, and I don't care how many blue-ribboned cows you've gaped at!'

'What is in it?' asked Villa.

'Money—money!' It didn't matter if his secret came out now. In this insane place, the cautious habits of half a lifetime slid away. 'The best haul I'd made this year. The contents of the safe of Roscoe & Bates, that's what was in it! Better than twenty-two thousand in good, hard cash!'

'The contents of a safe?' asked Calvin. 'You mean you were a messenger, taking it somewhere, and got on that roller coaster with——'

Adam laughed abruptly. 'No, he wasn't a messenger,' he said. 'He wasn't any messenger. He's a safe-cracker. Mr. Watkins, what good do you think it'd do you in here?'

'We'll get back.'

'You're a safe-cracker?' asked Mrs. Full, her pale face lengthening with horror, disgust and fear. 'A criminal?'

'In a manner of speaking, ma'am,' said Tom Watkins, 'I am.'

'I'll be hanged,' said Summersby. 'And you accused me of stealing your loot. I ought to butter you all over the wall.'

'You try it, you overgrown galoot. I didn't do a hitch in the Philippines for nothing.' Watkins smoothed back his hair, which was dangling into his eyes. 'Sure, I'm a safe man. Don't worry, Mrs. Full, that doesn't mean I'm a thug.' She looked scared.

'That's right,' said Adam, still chuckling. 'This boy's the aristocracy of crime. You don't have to worry about your purse. He only plays around with big stuff.'

Tom grinned. 'I'll bet you even know why I was on the coaster.'

'Sure. You were hiding out.'

'That's it. If I kept out of sight till dark I was okay. They were out for me, because my touch is known; but who'd think of checking an amusement park?' He turned as Calvin made a noise in his throat. The Vermonter was a study in outraged sensibilities.

'You—you swine!' he said, like a Victorian hero facing the villain. 'You stole that money——'

'My morals and your morals, Calvin,' said Watkins as genially as he could, 'are probably different, but it doesn't make a whale of a difference now, does it?'

Full turned to his wife and began to mutter to her.

Villa said, 'I don't like crooks. I run a respectable stand and I am an honest man,' and scratching his hand where the healed burn was, he turned away likewise. Summersby was sitting on the tyre, and only Adam looked sympathetic. The boy wasn't crooked, that was plain, but Watkins had the glamour that a bigtime thief has for the young, the fake aura of Robin-Hoodism.

He shook his head. He'd had to spill it. For a while they'd trusted him and now he was a pariah.

The food panel opened and something plumped in. Watkins glanced at his watch. Ten o'clock Saturday. He went over to the food.

It was a big, glossy chocolate-brown vulture with a blue head.

'Well,' said Adam. 'Well, now, I don't know.'

'They pulled a boner this time,' said Watkins. 'Unless it's part of the conditioning.'

Villa picked it up. 'It weighs many pounds. It's warm, just killed. I don't want any of it.' He dropped it on the straw. 'With my spices, perhaps; but not cooked on that grill, without sauce and spice. Aargh!'

Watkins thought, 'Amen to that.' He rubbed the sandy bristles on his chin. No razor or soap here. It dawned on him that he was thirsty, and he went to the fountain. As it always did when he bent over to drink, the curious web of silver strands in the corner caught his eye. There were so many puzzles about this damned lab that he despaired of ever solving all of them.

After fifteen minutes, the wall opened. They went out, Villa carrying the vulture. He flung it at the feet of the chief scientist, who was there with two associates.

'No!' he bellowed up at the creature. 'We do not eat this!' He articulated slowly, clearly, as though to a foreigner with a slim knowledge of English. It picked up the great bird and regarded it closely, then without warning threw it at one of the other giants.

The vulture caught the creature on the side of the head and knocked it off balance. Falling to its knees, it bleated out an angry sound and dived for the boss's legs. They went down together in a gargantuan scrimmage that made the humans dance backward to avoid being smashed by the thick swinging arms.

Tom Watkins walked off, unimpeded, to look for his briefcase. It was nowhere in the lab. He cursed bitterly. Twenty-two grand up the spout.

The head scientist, having chastised the other, left the room. Watkins had a glimpse of another room fully as large. Shortly the creature returned, carrying in one arm a load of wood chips, and in the other a bulgy, leathery thing that turned out to be a partially stunned octopus, still dripping the waters of an unknown ocean.

The humans killed it, rebuilt their grill (larger this time), and cut up the octopus and cooked and ate it. It wasn't so bad.

After a dragging day, they were locked into their box—no one had a chance to jam the door for the giants were watching them closely—and shortly afterward a load of raw vegetables was dumped in.

Watkins paced the floor after he had eaten, waiting for the sleep gas, determined to combat it if he could. When the drowsiness came, he walked faster. It didn't do any good. Powerless, he felt himself sinking to the floor.

Mrs. Full kept close to Calvin all through Sunday. They had been here since Thursday, all these men without women. The Mexican seemed all right, but you never knew.

Another facet of the same problem was the fact that she and Calvin were supposed to be on their honeymoon. She faced it: she was frustrated. She wanted a honeymoon, no matter what sort of prison they were in. So after their first meal on Sunday, she asked Calvin to fix up a private apartment in their prison.

With various materials, plastic blocks and the different sizes of slabs, and some screens of translucent fabric she had dug up in a corner, he made a walled-off compartment just large enough for two.

Then one of the scientists looked in, saw what was doing, and promptly knocked it down.

Adam, who had been helping in the latter stages, squinted at the ceiling of the box. 'You know, Mrs. Full, I think they can see us through that. If it's opaque to us, it still might be transparent to them; like a mirror, I mean, I've seen them at home, mirror on one side, window from the other. And if they want to observe us all the time, then this private cell of yours would make 'em mad.'

'But *it* had no roof,' she objected.

'That's right.' He shook his head. 'Another theory gone poof.'

'I'll build it again,' said Calvin stubbornly, and did so. This time the giants left it alone. He and Adam made a screen for the sand box too, and built a permanent grill for cooking.

VIII

By Tuesday they were all in a state of anxiety and scarcely-contained rage. Surveillance was casual, often non-existent, yet not once had they been able to block the wall of their prison or open the great door of the laboratory. Circumstances, chance, fate, something had stopped them every time.

There were three giants in the lab today. Sometimes there would be one of them, sometimes as many as five; but always there would be the one who had first removed them from the box, who seemed to be the head scientist, giving orders, bullying the others in the queer emotional way of these creatures. Today there were three. Usually, when they let the humans out, the lab was clean and orderly. The sloppy scientists had very efficient janitors, thought Adam. This time, however, the place was a shambles.

Out in the lab, there rose the honking sound of pain and anger—some of the noises they made, especially the commands, were recognizable now—and a sharp slap. Then Mrs. Full hurried into the box, carrying a number of two-foot-square slabs under her arm.

'What happened, ma'am?' asked Adam.

'Watkins played a few bars of real music on that device, and the brutes hit him.' She laid down the slabs. 'Our harmonies seem to cause them actual pain. They held the sides of their heads where ears ought to be, and shook themselves and made those hideous noises.'

'They hit me when I sang the other day,' said Adam, 'remember?'

'That's right. Look here.' She sat down and pulled one of the thick slabs on to her lap. 'I found these under a shelf out there. I wondered why they had been up there, when so many stacks of them just sit around on the floor.'

'I never saw any like these, ma'am.'

'Watch what happens when I push this ridge upwards, Adam.'

She pressed it and the slab, at first gay orange, turned pale blue; on it appeared three lines of squiggly characters, like a cross between Arabic writing and Egyptian hieroglyphics.

'A magic slate!' said Adam.

She pushed the ridge again. The writing disappeared, and out of the slab leered a bull gorilla, paws on chest, eyeing Adam with beady, ridged-browed malevolence. It took a second for sanity to convince him it was only a picture: three-dimensional, on a two-dimensional sheet of plastic, but so real he half-expected the beast to charge out at him. 'What about that?' she asked.

He hit his thigh with a fist. It was a photograph, he imagined, but made by a process so far ahead of anything humanity could produce that it seemed he might glimpse whatever was behind the gorilla if he put his eyes down to the side of the slate. 'Gosh!' he said, afraid to swear in front of her. 'Isn't that something!'

'It's a book,' she said, 'an album of photographs. Look here.'

The next picture was an equally miraculous one of half a dozen monkeys sitting on a tree trunk. Adam looked at it, then at the farthest trunk in their box of a room. Undeniably it was the same one.

Under the picture was a line of squiggles that probably spelled out the scientists' equivalent of 'monkeys'.

'They were here, in this place,' said Adam. 'The giants must have experimented on them too.' He turned his eyes up to the woman and saw that she was white and drawn.

'What happened to them?' he asked. 'There aren't any monkeys here now.'

'Exactly,' she said. She put on the next picture, and after a moment the next.

Dogs greeted his eyes, so real he could almost hear them pant; a cow gazed stolidly at him; a cheetah sat on a mound of straw with head cocked inquisitively; two cockatoos perched in rigid still-life on the silver rod of the prison box.

'What happened to them?' he asked again.

'The experiments ended,' she said.

Then there flashed out a thing like a blue sponge with legs, a thing which sat in the cat's-cradle they had speculated so much about. From its centre two ruby eyes blazed. *That* never came from Earth! Mars or Venus, maybe, or a planet so far from Earth that it bore no name. Adam said as much, his voice quavering.

She stared at him. 'If that was here, in this box, then *where are we?*'

He could not even guess.

The last picture in the slate was a group portrait of himself, the Fulls, Summersby, Watkins, and Porfirio Villa.

When was that taken? They were sitting in a circle on the straw, eating something. Peering closely, he thought it must be the vegetables. Sunday night, then.

'They must have taken it through the food panel,' he said. 'Are there any more pictures?'

'That's all I've looked at.'

Calvin came in. She handed him the first 'book' and showed him how to operate it. When he came to the monstrosity in the web his eyes widened. 'What is it?' he asked.

'A guinea pig, like all the others, including us,' his wife said.

'The tree trunks are explained now,' said Adam, half to himself. 'The sand box, too. That isn't a scientific treatise. I guess it's more of a memento, a record of us all. 'Us and the monkeys,' he said. 'Gosh!'

She took the next big slate on her lap. It was lavender.

The first few pages to appear were covered with the curious writing, very large and only a few words to a page. Then came pictures of many things, not photographs but drawings and paintings in vivid colour. There were portraits of the tall creatures themselves, in various settings, some outdoors in a landscape that was predominantly scarlet and green; there were group scenes in which they ate odd-looking foods and walked down blue pathways and examined strange pets and familiar animals. Under each picture was a short grouping of squiggles, marks and scribbles.

'Can that be a science book?' asked Calvin, leaning over his wife's shoulder. The beings were pictured as simply as possible, in no minute detail whatever, and their activities were of the most prosaic sort.

This pattern was followed through page after page—a picture (some of them were of things so alien they could not be placed), a single character, then a short word and another, long or short. After seeing a dozen of them, Adam noticed that the large character was always repeated at the beginning of the last word.

Suddenly the whole business clicked into focus. The whole damned deal, the lab, the scientists, the experiments and the meaning of the magic slates. This last slate was no more suggestive than many other things; it was simply the final push that sent him headlong into terrible knowledge.

Desperately, he went over it all in his mind, while the Fulls spoke in low tones. He was shivering now. He was more terrified than he had ever been before.

The punishments, the high stool and the arbitrary cuffs and swats; the gadgets, the mazes, the puzzles; were they all a part of a scientific experiment conditioning to neurosis? They were not.

Adam had found the only possible answer. The fourth slate had given it to him, although a hundred hints of it had shown up every day.

He addressed Mrs. Full. She was a little sharper than her husband, and this was more in her line. He wanted to make her discover the same answer. He had to *know* it was right.

'Ma'am, you know what this is?'

'No, Adam.'

'Look here. See this big letter, repeated at the first of this word?'

'Yes.'

He flipped a few 'pages' past. 'It's the same with all of them, you see? And the middle word is always the same—four curly letters. You know what that middle word is?'

'No, Adam.'

'It's "stands for" or "means". He stared at her. 'Get it?'

She thought an instant. 'Of course. Adam, that's very clever of you.' She hadn't seen the implication.

' "Stands for"?' Calvin repeated.

'A stands for Apple,' explained Mrs. Full. 'Or A stands for Airship, or whatever it might be. It's an alphabet book, dear.'

She still hadn't caught it. 'Remember when Mr. Full built the cubbyhole here,' Adam said, 'and the giant knocked it down? Why was he angry?'

'I suppose they wanted to observe us without any hindrance.'

'No, ma'am,' he said with conviction. 'That was simple frustration. They aren't scientifically disappointed if they can't see; they're just frustrated. Think of the punishment we get, slaps, the dunce stool.'

'As though we were children,' she said.

'Exactly. Now, here are these books—an alphabet book, and these others. What age would you say they're for? You taught kindergarten, you said.'

'I'd say for fairly bright children about five or six years old.'

'Or for us,' said her husband, 'when they start to teach us their language.'

'They are children's books, though, with short sentences and the gaudy pictures our own children love.' Mrs. Full stared at Adam. Her brown eyes widened. 'Nursery books . . . .' she said slowly. 'Instability to the point of insanity, if you found it in adult humans. Sloppiness and inefficiency, when these machines point to a high degree of neatness of mind. Wandering attention, inability to concentrate for long periods. Tantrums over nothing. Cruelty and affection mixed without rhyme or reason.' She took him by the arm, her fingers strong with fear and urgency. 'You've guessed something. Tell me, Adam.'

He was filled with panic, with a fearful knowledge that he could scarcely bear without shrieking.

'These machines,' he said, 'aren't scientific testers, they're toys.'

'Yes?' she said.

'We aren't guinea pigs. We're—we're pets. They've had other animals, from Earth and from God knows where, and now they have people.'

'Yes! Go on, say it.' She thrust her face up to his.

'Those twelve-foot "scientists" are kids,' he said. Then he stopped and deliberately got his cracking voice under control. She was as frightened as he was but she wasn't yelling. 'It's the only answer. They're about five years old.'

Calvin frowned. 'If that's true, we're in trouble.'

'You're damn right!' said Adam. 'A kid doesn't take

care of a pet the way a scientist takes care of a guinea pig or a white rat. If it annoys him, he's liable to pick it up and throw it at a wall! I might get my head torn off for singing, or you could be pulled apart for making a mistake with one of those toys.'

'Some children tear the wings off butterflies,' said Mrs. Full. She stood up. 'I'll go and tell the others,' she said firmly. 'It doesn't seem to me that we have much time left.'

She went out. In about five minutes everyone had come into the box but Watkins, who was playing the colour organ. They discussed the discovery in low voices, as though the alien children might be listening; Villa and Summersby examined the slates. After a while Watkins was pushed in, looking rather worn and frayed. Adam was standing in the far corner under the silver web. He saw the wall start to slide shut, remembered his wedge, and tried to see if it was still in place at the bottom of the wall.

He couldn't see it. Maybe it blended with the colour behind it, or maybe somebody had accidentally kicked it out of place.

The wall slid shut.

IX

These people had drawn Summersby into their trouble against his will; the situation was so bad that he could no longer tell himself he didn't give a damn. He had a bad heart but couldn't turn his back on these poor devils because of that. It was stupid and selfish. He felt sorry for them. He was uncomfortable with them, as he always was with standard-sized people, and he would still repel any attempt on their part to get close to him; but he was chastened by what he had been through. He recognized that.

It was all very well to say he didn't care where he died, but it would be a lot more dignified to do so as a free man, rather than as a harried rabbit. If he were killed trying to escape, it would be endurable. But if his heart gave out while he was trundling up and down the nursery in that ridiculous little auto thing, his last breath would be a bitter one.

Adam had just said, 'I laid a rod across the sill there.' Summersby walked to the wall, which appeared to be closed as usual. Just as he came to it, he caught the sheen of metal in a thin line up the corner, and knew that he was seeing part of one of the machines in the nursery. The rod had held the door.

Something moved outside; he could hear the dull slap of flat feet. They were going to be fed. He strolled away from the corner, saying quietly, 'It worked, Adam. Don't check it now, though.'

The small panel opened and one of the garishly hued platters was put in, loaded with a wriggling, seething mass of grubs and half-dead locusts.

'Supper?' cried Villa. 'This is supper? Do they think we are a lot of African natives?'

'Well,' said Adam, 'I guess they were fooled by me.' It was the first time he had made any sort of joke about his colour. Possibly, thought Summersby, he's becoming one of the group, as I am. Summersby felt chastened.

No one cared to sample the insects. They walked away from the platter and hoped that their captors would see the refusal and give them something else, but nothing was pushed in. After a quarter of an hour Watkins said, 'Think it's safe to have a try at the door?'

'No,' said Summersby. 'They'll be pumping in the sleep gas pretty soon, and we don't know whether they do it from outside the nursery or outside this box.'

'That's right,' said Calvin.

'They filled the nursery with it once,' went on Summersby 'but it seems logical to think they could also let it into this room alone. Maybe it works on them; if it does, then they wouldn't flood the nursery with it every night, because the adults have to come in and clean the place up.'

'A clever thought, Mr. Summersby,' said Mrs. Full.

'I'm going to stand by the crack and try to get enough air to stay awake; then when I think the coast's clear, I'll shove the door open and scout around. If I find a way out, I'll come back and drag you into the nursery and wake you.'

'Why are you saying all this?' asked Villa suspiciously. 'No, Mr. Big Man! I think you wouldn't come back. You don't like us.'

Watkins, evidently on edge from his mauling by the children, whirled on the Mexican. 'Oh, shut your yap! The guy's doing you a favour.' Then he said to Summersby, 'I'll come along. I'm not saying you'd run out on us, but I know locks and I might be able to help you if you run into trouble.'

'Come on along, then,' said Summersby. He put an eye to the thin slit. 'Here comes one of them. It's the head scientist.' He grinned. 'The kid who owns us, who lives in this house and invites his little pals in to play with his toys and his pets.'

The monster disappeared. Presently Watkins said, 'It's in. I'm sleepy.'

Summersby stretched as tall as he could and put his mouth and nose to the crack, trying to breathe only what air came through from the nursery. He saw the enormous child pass on its way to the door, and shortly the sound of its heavy feet stopped. He felt drowsy, his eyelids flickered. He beat his hands together, sucking in air from the opening. Villa started to snore.

Watkins said, 'I'm about done, Summersby.' He was kneeling at the crack below Summersby. In a few seconds he rolled over on the straw.

When did the adults come in to clean up? Summersby didn't dare wait much longer. Possibly they wouldn't come till morning.

He had to chance it. He forced his fingers into the gap and heaved. He propped one foot against the adjoining wall, dug his hands as far into the breach as possible, and hurled himself backward. The big door jolted an inch, hung, then slid back a couple of feet. He swung around and jammed himself through the aperture into the enormous room and the wall moved silently back into place; this time the rod was not there, and when the wall stopped, there was no crack at the corner. Summersby realized he must have kicked the rod aside when he slid through. Watkins was inside, asleep.

Summersby breathed deeply, and the effects of the sleep gas died, so that he was wide awake. He ran to the great door of the play-room, whose lintel towered twenty feet from the floor. Hastily he tossed together apparatus, boxes, toy blocks, until he had made a pile five feet high.

Scrambling up this, the things sliding under his feet, he waved an arm above his head in the place where he believed the electric-eye beam to be. Then the pile collapsed, and he fell into it, giving one knee a terrific crack and skinning his knuckles. The door glided open.

The next huge room was deserted and the soft bluish light was dimmer here than in the nursery. This place was far less cluttered, containing no more than a big yellow machine, a gigantic table and two six-legged chairs. There was a picture on the wall, the size of a barn's side, which he did not stop to look at.

The opposite door was open. The third room was a dining-room with two tables and a number of chairs, these of metal with eight legs each. Luckily, there was no one in it.

In the next room—all four were in a straight line, and he thought, either it's a long narrow house, or else it's as big as Rockefeller Centre—there were a number of gadgets, colourful and complex like the children's toys, but of different construction. He glanced at them but did not pause until he came to the next door.

It was closed. He presumed its opener beam would be in the same place as that of the play-room, and looked around for something to stand on.

He shoved at a couple of things, but they wouldn't budge. The only possibility was a big square brown box, set twelve feet off the floor on one of their mammoth tables. It was of a size to accommodate half a dozen cows, but looked as though it might be of flimsy enough material, plastic probably, to push off the edge, to fall exactly where he needed it.

He dragged a chair over, climbed up on its seat and then on to the table. He saw at once that the box would be immovable. An affair that might be a dynamotor was attached to one side, various objects were sticking out of the other and stacks of thick coils were piled on top. He was turning away, when his eye was attracted to a square plate among the things on the right side of the box. Its surface shone under the blue light, and he thought he saw the pinpoint twinkling of stars in it.

On a hunch, he walked over to it. He knew quite a lot of astronomy and if this happened to be a telescope, he might be able to determine their location.

The field of the plate was full of stars, but in patterns he had never seen. It was not a painting, for the stars twinkled.

A huge dial beside the plate had a pointer and scores of notches, each labelled with squiggly characters. He turned the pointer experimentally. The screen blurred, showed a planet with rings: Saturn.

'Neat,' he said to himself, and turned the pointer another notch. He got a view of a landscape, trees of olive green and crimson, seen from above. He tried other notches.

Finally, just as he had reminded himself that he had to hurry, he saw a familiar globe swim on to the glass. It was Earth!

What in hell . . . . ?

He pushed the pointer on, and was given another landscape, this time in Earth's colours, a meadow with a cow in it. He clicked the thing another notch and he got a star pattern again. He pushed it back to the cow.

He felt his heart thudding fast, too fast. There were other pointers, a little behind the first. He turned one slowly.

The cow grew larger until it almost filled the screen. Only when he could see nothing but its placid back did he realize that he was looking at this scene, as at the others, from *above*.

He tried a third pointer. The land whipped by beneath his gaze. He came to a city, the buildings reaching up to him in a wonderful illusion of depth.

Then it dawned on him what the machine was. He had found the answer to their last problem, and he had to get back to the box prison and thrash it out with all of them. There might be a salvation for them and there might not.

Leaving the screen showing the city, he jumped down

off the table and raced back through into the dining-room. Still there were no signs of any of the giants. He had crossed the threshold of the third room when he heard a door open on his right and dodged under the hanging shelf of the strange yellow machine, like a low desk covered with cogwheels.

A pair of feet, either of which would have outweighed a draught-horse, went past him; he dared not lean forward to see the rest of the creature, but it was undoubtedly an adult. It went into the playroom.

After twenty or twenty-five minutes, during which Summersby thought over the problem and decided that he couldn't find the solution alone, the giant came out of the playroom, crossed near his hiding place, and went out through a door. It was not in a hurry, so he decided it had not noticed his absence from the box.

He dragged a chair over to the nursery door. It was four times the size of Summersby's armchair at home, and eight times as heavy. As he was crawling up the leg to the seat, he recalled that he had a bad heart.

He intercepted the beam and opened the door. Having no more than half a minute to get through before it shut, he had to leave the chair where it was. He hoped none of the adults would realize that its position had been changed.

The playroom was clean and neat. Probably it would remain unvisited through the night. He went to the box and only then remembered it was shut tight. What did the children do when they opened it during the day? He had seen them at it. They laid their hands on top of the box, there on the left.

Hauling over enough junk to make a pair of steps, he got on to the roof of the box. There was a bar set into the coaming. He pressed it, leaned over, and saw the wall slide back. A second push returned it to its shut position. He opened it again, swung his legs over the edge, pressed once more and dropped. Snatching up a green block from the floor, he jumped into the box as the door was closing. He had just time to lay it across the threshold before the wall reached it and was held.

Trying not to breathe, Summersby picked up Watkins and slung him over his shoulder. He forced his fingers into the crack and heaved. Again he threw his weight against the wall.

Then he was buckling at the knees, trying desperately to bring his mouth next to the opening, but not quite making it.

'Describe it again,' said Watkins. 'Give me all the details you can think of.'

As Summersby went over what he remembered of the brown machine, Watkins tried to envisage it. He might not be able to handle it. To reverse a thing like that—when there'd be at least one or two principles he'd never heard of——

'How do you know that it's the instrument that brought us here?' he asked.

'It must be.' Summersby looked almost eager. 'It has those dials that focus it almost pin-point on any planet they want: I saw a few planets from a distance and close up. I saw a cow and a city on Earth. Then there's the big brown box. It's hollow—the door was half open. If they bring things, living things, from other planets, they need a receiving station large enough to take 'em. The box. It's logical.'

'It sure is.' Adam whistled. 'So we're on another planet. That was plain, if we'd thought about it seriously. No place on Earth could hide a race like this. Not with all the factories they must have to produce the toys.'

'Why couldn't we be inside the Earth?' asked Mrs. Full.

Watkins said, 'Summersby looked *down* on Earth. That argues another planet.'

'But how did they get us here? In two days?'

Watkins scratched his bristled chin and thought. 'It must have been instantaneous. Remember, we went through a quarantine and were healed of just about everything that was wrong with us. That must have taken a while.'

'The octopus was still wet,' said Adam, 'and the grubs and locusts were still kicking. They must focus that rig on Earth and push a button and here it is, like that. Instant transmission of matter.' He smiled weakly as though he were proud of the phrase, but he looked very frightened and unhappy.

Tom Watkins was scared, too, but not especially unhappy. For the first time in almost twenty years, he was free of worry about the bulls, the law. He only wished he knew what had happened to his loot.

'The planet,' said Calvin, 'whatever its name is, must have the same gravity and atmosphere as Earth. Same water, too.'

'That's right. So it's produced a race of critters with plenty of human characteristics,' said Watkins.

'Have they done this before?' asked Mrs. Full. 'I mean do you think we're the first to be snatched up?'

'No, I don't,' said Watkins, surprised that she was talking directly to him. 'People disappear all the time.'

The wall began to open.

'Here's the plan quick,' said Watkins. 'I've got to get out and find the machine, and see if I can fix it so it'll work backward, send us home. The rest of you create a diversion, keep the kids' minds off me.'

'What kind of a diversion?' asked Villa.

'If you were a kid with pets, intelligent ones, what would you watch them do for hours? Something unordinary—something you'd never imagine they'd do.' He looked at his watch. 'It's just ten. I never saw the gadget I couldn't figure out in two hours; if I'm not back by noon, you'd better come out, Summersby.'

'What if it's four-dimensional?' asked Adam.

'It's possible I can cook up a way to reverse its action anyway. There are some principles of electricity and mechanics that must be universal.'

'Shall we run the machines for them?' asked Mrs. Full. 'To distract the children?'

'They're used to that,' said Watkins. 'They bore easy. Suppose you're a kid with a normal regard for pets. You've had cats and dogs and rabbits and now you have monkeys. The monkeys are a lot smarter and more versatile, but they have their limits too. You get jaded with 'em. But one day they—' he snapped his fingers '—they start playing soldiers! They drill, stage mock battles, die and come to life, scrimmage—what happens then? You can't take your eyes off 'em!'

'That's it,' said Villa promptly. 'The children have gorillas, cows, they have never seen anything like war.'

'Maybe they don't know what war is,' said Adam. 'None of their toys show that war is ever waged by this race.'

'The toys of any people reflect their civilization in an unreliable and distorted way,' said Calvin rather stuffily. 'A visitor from Mars in one of our playrooms would conclude that we already have spaceships and ray guns, and that our usual clothing is chaps, sombreros, and space-suits.'

'They'll get the idea,' Watkins said impatiently. The giant children outside were bawling the word that meant 'Come!' He was in a hurry. 'Let's go,' he said. 'The four of you line up over there, catch the kids' eyes, and Summersby can boost me up to the beam. Then he'll join you.'

Watkins grinned, and dived behind the nearest many-coloured pile of gear the moment he saw the children weren't watching him. As he went toward the door, he heard Villa saying, 'My fourth cousin Pancho was a great man for war, so I will be general. Spread out in the thin line and be ready to march when I command.'

Summersby followed Watkins, and they came to the door. Watkins managed to get up on the big man's shoulders, and waved a hand above his head. Nothing happened.

'*Un, dos, tres,*' roared the Mexican down the hall. 'Begin!

Next time Watkins found the beam. The door glided aside. He dropped off Summersby's shoulders, jumped into the next room. A quick look showed him it was empty. As the door closed he heard Villa shouting hoarsely.

'Make bang noises for the guns. Fall dead, spring to life. We are mountain fighters of great skill. Climb on machines, drop off with bullets in your head, play you are——'

The door cut him off. Watkins started for the opposite door.

X

It was ten minutes to twelve. Summersby was panting like a spent hound. He had not exercised in months, not since the doctors had told him his heart was just about gone, and he was surprised that he hadn't keeled over before now. Dashing around playing guerrilla like some six-year-old! It had been a damn good idea, though. The giant children—there were two of them today—were still enthralled, lying on their bellies with their furry watermelon heads propped on fantastic two-thumbed hands.

Leaning against a pink plastic maze wall, puffing, he thought, I've almost grown to like them. Why?

Because for the first time since he was sixteen, John Summersby had to bend his neck back to look up at someone. These grotesque humanoidal beings were the only living things which did not make him feel overgrown, uncouthly out of proportion, a hulking lout. If a chair was too narrow for him, it would be like the head of a pin to one of these kids; if a fork felt uncomfortably small in his own hand, it would be tiny in one of those vast paws.

In their shadows, Summersby was a very small man. It was an unwonted sensation, the most satisfying he had ever experienced.

He looked at them out there, as they lay watching Mrs. Full and Adam mowing down Calvin and Villa with imaginary Brownings. He grinned, felt his lips curve in the unaccustomed grimace, and thought with no particular bitterness that he was getting mellow in his last days.

At five to noon the door opened. Summersby, seeing its silent motion, left off the mimic gunplay and started for the wall. The safe-cracker—Watkins—came running down the middle of the room, yelling.

'Come on, everybody.'

'Come on?'

The two giant children were on their feet, uncertain; they didn't realize Watkins had been out of the room.

'The adults spotted me!' he roared, swinging his briefcase wildly: where had he found that? 'They're after me!'

Summersby let out an involuntary grunt when through

the twenty-foot door came an eighteen-foot creature. This was an adult: leaner in the body, broader of hand and thicker of limb, wearing trouserlike garments and a flaring jacket of royal purple caught by a ruby bar. It advanced calmly into the hall, clumping flatfooted in three-yard strides. From its heavy-lipped mouth came noises like a whole orchestra in need of tuning.

'Hwhrangg!' it cried, waving its hand in the air. 'Breemingg!' It appeared to be soothing the children, telling them that Daddy was here.

Mrs. Full, on the control platform, screamed. Summersby stepped out irresolute. The coloured boy stood stunned, but Porfirio Villa, afire with the heady make-believe carnage of the afternoon, was quick to act. A dozen waddling leaps, a swift swing of his legs over the side, and the Mexican landed in the little red vehicle with the vast control board, the car that only he had been able to master. Pressing buttons, pulling plungers, sliding levers, he whirled it around and sent it at the towering adult.

The creature skipped out of his way, blaring anger. Villa came about sharply, gunned his 'motor'—if it was that—and rammed the gigantic enemy on the leg. As Villa's car overturned, the creature fell at full length, with a crash like an elephant dropping out of a tree. It contracted its body and gripped its ankle with both hands, honking dismally.

Summersby was running. He skidded up to the grovelling Villa, yanked him to his feet and shoved him out of range of the injured adult. The two children had broken into the barks that were their equivalent of weeping, one drawing its goading rod. Summersby crouched, went toward it, hoping to bring it down before it stunned him. As he came within diving range, though, the orange airship streaked over his head and jammed its nose into the child's belly. It folded over with a whoosh, grabbing its middle, as the toy wobbled off in eccentric flight.

Mrs. Full, the expert at flying the miniature vessel, had acted just in time. Now her husband hauled her off the seat and rushed her toward the door.

The remaining child stood in the middle of the floor, staring at its groaning, breathless playmate and at the maimed adult, honking to itself. Skirting it, the humans made for the door as fast as they could go.

Summersby overtook Watkins. 'I found it okay,' panted the safe-cracker.

'Can you work it?' They were through the door now, the two of them in the lead, running across the first of the rooms.

'There were other adults,' said Watkins. 'Three or four saw me. I don't know where they went.'

'Can you work it?'

'The matter transmitter?' He grinned briefly. 'Sure.'

The doorway before them was crowded by several of the giants. They came through, not hurrying, talking rather placidly; their movements had the swiftness of the children's without their jerkiness. In their hands were green goads. They pointed and came down upon the humans.

'Scatter!' yelled Summersby, and dodged under the shelf of the machine where he had taken cover last night. He went to the end. In seconds they would be peering under the shelf, spotting him, thrusting in their shockers and laying him out. And, damn it all, he cared! He didn't want to be stopped when so much of the fight was won. His heart might stop, he couldn't help that, but till it did he wanted to go on fighting. Balling his fists, he started to leave the sanctuary. Then he heard Adam Pierce begin to sing.

He had a high tenor voice, mellow with a sweet touch of huskiness in it, and he was singing 'Drink to Me Only' at the top of his lungs.

He hadn't gone crazy! Summersby remembered the punishments they had endured for making harmonious noises on the musical toy, the slap Adam got for singing. Adam had thought of the only weapon they could use now—*song!*

'Or leave a kiss within the cup,' roared Summersby, and without further thought walked into the room. Watkins chimed in, breathless but true of pitch.

Three eighteen-foot adults were standing there. Vast hands were pressed to bulbous heads, and agonized croaks came from gaping mouths. What weird auricular structure could cringe like this from a simple song? It did, and that was enough.

Mrs. Full clutched Summersby's arm. 'One of them struck Calvin with his prod.'

'Where is he?'

'Near that door.'

Beginning to sing again, Summersby raced up to the prone milk-inspector, picked him up and slung him, limp as a dead doe, over his shoulder. The others were gathering. He motioned them forward, and, as Watkins joined him, ran on.

'Where'd you find your case?'

'On a table. Hope the dough is all in there.' He glanced back. 'They're coming. We're racking 'em but they're game.'

They reached the midpoint of the third room, the dining-hall, as one of the beings staggered through the door behind them. It had lost its goad and was flattening its hands on its skull as Adam and Mrs. Full swung into

'Dixie.' It came at them like a drunk, unable to navigate a straight course but determined to reach them. It'll stamp on us, thought Summersby, easing back a little on his arm. It only has to come down once or twice with that Cadillac-sized foot and we're squashed ants. He sang.

'To live and die in . . . . '

The second brute appeared, lurched, caught up a flat plate and skimmed it at them. It was as big as a bath-tub. 'Drop!' cried Summersby, and as he went down on one knee, he felt the wind of the trencher's passing ruffle his hair.

The next door was closed. Summersby slammed himself flat against the wall and Adam, cat-like and fast, scrambled up over him, stood on his shoulders and broke the controlling beam. The aliens came down the room like two epileptic furies. 'Sing!' said Watkins. 'Everybody!' The door slid aside with maddening slowness.

'Try a fast one,' said Mrs. Full. ' "Blow the Man Down".' It was a funny suggestion, coming from her.

'As I was a-walkin' down Paradise Street . . . . ' they yelled in unison.

The third monster entered the dining-room, caught the full blast of their five voices (Calvin was still out, but Villa was giving a rum-tum-tum accompaniment), and sank to its knees, shaking its head as though it had been coshed. One of the others made a desperate leap at them. 'Melodies affect its organ of equilibrium,' Summersby thought. 'The poor thing's in agony. "I says to her, Lollie, and how d'ye do . . . ." '

They were through the doorway now. A last pursuer was reeling after them, green rod still held in one shaking hand. Its rust-red eyes were bulging out from their deep pits, and it made guttural, creaking noises.

'Down at the end,' said Watkins. 'The brown box.'

'Did you fix it?' asked Summersby.

'I think so. We have to take a chance. I guessed at a few things, but I think it'll work. Unless one of our big pals has mucked up my improvements.'

It was twenty yards away; but so was the last of the monsters. Summersby changed Full to his other arm and added his voice to the general clamour for a bar or so, then asked Watkins the question that had been nagging at him. 'Can we all go? Or does somebody have to send the others?'

'I'll send you. I'm not too sure I can get through. The dials and focusing lenses are on the outside, you know.'

'I'll work it then.' They were at the table; Summersby dropped Full and helped Adam shove a chair to the table. Mrs. Full and Villa were singing 'Quiereme Mucho' in Spanish, their voices a trifle hoarse by now.

'I'm damned if you will,' replied Watkins. 'It'd take me ten minutes to teach you how to work the transmitter. Think we have ten minutes?'

The giant was standing still, pawing the air. It would not give in to its pain and dizziness. If it fell now it might hit them, it was so close.

'You've *got* to show me,' said Summersby urgently. 'I have a bad heart. I'm due to die in a month or two.'

Watkins stared at him. 'Don't make me laugh. Do you think you went through the past hours with a rotten ticker?'

'It's true. I'm just waiting to die. You're no more than thirty-eight or so, and you've got twenty-two thousand dollars there,' he said, gesturing at the briefcase. 'I don't give a damn about your morals. You're a decent fellow and you ought to have this break.'

Watkins snarled, as he gave the valiantly singing Mrs.

Full a hand up to the chair seat, 'You think I have a martyr complex? You think I *want* to stay here? I'm elected, that's all! I haven't the time to teach you to work it! Your heart's fixed up the same as Adam's eyes and Calvin's sinus. Go back to your woods. You're okay.'

'No,' said Summersby, with stubborn rage. 'I'm sick of waiting to die. That's why I took the coaster ride. That's why I wanted——'

'You're nuts. Hand up old Calvin.'

The monster took two wobbling steps toward them. They were all on the chair, then clambering on to the table. Watkins swung open the door of the brown box. 'Fast,' he said urgently. 'Fast!'

Adam had Calvin by the armpits: he lugged him into the dark interior. Villa jumped in, Mrs. Full following. Summersby confronted the safe-cracker.

'Show me how to work the machine. I don't believe they could mend a bad heart.'

Watkins pushed the briefcase at him with so unexpected a motion that Summersby took it automatically. 'Send it to Roscoe & Bates, if I don't turn up. I guess I can't use it here.' He put a hand under his coat. 'Go on.'

'No!'

Watkins drew a gun, a small steel-blue thing that looked as wicked as a rattler. Summersby had had no idea that he was carrying it. 'Hop in, tall man,' said Watkins, grinning. 'You're holding up the works.'

Summersby backed away and stood in the door of the box. He could jump Watkins but if the mechanism were so complex, he would only doom them all. 'You're out of your head,' he said.

'Sure!'

Abruptly above the safe-cracker towered the fantastic

form of their forgotten enemy, reaching for them, one hand still to its head. Summersby inflated his lungs.

'Should auld acquaintance be forgot,' he roared tunefully, 'and never brought to mind!'

Everyone joined him. It was a startling cataclysm of sound even to Summersby. The alien tottered, hand outstretched; its mouth fell open, its eyes popped, violet blood coursed from one nostril; it clawed the air, honked grotesquely, and pitched forward, half on and half off the table, where it lay gurgling. A spot on the side of its skull, about the width of a gallon jug, on which the hair grew sparse and gray, pulsed as though there were no bone beneath the skin. Its ear, thought Summersby. Maybe the thing will die. Then Watkins is a gone goose, if he stays. He was about to lunge at the steady gun-hand but Adam and Villa yanked him backward into the box. Adam was crying.

'Try and come too, Mr. Watkins, try and come too,' he said.

Watkins laughed and waved the gun. 'Be seeing you.' Then he tossed the weapon into the box and slammed the door.

XI

There was darkness, then bright sun. They stood on a street corner, and Summersby could read the signs as plainly as Watkins must have read them in the focusing lens of the matter-transmitter on the unknown planet.

Broadway and 42nd Street. The five of them had clicked into being on the busiest corner of New York.

'That old crook,' said Adam, gulping. 'He focused us here for a gag.'

'I look *awful*,' gasped Mrs. Full, and Summersby, glancing at her, agreed. She had lost weight; and her skirt and blouse were mussed up, to say the least. All the men needed shaves. Calvin Full, recovering gradually from the shock of the goad, and still supported by Villa, looked like a drunk.

Adam addressed Summersby. 'Will Watkins be along too?'

'I don't know,' said Summersby. 'I hope so.'

'My chili stand!' shouted Villa, suddenly awakening to the fact of New York about him. Pushing Calvin to Adam, who grasped him by an arm, the Mexican waved hurriedly. 'Come and see me,' he said to all of them. 'I'll give you a bowl free.' He hastened away into the crowd.

'We've got to see about our clothes at the hotel,' said Mrs. Full. She sounded apologetic. 'I hope we'll see you again, Adam and Mr. Summersby.'

'I doubt it,' said Summersby. He looked at Calvin. 'Coming out of it?' he asked.

'Thanks,' said Calvin, nodding. He took his wife's hand. 'Gave you my address, didn't I?'

'I have it,' said Summersby.

'Well, good-bye,' said Mrs. Full.

'You did a fine job up there,' said Adam. 'I'm proud to have known you, ma'am.'

'Thank you, Adam. Good-bye.' They were gone.

'I suppose you'll be going too,' said Adam wistfully.

'I guess so. You'll go home?'

'I guess so,' Adam repeated. 'My folks will be sore. They'll never believe such a story. They'll think I ran wild or something.'

Summersby, still looking upward, and wondering if he could be staring blindly at the planet which Watkins must be trying to leave now, put a hand on his heart. They did fix up everyone else. He laughed. It was the first time he had laughed normally in seven months. 'I could get into the rangers again,' he said. 'Adam, I've got to see a doctor. I've got to find out something.'

'Yes, sir,' said Adam unhappily. Summersby looked at him. 'Really worried about your folks?'

'Yes, sir.'

'I'll come with you and tell them.'

'Mr. Summersby, you're a gentleman.'

'No,' said Summersby, 'no.'

'Yes, sir, you are. Can we wait just a minute more? Mr Watkins might be along any minute now.'

'We'll wait.'

After a while Adam, shuffling his feet, kicked something, bent down and picked it up. It was the safe-cracker's gun. 'I didn't think he'd carry one,' said the boy. He looked closer at it.

'What is it?' Summersby shifted the briefcase and held out a hand. Adam laid the weapon in his palm. 'He must have won it at the park.'

Summersby held it up. It looked like a small automatic of blued steel, but it was plastic. He turned it over. A pencil-sharpener.

Summersby grunted. 'A toy,' he said, giving it back to Adam. 'A kid's toy.'

LAST AND FIRST MEN

OLAF STAPLEDON

Olaf Stapledon was a lecturer in English literature, but had a knowledge of biology which was well up to date when he wrote Last and First Men *in 1930. Recent work, though often spectacular (as in the case of DNA), has really altered little on the scale on which he here chose to let his fertile imagination run. For his book is no less than an imaginary history of the many ways in which the human race might change and mutate over vast periods of future time. It would be bound, so he felt, to change through the effects of external pressures, and because of events such as large-scale changes of climate—perhaps a slow change from a new ice age to a new period of great heat involving the melting of the polar ice-caps which in turn would produce immense areas of flooding. Then there might well be microscopic changes and developments such as the evolution of new viruses and bacteria, some helpful, some disastrous; also there might be combats with extra-terrestrials.*

The First Men of his title are ourselves—Homo Sapiens. We fight each other and we end in Dark Age, while our successors, the Second Men, flourish for many ages but are destroyed by Martians.

The Third Men, with a part only of whose history the following pages are concerned, he imagines as attractive humanoids, not very tall, slightly built, lively, with a 'sunny brown' skin, covered with a luminous halo of red-gold hairs, 'which on the head became a russet mop'. He describes their golden eyes as 'more enigmatic than profound', their faces as compact and rather cat-like, their ears as proportionately larger than those of a cat and 'expressive both of temperament and of passing mood'. They took a pride in these elegant erectile ears which were 'delicately involuted', of a silken texture, and very mobile', while their hands were lean and dextrous. Rather emotional, the Third Men were short-lived, with a brief childhood and maturity. They were apt to die of old age at about sixty, but rarely reached that age for, in later life, they preferred to live dangerously, greatly disliking decrepitude and senility. They were extremely successful cultivators and had enough knowledge of other technologies to live in comfort and even luxury, but what they lived for was what Stapledon calls 'vital art'. They were, that is to say, passionate plant and animal breeders and one of their chief aims was to produce—for use or for fancy—new species of plant and animal. With both they had a vivid sympathy, which in former ages would have been thought of as uncanny, but which helped them to reach a very high standard of biological control. All the Third Men were at one in this passion for vital art, but individuals and groups varied very much in the ways in which they exercised it. As with us, fashion played its part:

To own many and noble beasts, whether they were economically productive or not, was ever the mark of respectability. The vulgar, indeed, were content with mere numbers, or at most with the conventional virtues of the recognized breeds. But the more refined pursued and flaunted certain very exact principles of aesthetic excellence in their control of living forms.

In fact, as the race gained biological insight it developed a very remarkable new art, which we may call vital art. This was to become the chief vehicle of expression of the new culture. It was practised universally, and with religious fervour; for it was very closely connected with their belief in a Life God. The canons of this art, and the precepts of this religion, fluctuated from age to age. There was almost universal agreement that the practice of vital art was the supreme goal, and should not be treated in a utilitarian spirit, but there were two conflicting sets of principles which were favoured by opposed sects. One mode of vital art sought to evoke the full potentiality of each natural type as a harmonious and perfected nature, or to produce new types equally harmonious. The other prided itself on breeding monsters. Thus a bird was produced which could fly faster than any other bird; but it could neither reproduce nor even feed, and therefore had to be maintained artificially. Sometimes, on the other hand, certain characters incompatible in nature were forced upon a single organism, and maintained in torturing equilibrium. One much-talked-of feat was the production of a carnivorous mammal in which the fore limbs had assumed the structure of a bird's wings, complete with feathers. This creature could not fly, since its body was wrongly proportioned. Its only mode of locomotion was a staggering run with outstretched wings. Other examples of monstrosity were an eagle with twin heads, and a deer in which, with incredible ingenuity, the artists had induced the tail to develop as a head, with brain, sense organs, and jaws. In this monstrous art, interest in living things was infected with sadism through the preoccupation with fate, especially internal fate, as the divinity that shapes our ends. In its more vulgar forms, of course, it was a crude expression of egotistical lust in power.

However, the supreme aim of the dominant, perfection-seeking movement was to embellish the planet with a very diverse fauna and flora, with the human race as at once the crown and the instrument of terrestrial life. Each species, and each variety, was to have its place. Each was to be internally perfected to its function and its capacities must be in true accord with one another. But the supreme aim was not concerned merely with individual types, but with the whole vital economy of the planet. Thus, though there were to be types of every order from the most humble bacterium up to man, it was contrary to the canon of orthodox sacred art that any type should thrive by the destruction of a type higher than itself. In the sadistic mode of the art, however, a peculiarly exquisite tragic beauty was said to inhere in situations in which a lowly type exterminated a higher. There were occasions in the history of the race when the two sects indulged in bloody conflict because the sadists kept devising parasites to undermine the noble products of the orthodox.

The great majority, however accepted the sacred canon. They might seek to enhance some extant type of organism, both by perfecting its capacities and by eliminating from it all that was harmful or useless. Or else, a more original and precarious work, they might set about creating a new type to fill a niche in the world which had not yet been occupied. They would select a suitable organism and seek to remake it upon a new plan, striving to produce a creature of perfectly harmonious nature precisely adapted to the new way of life. In this kind of work sundry strict aesthetic principles must be observed and the ultimate work of art must be an ever more subtle garment of living forms for the adornment of the planet.

Much more was needed than the rule-of-thumb principles of earlier breeders. It took this brightest of the races of the third species thousands of years of research to discover the more delicate principles of heredity, and to devise a technique by which the hereditary factors in the germ could be manipulated.

Imagine, then, a planet organized almost as a vast system of botanical and zoological gardens, interspersed with agriculture and industry. In every great centre occurred annual shows. The latest creations were put through their paces, judged by the high priests of vital art, awarded distinctions, and consecrated with religious ceremony. There might be improved grains, vegetables, cattle, some exceptionally intelligent or sturdy variety of herdsman's dog, or a new micro-organism with some special function. But also there would be the latest achievements in pure vital art. Great sleek-limbed, hornless, racing deer, birds or mammals adapted to some hitherto unfulfilled role, bears intended to outclass all existing varieties in the struggle for existence, ants with specialized organs and instincts, improvements in the relations of parasite and host. And everywhere there would be the little unclad ruddy faun-like beings who had created these marvels. Shy forest-dwelling folk of Gurkha physique would stand beside their antelopes, vultures, or new great-cat-like prowlers. A grave young woman might cause a stir by entering the grounds followed by several gigantic bears. Crowds would perhaps press round to examine the creatures' teeth or limbs, and she might scold the meddlers away from her patient flock. For the normal relation between man and beast at this time was one of perfect amity, rising, sometimes, in the case of domesticated animals, to an exquisite, almost painful, mutual adoration. Even the wild beasts never troubled to avoid man, still less to attack him, save in the special circumstances of the hunt and the sacred gladiatorial show.

These last need special notice. The powers of combat in beasts were admired no less than other powers. Men and women alike experienced a savage joy, almost an ecstasy, in the spectacle of mortal combat. Consequently there were formal occasions when different kinds of beasts were enraged against one another and allowed to fight to the death. Not only so, but also there were sacred contests between beast and man, between man and man, between woman and woman, and, most surprising to the readers of this book, between woman and man. For in this species, woman in her prime was not physically weaker than her partner.

Almost from the first, vital art had been applied to some extent to man himself, though with hesitation. Certain great improvements had been effected, but only improvements about which there could be no two opinions. Extreme good health and considerable physical beauty became universal. Child-bearing was made a painless and health-giving process. Senility was postponed. The standard of practical intelligence was appreciably raised. Every individual knew the characteristics of his or her hereditary composition. Thus in courtship the young man sought to persuade his beloved that, with his help, she might bear children of a peculiar excellence. Consequently there was at all times going on a process of selective breeding towards the conventionally ideal type. This included health, cat-like agility, manipulative dexterity, musical sensitivity, refined perception of rightness and wrongness in the sphere of vital art, and intuitive practical judgement in all the affairs of life.

At length there came a time when more ambitious aims were entertained and the community set about remaking human nature. Unfortunately there were conflicting views about the goal. The orthodox desired only to perfect man's body, but upon its present plan, and to perfect his mind, but without seeking to introduce anything new in essence. His physique, percipience, memory, intelligence, and emotional nature should be improved almost beyond recognition; but they must, it was said, remain essentially what they had always been.

A second party, however, finally persuaded orthodox opinion to amplify itself. Man, they said, is a very noble organism. We have dealt with other organisms so as to enhance in each its noblest attributes. It is time to do the same with man. What is most distinctive in man is intelligent manipulation, brain and hand. Now hand is really outclassed by modern mechanisms, but brain will never be outclassed. Therefore we must breed strictly for brain, for intelligent co-ordination of behaviour. All the organic functions which can be performed by machinery must be relegated to machinery, so that the whole vitality of the organism may be devoted to brain-building and brain-working. In spite of opposition, a small group of the governors themselves were determined to carry through the enterprise in secret.

THE FIRST OF THE GREAT BRAINS

They employed four methods, namely selective breeding, manipulation of the hereditary factors in germ cells (cultivated in the laboratory), manipulation of the fertilized ovum (cultivated also in the laboratory), and manipulation of the growing body. At first they produced innumerable tragic abortions. But at length something was produced which seemed to promise success. The dauntless experimenters succeeded at last in creating an organism which consisted of a brain twelve feet across, and a body most of which was reduced to a mere vestige upon the under-surface of the brain. The only parts of the body which were allowed to attain the natural size were the arms and hands. These sinewy organs of manipulation were induced to key themselves at the shoulders into the solid masonry which formed the creature's house. Thus they were able to get a purchase for their work. The hands were the normal six-fingered hands of the Third Men, very greatly enlarged and improved. The fantastic organism was matured in a building designed to house both it and the complicated machinery which was necessary to keep it alive. A self-regulating pump, electrically driven, served it as a heart. A chemical factory poured the necessary materials into its blood and removed waste products, thus taking the place of digestive organs and the normal battery of glands. Its lungs consisted of a great room full of oxidizing tubes, through which a constant wind was driven by an electric fan. The same fan forced air through the artificial organs of speech. These organs were so constructed that the natural nerve-fibres, issuing from the speech centres of the brain, could stimulate appropriate electrical controls so as to produce sounds identical with those which they would have produced from a living throat and mouth. The optic nerves were induced to grow out along two flexible probosces, five feet long, each of which bore a huge eye at the end. The natural lens could be moved aside at will, so that the retina could be applied to any of a great diversity of optical instruments. The ears also could be projected upon stalks, and were so arranged that the actual nerve endings could be brought into contact with artificial resonators of various kinds, or could listen directly to the microscopic rhythms of the most minute organisms. Scent and taste were developed as a chemical sense, which could distinguish almost all compounds and elements by their flavour. Sensory pain was to have been eliminated from the organism altogether; but this end was not achieved.

The creature was kept alive for four years. But though at first all went well, in his second year the unfortunate child, if such he may be called, began to suffer severe pain, and to show symptoms of mental derangement. In spite of all that his devoted foster-parents could do, he gradually sank into insanity and died. He had succumbed to his own brain weight and to certain failures in the chemical regulation of his blood.

We may overlook sundry vain and long-term attempts which were made to repeat the great experiment more successfully and pass on to the first true individual of the fourth human species. He was produced in the same artificial manner as his forerunners, and was designed upon the same general plan. His mechanical and chemical machinery, however, was far more efficient; and his makers expected that, owing to careful adjustments of the mechanisms of growth and decay, he would prove to be immortal. His general plan, also, was changed in one important respect. His makers built a large circular 'brain turret' which they divided with many partitions, radiating from a central space, and covered everywhere with pigeon-holes. By a technique which took centuries to develop, they induced the cells of the growing embryonic brain to spread outwards, not as normal hemispheres of convolutions, but into the pigeon-holes which had been prepared for them. Thus the artificial 'cranium' had to be a roomy turret of ferro-concrete some forty feet in diameter. A door and a passage led from the outer world into the centre of the turret, and thence other passages radiated between tiers of little cupboards. Innumerable tubes of glass, metal, and a kind of vulcanite conveyed blood and chemicals over the whole system. Electric radiators preserved an even warmth in every cupboard, and throughout the innumerable carefully protected channels of the nerve fibres. Thermometers, dials, pressure gauges, indicators of all sorts, informed the attendants of every physical change in this strange half-natural, half-artificial system.

Eight years after its inception the organism had filled its brain room, and attained the mentality of a new-born infant. His advance to maturity seemed to his foster-parents dishearteningly slow. Not till almost at the end of his fifth decade could he be said to have reached the mental standard of a bright adolescent. But there was no real reason for disappointment. Within another decade this pioneer of the Fourth Men had learned all that the Third Men could teach him, and had also seen that a great part of their wisdom was folly. In manual dexterity he could already vie with the best; but though manipulation afforded him intense delight, he used his hands almost wholly in service of his tireless curiosity. In fact, it was evident that curiosity was his main characteristic. He was a large bump of curiosity equipped with most cunning hands. A department of state had been created to look after his nurture and education. An army of learned persons was kept in readiness to answer his impatient questions and assist him in his own scientific experiments. Now that he had attained maturity these unfortunate pundits found themselves hopelessly outclassed, and reduced to mere clerks, bottle-washers, and errand-boys. Hundreds of his servants were for ever scurrying into every corner of the planet to seek information and specimens; and the significance of their errands was by now often quite beyond the range of their own intelligence. They were careful, however, not to let their ignorance appear to the public. On the contrary, they succeeded in gaining much prestige from the mere mysteriousness of their errands.

The great brain was wholly lacking in all normal instinctive responses, save curiosity and constructiveness. Instinctive fear he knew not, though of course he was capable of cold caution in any circumstances which threatened to damage him and hinder his passionate research. Anger he knew not, but only an adamantine firmness in the face of opposition. Normal hunger and thirst he knew not, but only an experience of faintness when his blood was not properly supplied with nutriment. Sex was wholly absent from his mentality. Instinctive tenderness and instinctive group-feeling were not possible to him. The heroic devotion of his most intimate servants called forth only cold approval.

At first he interested himself not at all in the affairs of the society which maintained him, served his every whim, and adored him. But in time he began to take pleasure in suggesting brilliant solutions of all the current problems of social organization. His advice was increasingly sought and accepted. He became autocrat of the state. His own intelligence and complete detachment combined with the people's superstitious reverence to establish him far more securely than any ordinary tyrant. He cared nothing for the petty troubles of his people, but he was determined to be served by a harmonious, healthy, and potent race. And as relaxation from the more serious excitement of research in physics and astronomy, the study of human nature was not without attractions. It may seem strange that one so completely devoid of human sympathy could have the tact to govern a race of the emotional Third Men. But he had built up for himself a very accurate behaviouristic psychology; and like the skilful master of animals, he knew unerringly how much could be expected of his people, even though their emotions were almost wholly foreign to him. Thus, for instance, while he thoroughly despised their admiration of animals and plants, and their religion of life, he soon learned not to seem hostile to these obsessions. He himself was interested in animals only as material for experiments. In this respect his people readily helped him, partly because he assured them that his goal was the further improvement of all types, partly because they were fascinated by his complete disregard, in his experimentation, of the common techniques for preventing pain. The orgy of vicarious suffering awakened in his people a long-suppressed lust in cruelty.

Little by little the great brain probed the material universe and the universe of mentality. He mastered the principles of biological evolution, and constructed for his own delight a detailed history of life on earth. He learned, by marvellous archaeological technique, the story of all the earlier human peoples, and of the Martian episode, matters which had remained hidden from the Third Men. He discovered the principles of relativity and the quantum theory, the nature of the atom as a complex system of wave trains. He measured the cosmos; and with his delicate instruments he counted the planetary systems in much of the remote universe. He casually solved, to his own satisfaction at least, the ancient problems of good and evil, of mind and its object, of the one and the many, and of truth and error. He created many new departments of state for the purpose of recording his discoveries in an artificial language which he devised for the purpose. Each department consisted of many colleges of carefully bred and educated specialists who could understsnd the object of their own department to some extent. But the co-ordination of all, and true insight into each, lay with the great brain alone.

When some three thousand years had passed since his beginning, the unique individual determined to create others of his kind. Not that he suffered from loneliness. Not that he yearned for love, or even for intellectual companionship. But he needed the co-operation of beings of his own mental stature. He therefore designed, and had built in various regions, turrets and factories like his own, though greatly improved. Into each he sent, by his servants, a cell of his own vestigial body, and directed how it should be cultivated so as to produce a new individual. At the same time he caused operations to be performed upon himself, so that he should be remade upon a more ample plan. Of the new capacities which he inculcated in himself and his progeny the most important was direct sensitivity to radiation. This was achieved by incorporating in each brain-tissue a specially bred strain of Martian parasites. These henceforth were to live in the great brain as integral members of each one of its cells. Each brain was also equipped with a powerful wireless transmitting apparatus. Thus should the widely scattered sessile population maintain direct 'telepathic' contact with one another.

The undertaking was successfully accomplished. On the highest mountains were super-astronomers with vast observatories, whose instruments were partly artificial, partly natural excrescences of their own brains. In the very entrails of the planet others, specially adapted to heat, studied the subterranean forces, and were kept in 'telepathic' union with the astronomers. In the tropics, in the Arctic, in the forests, the deserts, and on the ocean floor, the Fourth Men indulged their immense curiosity; and in the homeland, around the father of the race, a group of great buildings housed a hundred individuals. In the service of this world-wide population, those races of Third Men which had originally co-operated to produce the new human species tilled the land, tended the cattle, manufactured the immense material requisities of the new civilization, and satisfied their spirits with an ever more stereotyped ritual of their vital art. This degradation of the whole race to a menial position had occurred slowly, imperceptibly. But the result was none the less irksome. Occasionally there were sparks of rebellion, but they always failed to kindle serious trouble; for the prestige and persuasiveness of the Fourth Men were irresistible.

For some three thousand years the Fourth Men pursued their research with constant success, but at last progress began to be slow. It was becoming increasingly difficult to devise new lines of research. True, there was still much detail to be filled in, even in their knowledge of their own planet, and very much in their knowledge of the stars. But there was no prospect of opening up entirely new fields which might throw some light on the essential nature of things. Indeed, it began to dawn on them that they had scarcely plumbed a surface ripple of the ocean of mystery. Their knowledge seemed to them perfectly systematic, yet wholly enigmatic. They had a growing sense that though in a manner they knew almost everything, they really knew nothing.

The normal mind, when it experiences intellectual frustration, can seek recreation in companionship, or physical exercise, or art. But for the Fourth Men there was no such escape. These activities were impossible and meaningless to them. The Great Brains were wholeheartedly interested in the objective world, but solely as a vast stimulus to intellection, never for its own sake. They admired only the intellective process itself and the interpretative formulae and principles which it devised. They cared no more for men and women than for material in a test-tube, no more for one another than for mechanical calculators. Nay, of each one of them it might almost be said that he cared even for himself solely as an instrument of knowing. Many of the species had actually sacrificed their sanity, even in some cases their lives, to the obsessive lust of intellection.

As the sense of frustration became more and more oppressive, the Fourth Men suffered more and more from the onesidedness of their nature. Though so completely dispassionate while their intellectual life proceeded smoothly, now that it was thwarted they began to be confused by foolish whims and cravings which they disguised from themselves. Sessile and incapable of affection, they continually witnessed the free movement, the group life, the love-making of their menials. Such activities became an offence to them, and filled them with a cold jealousy, which it was altogether beneath their dignity to notice. The affairs of the serf-population began to be conducted by their masters with less than the accustomed justice. Serious grievances arose.

The climax occurred in connection with a great revival of research, which, it was said, would break down the impalpable barriers and set knowledge in progress again. The Great Brains were to be multiplied and the whole planet devoted far more strictly to the crusade of intellection. The menial Third Men would therefore have to put up with more work and less pleasure. Formerly they would willingly have accepted this fate for the glory of serving the superhuman brains. But the days of their blind devotion were past. It was murmured among them that the great experiment of their forefathers had proved a great disaster, and that the Fourth Men, the Great Brains, were mere abortions.

Matters came to a head when the tyrants announced that all useless animals must be slaughtered, since their upkeep was too great an economic burden upon the world-community. The vital art, moreover, was to be practised in future only by the Great Brains themselves. This announcement threw the Third Men into violent excitement, and divided them into two parties. Many of those whose lives were spent in direct service of the Great Brains favoured implicit obedience, though even these were deeply distressed. The majority, on the other hand, absolutely refused to permit the impious slaughter, or even to surrender their privileges as vital artists. For, they said, to kill off the fauna of the planet would be to violate the fair form of the universe. It would be an outrage to the Life God, and he would surely avenge it. They therefore urged that the time was come for all true human beings to stand together and depose the tyrants. And this, they pointed out, could easily be done. It was only necessary to cut a few electric cables, connecting the Great Brains with the subterranean stations. The electric pumps would then cease to supply the brain-turrets with aerated blood. Or, in the few cases in which the Great Brains were so located that they could control their own source of power in wind or water, it was necessary merely to refrain from transporting food to their digestion laboratories.

The personal attendants of the Great Brains shrank from such action; for their whole lives had been devoted, proudly and even in a manner lovingly, to service of the revered beings. But the agriculturists determined to withhold supplies. The Great Brains, therefore, armed their servitors with a diversity of ingenious weapons. Immense destruction was done; but since the rebels were decimated, there were not enough hands to work the fields. Some of the Great Brains, and many of their servants, actually died of starvation. And as hardship increased, the servants themselves began to drift over to the rebels. It now seemed certain to the Third Men that the Great Brains would very soon be impotent, and the planet once more under the control of natural beings.

But the Great Brains were not yet beaten. They managed to bring forward and to multiply a strain bred from some aberrrant individuals among the Third Men. These were highly suggestible, and it was by means of this mediumistic stock that the Great Brains consolidated their position.

They produced a race of living and even intelligent near-machines whose will they could control absolutely, even at a great distance. For the new variety of Third Men was 'telepathically' united with its masters.

Thus at the last moment the Great Brains were able to put into the field an army of slaves, which they equipped with the most efficient lethal weapons. In a few months all the Third Men, save the new docile variety, were destroyed; except for a few specimens which were preserved in cages for experimental purposes. And in a few years every type of animal that was not known to be directly or indirectly necessary to human life had been exterminated. None were preserved even as specimens, for the Fourth Men, the Great Brains, had already studied them through and through.

But though the Great Brains were now absolute possessors of the Earth, they were after all no nearer their goal than before. The actual struggle with natural species had provided them with an aim; but now that the struggle was over, they began to be obsessed once more with their intellectual failure. With painful clarity they realized that, in spite of their vast weight of neural tissue, in spite of their immense knowledge and cunning, they were practically no nearer the ultimate truth than their predecessors had been. Both were infinitely far from it.

For the Fourth Men, the Great Brains, there was no possible life but the life of intellect; and the life of intellect had become barren. Evidently something more than mere bulk of brain was needed for the solving of the deeper intellectual problems. They must learn somehow to remake their own brain-tissues upon a new plan. With this aim, and partly through unwitting jealousy of the natural and more balanced species which had created them, they began to use their captive specimens of that species for a great new enterprise of research into the nature of human brain-tissue. It was hoped thus to find some hint of the direction in which the new evolutionary leap should take place. The unfortunate specimens were therefore submitted to a thousand ingenious physiological tortures. Some were kept alive with their brains spread out permanently on a laboratory table, for microscopic observation during their diverse psychological reactions. Others were put into fantastic states of mental abnormality. Others were maintained in perfect health of body and mind, only to be felled at last by some ingeniously contrived tragic experience. New types were produced which, it was hoped, might show evidence of emergence into a qualitatively higher mode of mentality; but they succeeded only in ranging through the whole gamut of insanity.

The research continued for some thousands of years, but gradually slackened, so utterly barren did it prove to be. As this frustration became more and more evident, a change began to come over the minds of the Fourth Men.

They knew, of course, that the natural species valued many things and activities which they themselves did not appreciate at all. Hitherto this had seemed a symptom merely of the low mental development of the natural species. But the behaviour of the unfortunate specimens upon whom they had been experimenting had gradually given the Fourth Men a greater insight into the likings and admirations of the natural species, so that they had learned to distinguish between those desires which were fundamental, and merely accidental cravings. In fact, they came to see that certain activities and certain objects were appreciated by these beings with the same clear-sighted conviction as they themselves appreciated knowledge. For instance, the natural human beings valued one another, and were sometimes capable of sacrificing themselves for the sake of others. They also valued love itself. And again they valued very seriously their artistic activities; and the activities of their bodies and of animal bodies appeared to them to have intrinsic excellence.

Little by little the Fourth Men began to realize that what was wrong with themselves was not merely their intellectual limitation, but, far more seriously, the limitation of their insight into values. And this weakness, they saw, was the result, not of paucity of intellective brain, but of paucity of body and lower brain tissues. This defect they could not remedy. It was obviously impossible to remake themselves so radically that they should become of a more normal type. Should they concentrate their efforts upon the production of new individuals more harmonious than themselves? Such a work, it might be supposed, would have seemed unattractive to them. But no. They argued thus. 'It is our nature to care most for knowing. Full knowledge is to be attained only by minds more broadly based than ours. Let us, therefore, waste no more time in seeking to achieve the goal in ourselves. Let us seek rather to produce a kind of being free from our limitations, in whom we may attain the goal of perfect knowledge vicariously. The producing of such a being will exercise all our powers, and will afford the highest kind of fulfilment possible to us. To refrain from this work would be irrational.'

Thus it came about that the artificial Fourth Men began to work in a new spirit upon surviving specimens of the Third Men and thus to produce their own supplanters.

Stapledon calls the handsome and indeed glorious beings that the Great Brains now produced the Fifth Men.

Since they were to have the greatest possible brain area compatible with mobility and independent function, the rest of their organisms had to be proportionately large. In fact, a race of magnificent Titans was gradually bred, though the Great Brains took care that their bodies should not be so huge that they would be hampered by their own weight or, by the necessity of having bones so massive as to be unmanageable.

Stapledon obviously sees the production of these Fifth Men with their splendid looks and their fine balance of feeling and intelligence as the climax of his long tale. He imagines them, however, as having been followed by many other races of humanoids, some of them, such as those who took to the air and those who went back to the ocean, very attractive. But the reader will probably end his book feeling that it was really these splendid Fifth Men that the author loved.

THE ANARCHIST: or
THE DOOM OF THE GREAT CITY

DOUGLAS FAWCETT

The Anarchist *is a remarkable example of nineteenth-century S.F., which turned up in a junk shop in Stoke-on-Trent; it must, judging by other dates, have been written before 1892. If the reader finds some of the technical and political details old-fashioned, let him not be too sure. There is something uncanny in the author's vision of certain not impossible political developments which fortunately never evolved. Conrad's* Through Western Eyes *shows this anarchist crew as credible.*

For technical points see, for instance, note on p. 390.

It was after having completed a series of hazardous and adventurous travels in Africa and South-west Asia that I returned to London.

To a bachelor uncle, an inveterate politician, I owed much of my later enthusiasm for reform, but when I grew up and inherited his entire property from my uncle my first passion had been for travel—the more dangerous the better.

But this time, when I got back, I found that all the time while I had been seeking adventure there had been a new world of experience, the world of politics at home, close at hand. I had by now seen 'many cities and men', and, in London, the hydra-headed problems of civilization began to enthral me. It was a time of strife, and I soon threw myself into politics with the same zeal which had carried me through the African forests, or over the dreary burning sands of Arabia.

I became, first a Radical Liberal of my old uncle's

school, then an advocate of Labour and after a short apprenticeship was adopted by my party as their parliamentary candidate for Stepney.

London, even in the early 1890s (the time of which I write), was a bloated, unwieldy city, an abode of smoke and dreariness, and moreover, at this time, its more prosperous inhabitants were startled from time to time by the angry murmurs of labour—of the disinherited. This Colossus of cities held nearly six million souls, and the social problems were intensifying. I myself, as an evolutionary socialist, was averse to barricades. What man or Convention could beat out a workable constitution with streets slippery with blood, with factories and workshops wrecked, and perhaps a starving populace? So I was opposed at Stepney by an extremist revolutionary Socialist, as well as by the sitting Conservative member. My chances of election were poor, but I meant to battle vigorously.

One evening when I was preparing some notes for one of my Stepney meetings, a caller arrived, a certain John Burnett, a journalist and agitator, a man of extreme opinions, a stalwart individual with an appearance to match—that is with a thick black beard and a singularly resolute face. He believed only in voluntary association of individuals—no law, no force: such were his substitutes for the regulating legislation of socialists like myself. But meantime he proposed violence; force was to be his watchword. He made no secret of the fact that he meant to wage war against the existing social system. Though strongly opposed to his theories, I was attached to the man. He talked loudly, but, so far as I knew, his hands had never been stained with crime. Further, he had once saved me from drowning at great risk to himself, and he had contracted a warm affection for his debtor. Burnett was a marked man, and moderate as were my own views, the authorities apparently considered that they might be a blind. This possibility had of late been officially recognized and I had reason to know that my rooms had been searched in my absence. However, as they found that I was guiltless of harbouring explosives or even subversive documents, the attentions of the police were becoming less frequent.

My anarchist caller seemed to be in a hurry and brushed aside my opening remarks on the political situation.

'Your parliamentary elections and your socialism are played out,' he said, pointing with a not unamiable grin to the notes for my speech.

'I've heard that before,' I said. 'It's rubbish! Compared with socialists you anarchists are only a handful of people of no account politically. To my mind, all your crusades, when they aren't absurd, seem criminal.'

'As you like,' he answered carelessly, 'but, you know, the world has had enough barking and the time for biting has come.'

'Rubbish,' I said again.

'Suppose,' he went on, 'it wasn't rubbish, because our people had some incalculable force behind them? Suppose, for instance, our leaders—the leaders of a few thousand only, I'll admit—possessed some novel invention, something that could make them virtual dictators?' He looked very hard at me as he spoke.

'Wasn't some sort of infernal invention the dream of Hartmann the dynamiter?' I responded. 'Now there's a typical case of something near genius wasted on anarchy! Your martyr tries to blow up a German prince and the Houses of Parliament and destroys one arch of a bridge and an apple-woman.'

'All men bungle sometimes,' growled the revolutionist, 'Hartmann with the rest—but that was ten years ago. He was young then. By the way, don't call people martyrs prematurely! You think, don't you, that he went down with that boat—the one in which he escaped?'

'What do you mean?'

'Just what I say.'

'I don't care,' I said, 'whether your Hartmann was drowned or not. If he's alive, I suppose that would be welcome news only to one person—his poor mother.'

Ten years earlier Hartmann had just failed to blow up the German Crown Prince while he was on a visit to London. By some mischance the mine exploded just after the carriages had passed over a bridge. My sneer about the apple-woman must not be taken too seriously, though it is quite true that one such unfortunate perished in the crash of the rent arch. Hartmann and Michael Swartz, his 'shadow', had escaped by boat to Holland, but the boat had gone down with, it was believed, everyone on her. I knew Mrs. Hartmann well and had been of help to her. She was a gentle, sad old lady who did good works in Islington, and I knew her well enough to know that the criminal life and the hunting to death of this son had come near to breaking her heart. Our link was a certain very charming young lady, Miss Lena Northerton, to whom I was unofficially engaged. I tell this because it was my feelings for Mrs. Hartmann and Lena's interest in her, added to my long acquaintance with Burnett, that involved me in the whole adventure.

Next time I saw Burnett—I shall not say where but can assure the reader that it was not in any public place—he was in the company of an elderly thick-set man whose face I found most unprepossessing; the small deep-set eyes had a bulldog obstinacy and the mouth was hard and cruel. Burnett introduced us.

'Here, Swartz, meet my old pal Stanley! He isn't one of us but you can trust him.'

I confess that I was taken aback at this introduction. It is seldom the sea gives up its dead.

'You don't seem much to like the look of him,' said Burnett, amused. Swartz laughed grimly.

'One does not meet celebrities like Herr Swartz every day,' I said, still staring at the man.

Swartz assured me that he and Hartmann had got off merely with a wetting. Then after a while, he began to talk wildly about world-domination by the anarchists.

'Your campaign is maniacal!' I told him, feeling nothing but contempt for such talk. 'How can a few incendiaries or dynamiters, ceaselessly dodging the law, hope to defy an organized State?'

It was then that Swartz began to rummage in his pockets. He produced a flat piece of silvery grey metal about two inches square, and one-tenth of an inch thick, which, when he handed it to me, proved to weigh no more than so much cardboard.

'Take my knife, it's steel. Hammer the thing! Test it,' said Burnett.

I could make no impression. 'What's it for?' I asked.

'You can't guess?' said Swartz condescendingly. 'It's the grandest of Hartmann's strokes! If you want to know more, and if Burnett vouches for you, on Saturday night, after you've addressed your idiotic election meeting, we three will meet and with luck you may see Hartmann as well. Would midnight in Kensington Gardens, by the pond to the left as you come in from the Queen's Road, suit you?'

I hesitated and began, instead of answering, to ask about the bit of metal. What was the secret? They refused to give me more of a clue than is contained in this marked passage in a book which Burnett took from his pocket:

'There is real impediment in the way of man navigating the air, and that is the excessive weight of the only great mechanical moving power hitherto placed at his disposal—steam. When science shall have discovered some moving power greatly lighter than any we yet know, in all probability the problem will be solved.'

I had long been, as I have said, accustomed to adventure. Indeed some of my entirely legal current parliamentary doings might be said to come under that head. The following Saturday's Stepney meeting proved to be an instance of this, for in an uproar my platform was stormed by the followers of my extremist opponent and the audience stampeded.

All the same I didn't answer directly; indeed hesitated for a long time about the proposed meeting in Kensington Gardens. At that time of night the gates would be locked and I should have to scramble over the high railings and would possibly have trouble with the police. Yet something sinister about the behaviour of the hecklers at the Stepney meeting and the real savagery of the row that developed when they stormed the platform, finally made me determine to keep the strange midnight appointment. Hartmann, remember, was a dynamiter who had already proved himself dangerous.

Because of both Burnett and old Mrs. Hartmann, I did not intend to call in the police, and yet someone clearly ought to try to find out what were these new plans at which Burnett and the much more sinister Swartz had hinted. What for one thing had that bit of grey metal to do with the matter?

If the reader thinks my final determination rash, I must remind him that this was a time of much unrest, with riots in many of our great towns, while in London mysterious handbills were appearing in unexpected places inciting the workers to violence. Somebody ought to find out what was up and I had a chance to do it. There was a further chance that, if I met them, I might (without giving Burnett away and without endangering Hartmann or even Swartz) be able to find out enough at least to give some sort of a warning in official quarters. How foolish any such hopes were to prove, the reader will judge.

Fortunately for me the sky was overcast when, near the Marble Arch, I dismissed my hansom and walked briskly along the Hyde Park side of the road and in the direction of Notting Hill.

Soon I thought I heard a scuffling.

'Over the railings!' whispered a voice from inside the Park. 'Quick, the police are on our track.' I recognized Burnett's voice.

I hesitated. They were not yet on my track!

'Will Hartmann be there?' I whispered, the demon of curiosity leading me as so often.

'Yes! But come on. Sharp!' I hesitated no longer. With Burnett's help I managed to get up and over the tall spiked railings. 'We're spotted,' Burnett whispered. 'For heaven's sake, man, run for it!'

I listened and heard the sound of someone behind us, apparently also climbing those railings. Good heavens, what a pickle, I thought. If I am arrested now, in such company, what a deluge of disgrace! So with Burnett I ran! I ran as I had never run before, but I was out of condition and the pace soon told on me.

'Keep your pecker up!' panted Burnett. 'Hartmann is waiting.'

Waiting? Yes, I thought, bitterly, waiting to be arrested with us. Half-dizzy now with fatigue I made one more desperate sprint . . .

'Here we are,' gasped my companion. It was dark and I could see nothing and, at that moment, my foot caught in a root and I fell heavily to the ground. All I remember after that is seeing two dusky forms rush up, and seeing Burnett wheeling round. Then, from some unknown spot, broke a salvo of revolver shots, a heavy body fell bleeding across my face, and I lost consciousness.

Where was I? What was certain was that I had a headache that was almost past endurance. I stretched out my hand and it touched something cold and hard. I opened an eye and saw two men bending over me. There was the sound of voices. I must be in a police cell and might have to expiate my misfortunes with shame or even death. Who was to believe my tale? Horrified, I gave utterance to a deep groan.

'There's not much up with your pal, Jack,' said a voice; 'give him some more whisky; he's knocked silly, that's all.'

What was this? I made a supreme effort and opened both eyes. The face of the man nearest me was the bearded face of Burnett, and, by all that is marvellous, by him was Michael Swartz!

'Here, take this,' said Burnett. I drank off what he offered mechanically and was soon sitting up. By the light of a dim lamp I saw that I was in a low small room about twelve feet square, with bare greyish-looking walls and a few slit-like openings near the ceiling. Chairs and a table of the same greyish colour constituted its furniture. Opposite was a low door through which blew gusts of chilly mist. Having made this rapid survey I turned in astonishment to my two stolid companions.

Swartz asked me how I had enjoyed my nocturnal run in the park. But I was too bewildered to answer. How could Burnett have carried me safe away, where could he possibly have brought me, what had become of our pursuers, where was the mysterious Hartmann and who had fired the shots?

'Where on earth am I?'

'You aren't on earth at all,' was the answer, and the two burst into a hearty laugh. 'Nor in Heaven,' added the speaker.

'Come, a truce to humbug! Am I in London, on the river, in an anarchist's haunt, or where?'

'You are not in London but above it.'

I looked at the two wonderingly. A faint light was beginning to break on my mind. But no, the thing was impossible!

'Are you able to walk now?' asked Burnett. 'Come, Swartz, you take one arm and I'll take the other. We'll give Mr. Constitutionalist a lesson. Stanley, my boy, in all your days you never saw a sight such as I am going to show you now.'

'Thank you,' I replied, 'I will lean on you, Burnett. I can do without Herr Swartz.'

We moved across the room.

'Don't be nasty to the German,' whispered Burnett. 'He's the captain's right hand. It was he who knocked over your man just now and saved you from trouble. And now just look around you.'

We were standing in a sort of open bulwarked passage which evidently ran on for some length on either side of us.

'Look below,' said Burnett.

It was very dark outside, but far *below*, as it seemed, glittered innumerable specks like stars, a contrast to the cloudy pall above us. As I gazed down into the depths I became conscious of a dull murmur like that of whirling machinery, and I soon detected a vibration of the ledge on which my elbow rested. The truth rushed upon me.

I was being carried over London in some aerial craft conjured up by Hartmann the anarchist inventor!

Horrified by the potentialities of such a vessel, in such hands, I clung to Burnett's arm.

'I am, then, on——' I gasped.

'On the deck of the *Attila*,' put in Burnett. 'Behold the craft that shall hurl tyrannies into nothingness!'

But my thought was not of the tyrannies I had left, but of the tyranny to which this accursed ship might minister. Hartmann, they said, was remorseless.

'Yes,' growled a new voice hoarsely, 'I live for the roar of dynamite.' The rough-looking speaker's looks were as unpleasant as his words.

Swartz shouted a brutal parody of Tennyson's poem:

'The dynamite falls on castle walls
And splendid buildings old in story.
The column shakes, the tyrant quakes,
And the wild wreckage leaps in glory.'

'But, man,' I cried, turning to Burnett, 'would you massacre helpless multitudes? You, who hate tyranny, would you play the tyrant?'

He nodded an affirmative. I began to feel the helpless dismay with which one confronts an inevitable calamity. At that moment some disaster to the *Attila* would have been welcome.

'We don't argue here,' went on Burnett sulkily, 'we act. If you want argument, you must wait till you see the Captain. Disputes with us are useless.'

So even Burnett was becoming surly. The 'suspect' anarchist of Stepney was courteous and argumentative, but the anarchist of the *Attila* was dogmatic and brutal. It was best to humour him, for he might perhaps stand by me at a pinch. I tried to throw oil on the troubled waters.

'You used not to mind criticism,' I said.

'Those days are past', he said. 'The Captain will always talk, but we here are tired of it. We only exist now to act —when the word is passed. So drop all your homilies for the future'.

'Yes', put in the third man present out of the darkness. 'Fifteen years of revolutionary socialist talking and nothing ever done! But wait a few weeks and we on the *Attila* will have atoned wonderfully well for arrears.'

They laughed and left me to digest their advice.

For fully an hour I must have looked down on those twinkling lights with a horror beyond the power of words. It was as Burnett had said; Hartmann's dream was realized. The exile and outcast, with his crew, now enjoyed power such as a hundred Czars could not hope for. They were all proscribed men, loathing not only the landlord and the capitalist but also the passivity of the workers. They attacked not only the abuses and defects but the foundations of society.

What they meant to do with me was uncertain. But my relations with Burnett and various things that I had been able to do for Hartmann's mother, were sufficient to avert apprehensions of violence. My endeavour then henceforth must be to try to work on the mind of Hartmann. Burnett and Swartz had hinted that, though they were sick of argument, their Captain might not only talk but listen.

This new idea seemed to offer relief, even a gleam of hope, so meantime I began to peer about at my surroundings.

What was this *Attila*—this extraordinary invention? How built? How propelled? I had just begun to do more, to feel my way in the dusk along the open gallery on which I stood, when in the dim light I saw Burnett, who soon persuaded me that since the airship was sailing with all lights doused, to explore her before daylight was impossible.

So all I discovered that night was that the *Attila*, however extraordinary her construction and motive power or however shocking her mission, had nevertheless quite ordinary domestic accommodation. My berth proved to be rather like those of the second-class cabins on an ocean liner.

'By the way,' I said, as I was getting into my bunk and as Burnett was leaving me, 'what happened in the Park?'

'Quite simple!' he answered, looking well-pleased. 'When you fell, the two detectives were on us in a moment. I wheeled round, meaning to shoot, but it was all settled from up aloft, here. *Crack*, *Crack*, came from Swartz and Hartmann. Both men got it. One spun right round and fell across you (look, your coat is covered with blood). So Swartz and Hartmann had a nice bit of sport, for the *Attila* was floating about thirty feet above the trees. After that, they lowered a ladder. I climbed up and you were hauled up unconscious. Why did we take you on board?' Burnett answered my questioning look. 'We couldn't stop, and didn't fancy the idea of leaving you stunned and in the compromising company of two dead detectives. You knew too much. It was either shoot you or take you! The Captain was in your favour. I voted for you. Your theories are rather Utopian, but you may change.'

For a while I was silent.

'Then so far as my theories go,' I said 'I will confine myself to one remark. An airship may be used as well as abused.'

Burnett laughed. 'Don't forget to define your view of "use" to the Captain. I must be off on watch!'

Just before turning in I looked closely at a jug that stood on my wash-stand. It was of the silvery-grey colour which seemed ubiquitous. A sudden thought struck me. I emptied out that jug. Its weight seemed so absurdly small that I could hardly believe my senses. The mystery of the thin silvery-grey sample was explained. It was out of such materials that the body and fittings of the *Attila* were fashioned.

My little cabin was flooded with sunlight when I woke with Burnett looking in through the door.

'Where are we?'

'Over the North Sea. Get up sharp. The Captain wants to see you. I'll give you some grub when you're dressed,' Burnett said.

Dressed? Yes, but not in that coat; the blood on it seemed to me the mark of Cain. Stepping into the next cabin where Burnett and I were, so it seemed, to eat breakfast, I was struck by two things: the coldness of the air which I attributed to the height at which we were flying, and the silvery-grey colour of everything around me from the walls and floor to the dishes and mugs. Through the door, and framed in this dull silver, I could see a magnificent cloud-picture. Mass after mass of mist seemed shaped into the shifting images of fantastic turrets, battlements and mountains drifting by.

'Beautiful, isn't it,' said Burnett. 'But where's your coat, man? Oh I remember. I'll fetch you one of mine.' He was as good as his word.

It was not till after we had eaten that I said:

'You speak of Hartmann as your captain. What authority has he got?'

'The authority of the soul of this enterprise! A couple of days ago two Italians turned what we call rusty. Hartmann shot them both where they stood, and we supported his action.'

'How many are you aboard now?'

'Twenty-five . . . eight Germans, two Russians, one Italian (now), some Swiss and the rest English.'

All this time Burnett was being very frank with me, telling me how, through his various inventions, Hartmann had raised the money to build *Attila* in Switzerland, about their friends 'down below', and how their secrets were kept. However he told me very little about the technical side of things, saying that Hartmann would tell me as much as seemed good to him, 'as much as you can understand', said Burnett with a grin.

I must pass over the beauty of what I saw as we passed along the open gallery or deck, the one on which I had lingered last night. Light clouds hung above, and there were more clouds below. Here and there, through rifts in this cloud-floor, flashed the blue waters of the sea; a low autumn sun lighted the scene and, far away, a thin streak on the horizon showed a coast.

'We shall cross over to the land at a great height,' said Burnett, following my look. 'We keep private—*Attila* is not to be seen at present.'

As he spoke I looked aloft instead of down at the sea.

Attila's underparts had the shape of a graceful ship's hull. Some thirty feet above us her lines curved inwards and the hull itself ended in a flat, railed upper deck. Over this again, however, rose a forest of thin grey poles running up to and supporting a single vast flat oblong structure, which I can only describe as a sort of roof, and which seemed to play the part of a single wing and which was higher forward than aft. Of all this, however, I only at this moment had glimpses, for Burnett would not let me linger anywhere, and we had soon stepped through one of the many doorways that led to the interior of the ship.

There is no space either to describe the many alleyways,

crew-cabins, mess-rooms, and guard- and store-rooms that made up this interior, except to say that, as far as I could judge, *Attila*'s length must have been about 240 feet and her extreme breadth about a hundred. Broader at the stern, she narrowed to a sharp bow, and on this bow, like a horn on the snout of a rhinoceros, was a conning-tower. Along each of her sides were two or three small cannons made, as I saw, of the ubiquitous grey metal. Burnett told me that we had now reached the Captain's quarters which he called 'the citadel', and which seemed to be a fortress within a fortress complete with spiked defences and mounted machine-guns. Why cannon and machine-guns, I wondered, in a ship that, as Burnett had already told me, carried bombs filled with dynamite?

But Burnett's mood did not invite questions. 'The Captain will see you alone,' he said at last as he shut a grey metal door behind me.

Seated before a writing desk, studded with the knobs of electric bells and heaped with maps and instruments, sat a man with straight piercing glance and a high forehead. There was an independent look, a cruel hardness, a cold inflexible sedateness that seemed appropriate to the dread master of the *Attila*. As I advanced into the room, he rose, a grand specimen of manhood, standing full six feet three inches in his shoes. He shook hands more warmly than I had expected, and motioned me to a seat.

'You have heard about my mischance,' I began tentatively. 'I had merely hoped just to meet you for an hour.'

I felt he was weighing me in the balance.

'Those luckless detectives were certainly embarrassing,' he replied. 'Of course, you can understand why we were bound not to leave you. And now, are you sorry that you have seen the *Attila*?'

'On the contrary, I am lost in wonder. But look, sir, the thought of those unfortunate men haunts me, and our purpose fairly appals me.'

He listened; a man in his position can afford to be tolerant.

'Oh, the two detectives! Do generals dissolve into tears when two hostile sentries have to be shot or shrink from the slaughter which every campaign entails? Nonsense, sir!'

'But your war is not against this or that army or nation, but against civilization as a whole. You can scarcely justify that.'

'Easily! The victory in view is the regeneration of man, the cost, some thousands, perhaps hundreds of thousands, even millions of lives. The assailants are our own small but legitimate army. At the worst we shall shed no more blood than did a Tamerlane or a Napoleon.'

'The ideal may be a grand one, but your crew? Most, I will venture, love destruction for its own sake. Is Swartz a reformer?'

'My crew? Every man is selected by myself. Every man is an outlaw from society, and most have shed blood. They burn to revenge on society the evils which they have received. They are like the creatures generated in decaying bodies. They are the maggots of civilization, the harvest of the dragons' teeth sown in past centuries. It is the sins of this industrial age which have bred the crew of this death-dealing *Attila.*'

At last I asked him the question that had most puzzled me with this sort of 'army'. What next step did he plan?

'How,' I asked him, 'do you propose to conquer, even though you now have the *Attila*?'

'When I attack there will be outbreaks of violence in every great city in Europe. We have some 12,000 adherents in London (my first objective), many more in Paris. When *Attila* rains down a tempest of bombs, anarchists who make up our ground-force will fire the streets in all directions, rouse up the populace, and let pandemonium loose. In such confusion, order and precautions will be impossible.'

'You horrify me. And the object?'

'To wreck the present kind of civilization. We want no more "systems", or "constitutions". In the future men will effect everything by voluntary association, and especially abjure the foulness of modern wage-slavery. If such a state of things cannot be established at once, the *Attila*, and of course consorts of hers soon to be built, will sail the air. Some supervision must no doubt be exercised at first.' He broke off and then resumed: 'One word, Mr. Stanley, I ask you neither to join us nor to agree with us. Should you dislike this tour, at nightfall you shall be landed in France. My mother, whom I have just visited, tells me that you have been a good friend to her. I am your debtor for that and, least of all men, do I forget debts! If you stay, I only ask you never to interfere in anything you see in progress. Which is it to be?'

I hesitated. At last I looked him in the eye and said: 'I elect to stay. I can do no good by leaving, and by staying I shall at least have an absolutely unique experience.'

'Good!' he answered. 'Now come and see something of the *Attila*,' and with that he strode out on to the deck and I followed him.

'What was that land visible just now, Captain?' I asked presently.

'Holland. Tonight we shall cross France, and on to Switzerland. We shall stop over a forest not far from the Lake of Geneva, where some fifty delegates will meet us. After that we return to London.'

'For war?'

'For war.'

Down into the depths of the *Attila* we went, turning off at last into a passage brightly lit with the electric light. A rumble and thud of machinery broke on the ear and we stood in the engine-room of the *Attila*.

My readers are aware of the wonderful advances in electricity that were made in the early part of the twentieth century. In the mechanism of this engine-room the appropriation of the best modern inventions left nothing to be desired. Electricity, according to a newly introduced method, was being generated directly from coal; thus the force at the disposal of the aeronaut was colossal, and, what was even more expedient, obtained for a trifling outlay of fuel.*

I was soon on the way to solving the riddle of the *Attila*'s flight. The buoyancy of the vessel was that of an inclined plane driven rapidly through the air by a screw. Albeit light, she was, of course, under normal conditions, greatly heavier than the quantity of air she displaced. Desirous of probing the problem to the bottom I asked, pointing to the propeller shaft:

'What would happen supposing that shaft broke, or the machinery somehow got out of order?'

'We should fall, but very gradually at first, as long as our speed was fairly well maintained. The air-wing, as you

* An expert has drawn the editor's special attention to this passage for the author seems (in 1892) to hint at the Bacon fuel cell, an invention which has not yet (in 1966) gone into production.

An article in the *New Scientist* for November 4th, 1965, further corroborates this idea of anticipation for its author suggests that, for various reasons, a derivative of coal (coal-tar rather than coal itself) might one day be a source of power where lightness was important. This article ends with the sentence, 'Might we thus, in pleasant paradox, see coal, the venerable fuel, supersede petroleum in this advanced field?'

know, will only buoy us up on the condition that we move, and that pretty quickly. There are two spare steering screws to fall back on.'

'What if they stopped?'

'The sand-valves would have to be opened.'

'The sand-valves?'

'Yes. You have doubtless been surprised at the huge size of the *Attila*. Well, the main parts of the upper and middle portions of her hull are a succession of compartments filled with hydrogen at a high temperature. Below these compartments again lie the sand-reservoirs. When these are are three parts full the effect is to keep the *Attila* at about sea level, supposing, that is to say, that the screws are completely stopped. By releasing ballast we can regulate our weight. The secret of it all is the marvellous lightness of these walls. I am not free to tell you to what discovery that lightness is due.'

Hartmann went on to satisfy me about a number of other things: that a normal landing was possible, as well as the sort of hovering of which I had been a dazed witness in Kensington Gardens. Powerful springs fitted to landing wheels gave her, so he said, the sort of landing that an albatross makes, when with outspread, motionless wings, the bird comes down on to the ocean.

About the technique of making up the loss of the hydrogen which had had to be discharged on landing or other descent he was equally convincing. They apparently carried immense spare stores of the gas in tubes, kept under pressure of many thousands of pounds to the square inch.

Finally, he showed me what he called 'the magazine'—the hold in which the dynamite, in its containers, would soon be carried. This hold was fitted with racks and communicated with a trap-door. He seized a ring, lifted the trap and showed me the empty air, or rather the clouds and sea, below us. 'That opening will vomit disaster one day,' he said with satisfaction.

The Captain left me, with a few words of explanation, in the crew's quarters. His men wore no uniform except that each had a red stocking-cap of the kind that bargemen sometimes have. To my surprise they seemed quite friendly. They were proud of their ship and soon began to explain to me the process of what they called 'sanding up' and also of refilling the hydrogen reserves. These processes, they told me, would be the next thing on the *Attila*'s programme. They also described the technique of coming down in the dark. They would settle on to a spit of land off the Dutch coast—her secret depot among the dunes.

I must pass over the elegant way in which, later on, these manoeuvres were in fact performed, and the more sinister filling of the great magazine with dynamite-sticks and bombs. Neither have I space to tell of the beauty of the tranquil parts of our journeys, to Holland, and to near Geneva, or of the terror of the time when, over the North Sea and flying very high, we were caught in a thunderstorm with winds that rose to hurricane force, the drama being made more poignant by the spectacle on the raging waters below us of a dismasted and funnel-less passenger-steamer, which after tossing and wallowing broadside on among steep seas finally sank with all hands. A far worse sea-episode was on our return when, having 're-sanded' and taken in both ammunition and extra hydrogen, we deliberately sank a warship 'for practice'.

'I trust your nerves are in order, Mr. Stanley?' asked the Captain.

It was the morning of October 19th, that memorable

day in the history of revolutions. I had ascended to the upper deck. Some few yards in front of me the platform tapered off to a point at the convergence of the bow railings, and directly in front of this the hull sloped downwards and outwards to form the projecting ram. At the extremity of this rose the conning-tower. Amidships and astern hummed the forest of stays and props which hung us to the air-wing, clustering thick over the rounded boss of the citadel. We were flying over the coast and had just sighted Brighton through the haze,

Secrecy needing no longer to be observed, the *Attila* soon swept down like an albatross into the sight of men. Gliding at about two hundred feet above the water she must have presented a truly majestic spectacle. Certainly the esplanade and the beach soon buzzed with wonder beneath us, and, as we skimmed over the housetops beyond them, the street seemed to fill as if by magic. Thunders of applause rose behind us as awe regularly gave place to admiration.

'They will sound a different note tonight,' said the bitter Swartz, who was standing by me. The *Attila* flew on, always keeping about a hundred and fifty feet from the ground and deliberately courting the observation which she had so lately shunned. Of her purpose or ownership no sign, however, was given.

Now, for the first time in my life, I fairly revelled in the incense of my fellow-creatures' astonishment. At about ten o'clock we passed over East Grinstead and shortly afterwards crossed the boundary into Surrey.

And now there fell on me the shadow of the coming disaster. The faces of the crew were savage; even Burnett had lost his good comradeship and was surly. He asked with a sneer how I liked my position. Nettled, I told him that at any rate my hands would be free from bloodstains.

'The drama opens in an hour,' said the Captain as he passed on his way to the conning-tower. 'Within three days London will be in ruins, and Lord Macaulay's New Zealander will be able to commence his archaeological survey of an extinct civilization.'

'Is there no way of avoiding the horror of what you propose? In the name of humanity, Captain, I beseech you to pause! Think, if your schemes fail, as well they may! Think of the agonies which this awful resolve must breed! Think——'

'No more of this,' the Captain said sharply. 'London, I say just as Cato said of Carthage, London must be destroyed.'

'Thank heaven this will be no catastrophe of my making,' I replied. 'And now may I ask a rather leading question?'

He paused at this and answered:

'At the worst you can only be refused an answer.'

'Where will the first blow be struck?'

'Above the Houses of Parliament. A blank discharge from the cannon will warn all, after which my flag will be run out. We shall conduct the attack in three ways, by shell-firing and machine-gun fire, by dynamite in bombs and other containers, and by streams of burning petroleum. Meantime, our associates will be spreading devastation below. The Houses of Parliament, the City, and the West End will occupy us in turn.'

He turned and left me. I knew that I was as helpless as a bluebottle in a spider's web. Looking over the rail I could see that petroleum was being poured into tanks formed by fitting cross-walls into parts of the lower gallery. There were some eight of these along the bow-end of the vessel alone, and I trembled to think of the fearful mischief these hideous contrivances portended. Lamentations of this sort were, however, futile.

Casting a glance over the landscape I saw Caterham vanishing beneath us. We were now going at a higher speed and, in a short time—far too short to my thinking—were skimming over Croydon, Norwood Junction, and the Crystal Palace. We were now getting near our destination, and our altitude, recently raised to one of five hundred and fifty feet, was once again altered to one hundred and fifty. The speed, too, was soon reduced, till at last, gliding gracefully over Lambeth, we passed obliquely across Westminster Bridge.

The scene here beggars description. An enormous crowd, which had already massed for some great labour demonstration, was there to greet us and had usurped every available patch of standing room. Windows and roofs became animated, and vehicles of all sorts pulled up in batches and served as the vantage ground of excited groups. Probably the arrival at Brighton had been at once telegraphed to the newspaper offices, but to the majority we came as a complete surprise and at the outset it was clear enough that the airship inspired no terror. Cheers shook the air and the distant thunder of applause rumbled far away down the Embankment.

What mockery it was! The populace thought they were applauding an inventor and they cheered a ruthless destroyer! The hour had come, Big Ben's tower rose only twenty yards from us.

Suddenly, on board, a gong sounded ominously. It was the signal. Our four quick-firing guns vomited flame simultaneously, and before the crash had died away, a blood-red flag was fluttering at the stern. The crew yelled with excitement, for the *coup* was evilly romantic. The flag bore five ominous words—THUS RETURNS HARTMANN THE ANARCHIST.

The gunfire gave a shock never to be forgotten. The

cheering ceased in an instant, and in its place curses and howls rose up from the mob.

'Vermin!' yelled one of the crew. 'You will howl louder soon.'

The words had scarcely left his lips when the *Attila* was sharply propelled onwards, the force being such as to cause me to grasp the railing to save myself from falling. The object of this manoeuvre was evident. It was necessary to rise, now that we were recognized, and active operations were to commence. After a series of wheels the *Attila* climbed high above the clock tower and commenced to cruise about in large circles.

The gong sounded once more. Once more the quick-firing guns vomited flame and, mingling with their almost continuous roar, there now came a crash of appalling magnitude, shaking the very recesses of one's brain. Another and another followed, till the air seemed to beat in waves upon us. Then followed a rattle like that of a landslip. I looked over to start back with a shriek. Horror of horrors, the great clock tower had fallen on the crowd, crushing into jelly a legion of buried wretches and beating into ruins the whole mass of buildings opposite. Of the Houses of Parliament the pinnacles were collapsing and walls were being riven asunder as the shells burst within them.

With eyes riveted now to the massacre I saw clearings made by the shells and instantly filled up; house fronts crushing horses and vehicles as they fell; fires bursting out on all sides, and terrified police struggling wildly and helplessly in the heart of the press. The roar of the guns was continuous. I saw Burnett, black with grime, hounding his comrades on to the slaughter. I heard the roar of Swartz's bombs, and the crash of the burning and falling houses. Huge circles of flame raved beneath us. The *Attila*, drunk with slaughter, was careering in continually fresh tracts, spreading havoc and desolation everywhere.

The morning passed in horror but the afternoon and evening were wilder yet. The sky, overcast with clouds and black with uprolling smoke-wreaths, lay like a spotted pall over the blazing district. Around and within Westminster enmity could do no more and the *Attila* drew off, climbed upwards into the heavens and, hidden in the cloud masses, gave London a momentary respite. Hartmann wished to reserve the crew for the attack on the City. 'Paralyse this heart,' he said, 'and you paralyse credit and the mechanism of finance almost universally.'

The respite was not long, but during the whole time we kept well veiled within the angry zone of clouds. Burnett came up to speak to me, but I received him coldly enough. Swartz was 'surprised that I had no compliment' for him when 'even the Captain' was pleased. He remarked that the slaughter had been prodigious, that the Houses of Parliament were wrecked and the flames were carrying everything before them.

Towards four o'clock the *Attila* began to redescend. We were evidently not unexpected, for I made out soldiery in the streets and several detachments of artillery. How they expected to wing us I really don't know, for a moving airship hurling dynamite is neither an easy nor a pleasant target. Our descent stopped at the half-mile limit. There was no delay this time. The first and second bombs fell on the Tower of London, reducing it half to ruins; they were of the largest kind and terribly effective. Meanwhile the quick-firing guns played havoc at all points of the compass. As we rode over the heart of the City, that sanctum of capital with the Bank of England, the Royal Exchange, the Stock Exchange, lying helpless, the bombs fell in a tempest, shattering fabric after fabric, in a constant roar of explosions. The loss of life must have been terrible. Burnett, handling his gun like a practised marksman, sprayed St. Paul's, and Swartz's bombs did the rest. The crash of the infalling dome rose even above the general uproar. But for Burnett there was retribution. Hitherto, we had escaped being hit; the motion and height of the *Attila* were in our favour. But, as fate would have it, a volley of grape-shot now struck us. From the sides of the airship they rebounded (steel armour would have been more easily pierced) but a stray shot hit Burnett as he was gazing over the side through the smoke at the wreckage, and holed his throat. He fell back with a gurgle, the blood spurting from his carotid artery like jets from a siphon. In less than a minute he was dead.

I felt no ray of sympathy, for by this time I was dead to all feelings except those of helpless hatred for the anarchists and horror at the hideous slaughter below. Could I have killed Hartmann I would gladly have paid the price for it. But his day of reckoning was to come.

The death of Burnett drove the crew to frenzy; their curses were not those of men but of fiends. The fury that one blow of their despised victims should have told, goaded them into the mood of Molochs. The news flew to Hartmann, who returned a welcome answer. The yells around me were broken by a burst of laughter.

'What is it?' I asked, fearful of some new horror, full as the measure of crime now seemed.

'Wait and see!' was all the reply I got.

The *Attila* began to move at a high speed, and four of the men rushed down on to the lower deck. We were swooping on the City like a falcon. I was at the rail in a moment and, careless of uprushing shot and shell, bent over the side.

Down we swept again like a hurricane over yelling,

maddened throngs massed in Farringdon Street. Suddenly I heard a sharp cry. 'Stand off!'

A column of flame shot up our side, reddening the very bar I had been clutching and a stream of fire like a comet's tail drew out in the wake of the *Attila*. It was the contents of the first tank of petroleum pouring its flaming contents over the shrieking wretches below! For full fifty to sixty yards the blaze filled the roadway, and the mob, lapped in flame, were writhing and wrestling within it. A fiendish revenge was glutted.

By this time darkness should have been coming down rapidly, but there was too much light. I staggered to the stern. We were now circling over Fleet Street and the neighbourhood of the Strand. The fires lighted at Westminster in the morning had now increased and were carrying all before them, so that a crimson-yellow rim stretched all the way from Whitehall to Victoria, while on our right the City blazed. Now for the first time I saw that others were hurrying on the incendiary work below. There were visible blazing circles in South London over the river, blazing circles far away in North London. Hartmann's ground force had kept their faith and were active. I shuddered to think what these brutes or the mob might do. The West End was even now probably being looted and the worst passions would toll its death-knell. Suddenly I shook with terror.

I must explain that, in Holland while sanding up, we had picked up a member of Hartmann's London 'ground forces', and Hartmann had given me permission to send a letter by him advising my fiancée, Lena Northerton, and her parents to leave London for a day or two and to take old Mrs. Hartmann with them—giving, of course, no reason for such a strange bit of advice. This letter had been given to Burnett to pass on and now suddenly I began to doubt whether he had in fact remembered to do this. Kneeling by the body I ransacked the dead man's clothes and my worst fears were realized. In his breast pocket still lay the paper with the message.

I was frantic. Hartmann of course would not see me, but I managed to get the message to him that the warning to Lena, and consequently to his mother, had not been delivered. I told him to look below and to guess what their fate might be. I begged him to land me.

'The *Attila* can land no one,' came back a message in answer, 'but you may have my parachute. We cross Hyde Park shortly.'

The prospect of such an exit was gruesome, for I realized that the parachute descent, though bad enough, was not likely to be my greatest danger. This thought was reinforced by the fact that Hartmann had added to his gift of a parachute that of a revolver. The feel of the weapon in my hand helped to make me realize that, if I were seen coming down, I ran the risk of being instantly torn to pieces—or worse.

The process of being dropped was horrible, as I had feared it might be. First I had to go down a swinging rope-ladder from that trap from which the dynamite bombs had been dropped, then I had a parachute without a harness to which it was a case of clinging by one hand before letting go of the oscillating ladder.

I can scarcely bear, even now, to think of the moment when I kicked my feet free of the ladder. However, I was fortunate, I cleared it, cleared also the airship's wheels, the parachute bellied out, and, finally, the wind blew me not only clear of the trees, but of the terrified or brawling crowds with which the dark Park now swarmed.

So far I had been lucky. But now, if I were to reach Lena, I had to face the streets. As I got near the Bayswater

Road, I came upon crowds of fugitives from the fire and from the looting mobs. Aristocrats, plutocrats, and tradespeople were huddled into groups; many of the men carried weapons, and it was well for them and their convoys when they did so, for bands of ruffians were prowling round robbing, insulting, and murdering at random.

The terrible licence here boded no good for Lena and her parents, always supposing the Northertons had received no benefit from the guarded hints given by her son to Mrs. Hartmann. I had cause to fear that these hints must have been far too vaguely worded, in which case nothing was more likely than that they had been ignored. Who unless clearly warned would have looked for a revolution so sudden and mysterious as this? Hartmann had, I knew, visited his mother and had of course wished also to warn her of these impending horrors. He might well have robbed his well-meant caution of the emphasis and impressiveness it called for.

A bright light shot downwards trom the sky on a patch of buildings which were immediately lapped in flames. I understood; the drama was running its third act; the *Attila* had once again exchanged the part of dynamiter for that of an aerial *pétroleuse.* I joined the tumultuous yelling mob that flowed like a river in freshet along Bayswater Road in the direction of Notting Hill. What a gauntlet I had to run! The mansions lining the thoroughfare were being looted by the dozen and their inmates shamefully maltreated or butchered, while in many places the hand of the incendiary was crowning the work of destruction. It was opposite these last-mentioned places that the struggles of the mob were most arduous. After a house had been alight for some time, the passage past it necessarily became dangerous, but owing to the steady pressure of the mass of people from behind no one once entangled in the mob could hope to avoid it. Numberless deaths occurred by the mere forcing of the fringe of the crowd on to the red-hot pavements, and into the yellow and ruddy mouths of the outleaping jets of flame and these were terrible sights to witness.

One could get into the stream easily enough, but getting free of it was quite out of the question. On the one side I saw men and women crushed, trampled on, and suffocated against the railings. On the other I saw scores forced into the flames which their own comrades had kindled. The safest place was in the current that was now sweeping me along, a current which ran some three feet off the pavement on the left, a place fairly out of reach of the flames and blasts of heat from the houses on the opposite side. Right ahead of me from the Queen's Road Station downwards to Westbourne Grove the streets on both sides were being fired by bands of ruffians whose red stocking-caps, like those worn by the *Attila's* crew, told who they were. These were followed by armed companies of marauders. Not a soldier, volunteer, or policeman was visible. As I passed a shop vomiting clouds of smoke and sparks a miserable woman rushed out and clung to my knees in a frenzy, entreating me to save her. Two of the red-caps dashed after her in hot pursuit, but I lost no energy in parley. In less time than it takes to write of it I shot them down, and dragged my charge into the centre of the roadway.

'I can't stay!' I shouted. 'Work your way up the street into the crowd going to Shepherd's Bush. It's safer there.' Then I plunged once more down the street—between the fiery houses, over smoking stone heaps and rafters till, with singed clothes and almost stifled with smoke I found myself in Westbourne Grove. Here I saw a terrified horse lying between the poles of a splintered cart. I was going to shoot him out of mercy, when the thought struck me that he might be useful. Hastily loosening the harness, I helped the poor beast to rise, and jumping on his back galloped down the Grove. Within ten minutes I found myself on the pavement outside Lena's home: there tethering my horse to the railings, I leaped up the steps to the Northertons' door. Furiously I plied the knocker, and beat on the panels with my revolver-butt, till I heard old Northerton shout angrily through the letter-slot: 'Who's there?'

'Stanley, Arthur Stanley,' I answered, and the door instantly opened. 'Your wife and Lena?' I asked anxiously.

'My wife is inside, but we are in a fever about the child, she has not returned. She went out early this morning.'

'Where? D'you know the streets are a shambles?'

'My God! yes; but where she has gone we can't tell. The cook heard her say that she went to see an old lady in Islington.'

'What? Islington! Are you sure?'

'Yes, why?'

'Because I know the place. I can guess where she went. There's no call for panic; I'll start at once.'

'Godspeed,' he said. There was no time for questions.

I was out of the hall in a moment and in another had untethered and sprung upon the horse. It was in Islington that old Mrs. Hartmann lived.

I should perhaps explain at this point that, though Lena and I were engaged, the fact had so far been kept from her parents, who were much better off than I was ever likely to be, and being of the old school might also, we had supposed, not view their only daughter's marriage to a Socialist with much enthusiasm, though in fact Lena had long shared my opinions. They did not know this or that

Lena had for long been a friend and comforter to Mrs. Hartmann towards whose little Islington villa I was now trotting and cantering as fast as I could get the horse to go.

It was night now and the street-lamps were of course unlighted, but the glow of the innumerable fires cast a red and ghastly glow along all the streets. As I galloped through Marylebone I caught glimpses of the *Attila* wheeling far away over Kensington, still busy with her work of destruction.

It must have been ten o'clock by the time I reached Mrs. Hartmann's house. Throwing the reins over the railings and revolver in hand I made for its door.

The little ground-floor room which I knew well was full of people, but they were clearly not rioters. People had taken refuge there, among them a Sister of Charity and a number of small children. My entrance—unkempt, dirty and flourishing a revolver—naturally alarmed them. I looked round, just as alarmed as they were, for neither Lena nor old Mrs. Hartmann were to be seen and, in an agony, I asked where they were.

'Mrs. Hartmann is dying.' It was the Sister of Charity who answered. 'Miss Northerton is not hurt and is with her.'

So Lena was safe. The relief was so great that in my state of fatigue and with the need for immediate action over, I could have broken down there and then. However, it was not long before Lena and I were in each other's arms, and this restored me.

It was not till later, in fact till after Mrs. Hartmann's death, that I heard the story of how, knowing nothing of what was to happen, they had gone together to Westminster with the idea of seeing the great labour demonstration. When the *Attila* opened fire they had become involved in the panicking crowds. When Big Ben fell they had been trapped, the old lady fell, was trampled on and, as it proved, sustained grave internal injuries. With great difficulty Lena had managed with kindly help to get her clear and then to find a cart and bribe a driver. They had picked up various sufferers on the way, had at last managed to get clear of the central districts, and when Lena got her home she had had good hopes that Mrs. Hartmann was snatched from death. But haemorrhage had set in and, from fainting and weakness, Mrs. Hartmann had passed into a coma. She had however just had time to dictate a letter to her son, and had begged Lena to find some means either of transmitting it, or at least of getting its gist through as a message.

Mrs. Hartmann, of course, had no idea that it was her son who was the prime cause of the horrors she had seen (and incidentally of her death) but she guessed that he might in some way be mixed up in it and in her letter she begged him in the most pathetic terms to realize that his courses were wicked. She died about an hour after my arrival.

At last I was able to tell Lena of the extraordinary experiences through which I had passed in the few days since I had last seen her. Lena listened with the keenest interest and it appalled and astonished her that the son of the poor harmless friend whose eyes we had just closed should be responsible for such hideous slaughter and destruction; indeed at moments she seemed hardly to believe my tale.

'But did you not see the airship for yourself?' I asked

'No, we were hopelessly jammed up in the crowd near Whitehall. The wildest rumours were flying about, the crowd was murderous either from panic or because they were being harried by bands of men in red stocking-caps.'

That badge again, I thought. Through the window I suddenly saw a bright trail of light.

'Look, Lena! Look! There she is! Now will you believe me?' The airship sailed with her bombs flashing as they fell, and the streams of petroleum followed in rivers of fire. Lena gasped and we stood riveted with horror at the window. The *Attila* with her searchlight, her one electric eye, stood out sharply against clouds that were crimson from the glow of the fires. She was pouring out petroleum, and flames from the gutted buildings seemed to leap up to meet her; indeed she seemed mad with the irresponsibility of strength. With our recent experiences of the horrible consequences of such attacks fresh in our minds, we hardly dared to think of the effects of this renewal of the conflagration.

'If he is up there as you say,' said Lena doubtfully, 'what about that letter?'

'I shall do my best to deliver it' I answered grimly. 'May it bring some sort of repentance! Nothing else seems to move him. But there are other great cities . . . . here and on the Continent and he may not be slaked even yet.'

I thought of my horse again; he was the best means I had for getting Lena back to her parents. We waited a while but the *Attila* came no nearer, and so we mounted and with Lena behind me, we managed that strange ride across London.

The joy of her parents and their gratitude to me, whom they persisted in regarding as a hero and Lena's rescuer, was very great. In fact our midnight ride had been, in my estimation, only an affair of two people on one horse, for we had been unmolested. However their gratitude suited us very well as seeming to give me some claim to Lena and it was not long before they were in possession of our secret which had, it seemed, long been guessed by them.

But we two were exhausted, and though there seemed a lull in the air raid and though they would gladly have heard my story immediately, yet, with old Mr. Northerton and his manservant keeping vigil armed to the teeth, we gave way to our extreme fatigue. It was, then, not till next morning that the story of my adventures was told, and the astonishment of my hearers knew no bounds. They had wondered greatly at my absence, but were now of opinion that to have sailed the air in the *Attila* was a privilege the historian would grudge me. I answered that the spectacle of the great massacre was so far from being a privilege that the bare memory of it horrified me. Had I known what to expect I should have accepted Hartmann's offer and been promptly landed somewhere on the Continent.

My narrative having come to an end, we were speculating on the further outlook, when a tramp of feet arrested us and all four of us rushed to the window. A regiment of volunteers was marching briskly towards the Park, their bayonets flashing brightly in the sunlight. Had the forces of order rallied? Had the progress of the *Attila* been checked? I was soon in the street, greedy for information. Accosting an officer, I asked him what was the news. He said that the airship had ceased dropping petroleum, that a vigorous reaction had taken place, that the conflagrations were partly checked, while the 'ground' anarchists were being driven from the streets with bullet and cold steel. I ran back into the house, and, shouting the good news to old Northerton, enlisted him forthwith for an expedition. We would make our way to Hyde Park, and find out more from the crowds who would be sure to gather there.

Mrs. Northerton and Lena protested, but very little attention, I am afraid, was paid to them. Taking a satchel of provisions and a couple of flasks of claret with us, we left the ladies to brood over our temerity. Though it seemed improbable that chance would favour me, I stuffed into my breast-pocket poor Mrs. Hartmann's last letter. It certainly would not be my fault if her fiendish son failed to get it.

We followed the marching regiment till Westbourne Grove was reached. The heat, smoke, and dust here were intolerable, and whole clumps of buildings were still blazing. A stranger with whom we got into conversation told us that all through the night fires were being kindled in every direction by the airship. It had been discovered that hundreds, if not thousands, of confederates on the ground were pushing on this abominable work, and that these by inciting the mob to violence had greatly helped to swell the terrible list of catastrophes. He added that the airship had drawn off awhile and was wheeling idly around Hyde Park in wide circles, occasionally discharging her guns whenever the crowds grew dense. Meantime, order had been partially restored; the military had been called out; the police, at first helpless, had rallied; and volunteer regiments and special police corps were pouring on to the different scenes of action. Anarchists and rioters were being shot down in batches and it was believed that all co-operation with the airship from below had been at last extirpated. Then came an announcement which moved me to barely repressed excitement. The airship, during the early morning, had been seen to descend in the Park and to deposit four men, subsequently rising to her former altitude. The police were now searching for them in all directions, and it was said that their arrest was imminent.

'She is still hovering about over the park,' our informant concluded. As we hurried on, I began to think about all this. Swartz, I knew, had been prepared to descend. But why four for an errand for which one alone had been originally told off Perhaps despite the devastation he had caused, Hartmann was dissatisfied? After all his vast outlay of energy and material had not effected the ruin of as much as one-fifth part of the great city. Perhaps the resources of the *Attila* were becoming strained, and it was necessary to devise some new and less costly mode of attack. Of the lull in the work of the anarchist incendiaries Hartmann must early have got wind, but not knowing the cause of it, and anxious to secure a redoubled activity below—now so indispensable to his success—he had perhaps dispatched four of the crew to fan their energies into fury. That their efforts would be futile now seemed to me certain.

Just then a squad of soldiers passed by escorting some incendiaries, whose brutal faces, filthy with grime, filled us with loathing and anger. They were to be shot in a neighbouring mews. But these faces seemed unfamiliar to me—all alike of a low grade of ruffianism such as every great city breeds, but which never declares its strength till the day of weakness arrives. But suddenly one of the wretches who lagged somewhat behind the rest, received a sharp cuff from a soldier, and in the volley of curses that followed I recognized a well-known and long-detested voice. It was that of Michael Swartz who, bruised, handcuffed, befouled with grime and dirt, was being driven like a bullock to a slaughterhouse. How savage a despair must have goaded him in the last four minutes of his dark life!

After half an hour we found ourselves in Hyde Park. Our informant had not misled us. High above the grass circled the *Attila*; her graceful flight and vast bulk, her silvery grey sides, her long red flag streaming over the screwblades, her ramlike horned bow, and, above all, her now hideous repute, rendered her a weirdly conspicuous object. Old Mr. Northerton's face was a picture; the look he bent on me was one of unconcealed wonder at the airship and of deep respect for his would-be son-in-law, who had actually trodden its deck. He seemed fascinated by the air vessel, and lamented loudly that its conception should have lodged in so unworthy and fiendish a mind.

'Think what a good man might have effected for his kind, for their creature-comforts and commerce, for the cause of science and culture. A fleet of such ships would make England monarch of the nations and arm her with power to sweep away hordes of iniquities. War could be stamped out and universal arbitration substituted for it.'

'Until France or Russia began to launch similar fleets,' I answered, for it seemed clear enough that nations who could fight with armies and ironclads would have no insuperable prejudice against fighting with airships. In practice inventions of this character cannot be permanently kept secret.

There were few persons in Hyde Park, for the dread of the airship was universal. Her guns singled out crowds, and any symptom of their formation in the park speedily corrected itself. Outside the railings, indeed, there were plenty of onlookers, but there the military patrolled the streets, along with mounted police. I was told by a bystander that severe fighting was going on in East London, but that nothing serious of late was reported from the West End. This sounded all very well, but what, I asked, if the *Attila* was once more to reopen fire? How about the restoration of order then? Would regiments clear the streets under bomb showers, would police hunt down incendiaries in spite of petroleum? The man admitted that in that case chaos must follow, but all the same he reckoned the vessel was emptied.

'She can't hold much more stuff at any rate.'

I was gazing at the onlookers around us when a strange group caught my eye. Two men had just entered the Park, followed by a third with his hat pulled well forward over his brow. The two men in advance were talking excitedly.

Something in their faces riveted my attention and as they came nearer, I recognized three members of the crew. What were they doing here? My notion was that their mission had failed, that their associates were being shot down, and that they were now seeking a haven in the *Attila*. But was it possible that they could be picked up by the *Attila* in the broad light of day in the face of the crowd, police, and military? Whatever the explanation might be—one thing was clear, the chance for my letter had come! As one of them—a man named Norris—passed me I looked him full in the face—he grew pale as death, and I saw him feel for his revolver. Evidently he thought that I should denounce him. No such plan had crossed my mind. Hateful to me as were these anarchists, they had treated me well on the *Attila*. Honour shielded even the enemies of the human race from such scurvy return.

Brushing against Norris I whispered: 'A letter—for the Captain,' stuffing it dexterously into his hand at the same time. This action passed wholly unnoticed. Norris himself passed on hurriedly, directing his steps to the central portion of the park. I watched the three anarchists till they reached an almost deserted spot, about 400 yards off, and it then became evident that they were bent on signalling to the *Attila*. For aught I knew Hartmann in his conning-tower was even now sweeping the grass with his powerful field-glass.

I saw Norris produce something out of the breast of his coat. The three anarchists then lay down on the grass and seemed to be awaiting some answer. The device adopted was simple. To ensure notice they had agreed to exhibit a large yellow flag, and for security's sake they had unrolled this at full length on the grass, lying around it at the same time so as to screen it from observation. The problem remaining over was how the *Attila* was to get them safely on board. She was, perhaps, 250 feet above them at the moment, and the difficulty in such a situation seemed almost insuperable.

Suddenly a cry from Mr. Northerton arrested me. The airship was curving swiftly in and out, so as to trace a sort of descending spiral. Then when nearly over the flag she stopped almost dead, and seemed to be falling rapidly.

'It's falling! It's falling!' yelled Mr. Northerton. 'It's done for!'

But I knew better.

The *Attila* sank slowly to the ground. The police, military, and spectators outside and inside the railings rushed forward to the scene with loud cries of exultation. All were seized with the desire to vent their rage on the foe who now seemed to have lost his might. It was with the greatest trouble that I held Mr. Northerton back. He was carried away by the sight of the thousands streaming into the park and converging in masses on the fallen monster. They were now close up. Several rifle cracks told that the soldiers to the fore were already hotly engaged, were perhaps striving to storm the hull.

And then came a dread disenchantment.

As the rabble closed on the airship she gave a huge heave, her bow swinging over her assailants like the tilted arm of a see-saw. Next, the stern cleared the turf and the colossus rose majestically, rolling the while like some ship riding at anchor. The gnats who clung to her dropped off confusedly, and the whole multitude in her neighbourhood seemed bewildered with surprise and terror. Suddenly the *Attila* was enveloped in flame and smoke; the roar of her big pieces mingling with the cracks of the machine-guns and the rifle fire that spurted from the loop-holes in her armour. Lanes were cut in the crowd in all directions and a hail of bullets whistled past the spot where we stood, many claiming their victims around us. Discretion, not valour, was our choice. We made wildly for the outlets towards which the screaming mob rushed behind us, and, once through them, made our way rapidly down the street. Having run some few hundred yards we stopped and saw with dismay how narrow had been our escape. The *Attila* was still rising majestically with her quick-firing guns playing on the multitude as a hose plays on flames. The wretched victims were fighting for the blocked gates and outlets, bloody gaps opened and shut in their midst, and heaps of butchered and trampled bodies tripped up the frantic survivors as they ran. The picture lingers vividly in my memory: the cloudy pall above, the still smoking and ruined houses opposite the park, the heaving crowd with its multitudinous detail of slaughter and suffocation, the smoke-clad hull of the *Attila*, as it rose in angry majesty, its top peering like the Matterhorn through clouds. The sight would have moved the pity of a Borgia and glutted to the full the morbid aestheticism of a Nero.

But the massacre was short. When the airship had reached the height of about 150 feet she suddenly ceased firing, and began once more to circle with albatross-like grace. What was the motive for this strange suspension of hostilities? Possibly her munitions were failing, and the thought of departure with his grim project unaccomplished had forced Hartmann to husband his resources and await better opportunities for mischief at night. His state of mind must have been unenviable. That he had yet received the letter might, or might not, be the case. But in any case he had a gloomy prospect to brood over. The failure of his artillery and petroleum to effect the ruin he had contemplated was—from his standpoint—a catastrophe as was also the extirpation of the anarchist rising below. Of the success or defeat of the continental anarchists we had as yet heard nothing, owing to the disorganization of the usual channels of information, but seeing that the attack in London had failed, it was highly probable that it had withered away where there was no *Attila* to back it. In this event Hartmann's situation would be precarious. Defiant of human effort as seemed the airship it was nevertheless dependent on the maintenance of its communications with society—communications which had hitherto been kept up with the various continental anarchist groups. But in the failure things might come to such a pass that the *Attila* would be altogether without a base, and deprived of this her death from inanition was a mere question of time.

At this stage my speculations were cut short by a rush of fugitives down the street, and, unable to breast the torrent, we took the only possible course and flowed with it. Some way farther on, however, the panic began to ease down, until many stopped to gaze on the destroyer which sailed so contemptuously above them. Some even found their way back to the Park, anxious to do what they could for the wounded and dying wretches who littered the turf for an area of at least 300 square yards.

We were about to do the same when the road was summarily cleared by police and all further access to the park prohibited. We, with the others who were in the street, had to stop and as we did so we turned our looks aloft.

'The ship, or whatever you call her, seems quiet again,' observed an old gentleman who was standing near us.

'A calm before the storm, I am afraid,' I answered.

'When darkness comes . . .' observed another and left his sentence unfinished.

'Heaven shield us from this monster!' said my future father-in-law.

We watched in silence for a while. The airship's slow circling flight was at this moment bringing her nearer, and now many details of her structure were visible, as well as the fact that most of the crew seemed to be on deck.

'Yes, she is beautiful,' said Mr. Northerton, 'and just as you described her.'

She was closer now and in fact the crowd in the street soon judged that she was too close and had melted away. I ought to have seen to it that my future father-in-law should also look for some shelter but my eyes were fixed on one of the little figures visible on the deck—a man taller than the rest—in whom I thought I recognized Hartmann. Suddenly this man, whoever he was, levelled a pistol at one of the others, backed across the deck, fired the pistol and then, wheeling, hurled himself at one of the doors that led to the citadel. With a rush the gunners who were on his side of the deck made as if to follow him, only, after another shot from the revolver, to find that the door had banged in their faces. Then suddenly there was a blinding light and an explosion whose blast threw us down and shattered all the neighbouring window-panes. Before the echoes had died there rained down from the sky—the larger pieces planing slowly—a shower of shattered fragments of the light grey metal. The airship had gone. Of dynamite bombs or of the petroleum that she had carried there was none, only the grey metal, only the very structure of the ship herself.

Thus ended the *Attila*, mysterious as ever. What had happened in those last minutes will, I suppose, never be known. Had the crew mutinied because Hartmann had proposed some vindictive course that even they considered too mad, or had this been an accident or perhaps suicide?

Impossible to say, nor of course did Lena or I ever know whether Mrs. Hartmann's dying letter, which might have helped to turn him from the further destruction of cities, had ever reached her son.

What is certain is that Hartmann's plans had miscarried, that his beautiful *Attila* was now more homeless than the wandering albatross and that, in those last moments, he knew it.

The reader of today knows the story of London and of Britain in the next few weeks and months, how order was once more re-established, how the material wreckage of that dreadful twenty-four hours was slowly replaced, how, gradually, the country recovered from the shock and how from that time the great problems of labour and social justice became dominant.